Restored to Freedom from Fear, Guilt, and Shame

OTHER TITLES IN THE SEANET SERIES

Vol. 1
Sharing Jesus in the Buddhist World

Vol. 2
Sharing Jesus Holistically in the Buddhist World

Vol. 3
Sharing Jesus Effectively in the Buddhist World

Vol. 4
Communicating Christ in the Buddhist World

Vol. 5
Communicating Christ through Story and Song:
Orality in Buddhist Contexts

Vol. 6
Communicating Christ in Asian Cities:
Urban Issues in Buddhist Contexts

Vol. 7
Family and Faith in Asia:
The Missional Impact of Social Networks

Vol. 8
Suffering: Christian Reflections on Buddhist Dukkha

Vol. 9
Complexities of Money and Missions in Asia

Vol. 10
Developing Indigenous Leaders: Lessons
in Mission from Buddhist Asia

Vol. 11
Becoming the People of God:
Creating Christ-centered Communities in Buddhist Asia

Vol. 12
Seeking the Unseen: Spiritual Realities in the Buddhist World

VOLUME 13 IN THE SEANET SERIES

Restored to Freedom from Fear, Guilt, and Shame

Lessons from the Buddhist World

PAUL H. DENEUI, EDITOR

Restored to Freedom from Fear, Guilt, and Shame: Lessons from the Buddhist World
Copyright © 2017 by Paul H. de Neui
All rights reserved.

No part of this book may be reproduced, stored in a retrieval system, or transmitted in any form or by any means—electronic, mechanical, photocopy, recording, or otherwise—without prior written permission of the publisher, except brief quotations used in connection with reviews in magazines or newspapers.

Unless otherwise noted, Scripture quotations are from The Holy Bible, New International Version®, NIV® Copyright © 1973, 1978, 1984, 2011 by Biblica, Inc.® Used by permission of Zondervan. All rights reserved worldwide.

Scriptures quotations marked "ESV" are taken from The English Standard Version® (ESV®) copyright © 2001 by Crossway, a publishing ministry of Good News Publishers. All rights reserved. ESV Text Edition: 2011.

Scripture quotations marked "MEV" are taken from the Modern English Version. Copyright © 2014 by Military Bible Association. Used by permission. All rights reserved.

Scripture quotations marked "NRSV" are taken from the New Revised Standard Version Bible, copyright 1989, Division of Christian Education of the National Council of the Churches of Christ in the United States of America. Used by permission. All rights reserved.

Scripture quotations marked "RSV" are taken from the Revised Standard Version of the Bible, copyright 1952 [2nd edition, 1971] by the Division of Christian Education of the National Council of the Churches of Christ in the United States of America. Used by permission. All rights reserved.

Published by William Carey Library, an imprint of William Carey Publishing
10 W. Dry Creek Circle
Littleton, CO 80120 | www.missionbooks.org

Cover Image: *Forgiving Father* by Frank Wesley. Used by permission.

William Carey Library is a ministry of Frontier Ventures
Pasadena, CA 91104 | www.frontierventures.org

23 22 21 20 19 Printed for Worldwide Distribution

Library of Congress Cataloging-in-Publication Data
Names: De Neui, Paul H., editor.
Title: Restored to freedom from fear, guilt, and shame : lessons from the Buddhist world / Paul H. de Neui, editor.
Description: Pasadena, CA : William Carey Library, [2017] | Series: Seanet series ; Volume 13 | Includes bibliographical references and index.
Identifiers: LCCN 2016051995 (print) | LCCN 2016054263 (ebook) | ISBN13: 9780878085279 (pbk.) | ISBN10: 0878085270 (pbk.) | ISBN 9780878088737 (eBook)
Subjects: LCSH: Christianity and other religions--Buddhism. | Buddhism--Relations--Christianity. | Missions to Buddhists.
Classification: LCC BR128.B8 R47 2017 (print) | LCC BR128.B8 (ebook) | DDC 261.2/43--dc23 LC record available at https://lccn.loc.gov/2016051995

In memory of Gail Barber Klepel
Loving wife, mother, missionary and friend
Faithful servant of Jesus Christ

Contents

Introduction xi
Contributors xv

PART ONE
Understanding Fear, Guilt, and Shame Cultures

1. Beauty for Ashes: Culture, Conflict, and Reconciliation
   in a Buddhist Context 3
   Mary Adams Trujillo
2. Three Distinct Cultural Views of Reality and Its Relation
   to Our Missional Calling 31
   Steve Spaulding
3. "They Don't Feel Guilty!?!": Biblical Ethics and Morality
   in Honor-Shame Cultures 45
   Jayson Georges

PART TWO
Communicating in Fear, Guilt, and Shame Cultures

4. Suitable Messages for Fear, Guilt, and Shame
   Buddhist Cultures. 73
   Alex G. Smith
5. Transformational Mission in Fear Cultures in the
   Buddhist World and Beyond 103
   David S. Lim

6. How to Communicate the Gospel in a Shame Culture:
   Some Thoughts on the Skill of Japanese "Noh"............137
   Timothy Hwang Taeyun
7. Christian Observation of Buddhist Fear Expressed
   in a Devil Dancing Ceremony........................149
   G. P. V. Somaratna

PART THREE
Restoring to Freedom from Fear, Guilt, and Shame

8. Reconciliation Through Purification Rituals
   in Communal Cultures...............................175
   Cristian Dumitrescu
9. A Church Restored from Sin, Shame, and Fear
   in a Tibetan Context...............................193
   Christian Gabre
10. Seeking Social Reconciliation for India's Dalits
    Through Buddhism..................................219
    Sunil Sardar
11. Reconciling to Self, Others, and God?: The Gospel
    Responding to Fear, Guilt, and Shame in Thailand.........237
    Daniëlle Koning

*Restore to me the joy of your salvation
and grant me a willing spirit, to sustain me.
Psalm 51:12*

*It is for freedom that Christ has set us free.
Galatians 5:1*

Introduction

Do not be afraid; you will not be put to shame.
Do not fear disgrace; you will not be humiliated.
You will forget the shame of your youth
and remember no more the reproach of your widowhood.
For your Maker is your husband—
the Lord Almighty is his name—
the Holy One of Israel is your Redeemer;
he is called the God of all the earth.
Isaiah 54:4–5

Anxiety is common to every culture. The expression of it and restoration from it are also determined by every culture. What brings relief in one context may only aggravate anxiety in another. Those working interculturally face this challenge when the solutions that worked in their home contexts fail to bring desired results in the new location and often cause further damage. The hidden inner differences of our various worldview lenses best reveal themselves in times of crisis, when we don't understand why "the other" doesn't respond as we do. A teachable moment? Yes, but learning in the midst of crisis is difficult at best. Unfortunately the usual result of such unguided cultural encounters is a reinforcement of prejudicial stereotypes on both sides. What would happen if intercultural workers were to prepare themselves proactively for the inevitable and view future encounters of differing worldviews as enriching experiences rather than cultural time bombs waiting to explode? That is the purpose of this book.

Anxiety is given expression from out of the worldview where it is born. For many cultures, fear-orientation, guilt-orientation, and/or shame-orientation are major impacts upon the shaping and expression of individual and communally-held worldview. While all are present to a certain extent in every culture, this volume draws from the expressions and insights found from within the context of the Buddhist world. Understanding orientations differing from our own actually helps us understand more of ourselves. This is part of the enrichment resulting in the process of encounter. It is to this end that SEANET proudly presents *Restored to Freedom from Fear, Guilt, and Shame: Lessons from the Buddhist World*, volume 13 in its series on intercultural and inter-religious studies on Christian mission in Buddhist contexts.

This book was written primarily for western practitioners and intercultural communicators of the Christian faith who desire to understand more of cultures that are less guilt-oriented than their own. However, this volume will benefit all who seek to understand these three worldview motivations. While much has been written on shame and guilt-oriented cultures, the reality of fear as a major cultural orientation is only now beginning to be recognized within the West itself. In subtle ways, western worldview has been experiencing a major shift in this direction, particularly since 9/11. Evidence of this can be seen by a quick review of major themes found in current popular films, internet series, and even recent election results. Fear as cultural orientation joins guilt and shame in expressions easily seen in "others" but often unnoticed in oneself because, in the words of Edward Hall, "cultures hide more than they reveal" (*The Silent Language* 1959, 53). We require the lens of the world in order to better see ourselves and recognize our own cultural blindness.

This book joins the multitudes of others birthed out of a communal effort. To fail to acknowledge some of the important contributors would lead to major guilt and shame. First of all, the editor wishes to thank each of the eleven contributing authors whose names should really be on the cover of this book. Each has shared from his or her own personal experiences through quality research and missiological analysis to first present their work at the SEANET conference of 2016 and then to take the time to rewrite for publication. Thanks must also go to Emily Bourne, Tierney Rude, and Nathan Salinas, class participants from North Park Theological Seminary who traveled with me to Thailand, "adopted" the authors, and walked alongside them afterwards to make these final chapters possible. Special gratitude also goes to my faithful assistant Benjamin Wickstrom who not only did everything his fellow students did as listed above, but who also put in many extra hours reviewing and formatting the entire text several times along with many other details I fear I have forgotten. To Mary Trujillo and Anthony Zamble, your support and encouragement as colleagues and friends has made this effort worthwhile and the process much more life-giving. All of us at SEANET owe a great debt of gratitude to the fine staff of William Carey Library Publishers, who carry on the commitment of its founder Dr. Ralph Winter to the cause of SEANET. To Jeff Minard, Melissa Hughes, and all of your team of artists and editors, we thank and honor you!

The authors in this volume come from a wide range of ethnic, cultural, and professional backgrounds, but all have one thing in common. Each one is committed to making the restoration of freedom from fear, guilt, and shame found in Jesus Christ a reality for all the world's contexts including the Buddhist world. Freedom "from" brings with it the positive side of these three orientations: the freedom "to" empowerment, honor, and innocence. We use the word "restoration" believing that it is God's intention to restore all that was lost through fear, guilt, and shame back to the original freedom to power, honor, and innocence of relationships with the Creator, with humanity, with self, and within all of creation. To that end, we join our voices with that of the Psalmist,

> *Restore us, O God;*
> *make your face shine on us,*
> *that we may be saved.*
> *Psalm 80:3*

Paul H. de Neui
Chicago, Illinois, USA

Contributors

Paul H. de Neui is an ordained minister with the Evangelical Covenant Church. He and his wife served as missionaries with church planting and community development organizations in northeast Thailand from 1987–2005. He completed his PhD in Intercultural Studies at Fuller Theological Seminary. Paul has been involved in SEANET for over fifteen years. Presently he is the professor of Missiology and Intercultural Studies and the director of the Center for World Christian Studies at North Park Theological Seminary in Chicago, Illinois.

Cristian Dumitrescu is passionate to discover bridges that help people living in shame and honor cultures rediscover the beauty of the gospel through their local worldview and value systems. He earned his BA in Theology at the Romanian Adventist Theological Institute and a License in Theology at the Babes-Bolyai University in the same country. After serving as a pastor in post-Communist Romania, he pursued an MA in Religious Studies at Newbold College, near Oxford University in the UK. He also sought a PhD in Missions at Andrews University in the US, where he also taught for ten years. Dumitrescu raised awareness about the plight of immigrants in Europe long before the immigration wave of 2015–16. He has taught pastors in Indonesia, Myanmar, Mongolia, China, and Indochina and held evangelistic presentations on three continents. Cristian currently teaches and directs the doctoral programs at the Adventist International Institute of Advanced Studies in the Philippines and is an associate editor for the Journal of Adventist Mission Studies. He pastors a congregation located inside the Taal Volcano on Luzon Island where he lives with his wife and two daughters.

Christian Gabre grew up in Sweden and received a calling for Asia early on. He prepared himself with language study, outreach experience, and by earning a Master of Divinity degree from Örebro School of Theology. He later acquired skills in anthropology from Gothenburg University. He moved with his wife Lisette and their three small children to Central Asia in 1995, and then to Thailand in 2007. His heart is full and hands are busy with enabling, equipping and encouraging the growth of fellowships, with a particular focus on Tibetan Buddhist people groups. He has continued his study of languages, culture, and theology in very practical ways. In his leadership role for the network and association Central Asia Fellowship (CAF), he travels across Asia seeking to be an inspiration for prayer and unity, and to provide training and resources, which is the very essence of CAF. He and his wife live in Asia as happy, young grandparents, continuing to bless Asia.

Jayson Georges has served nine years in Central Asia. He has a Master of Divinity degree from Talbot School of Theology. He is the author of *The 3D Gospel* and *Ministering in Honor-Shame Cultures: Biblical Foundations and Practical Essentials*, and founding editor of www.HonorShame.com. He now resides in Atlanta, GA with his family.

Rev. Taeyun (Timothy) Hwang has been a missionary to the Philippines since 1981. He now serves as a missionary-at-large for the Global Mission Society, where he served six years training missionary candidates. He earned an MA and a PhD in Asian Studies and Philippine Studies from University of the Philippines. He has taken various positions in many schools in his mission fields. Presently he holds the position of chairman of the Board of Trustees for the Asian School of Development and Cross-Cultural Studies in Quezon City, Philippines.

Daniëlle Koning is from the Netherlands. She has a PhD in Anthropology and Sociology of Religion from Vrije Universiteit in Amsterdam, focusing on mission dynamics in so-called "immigrant churches" in the Dutch capital. Currently she works as both a researcher and mission practitioner in northeastern Thailand for Adventist Frontier Missions, a supportive ministry of the Seventh-day Adventist church. She is currently working on a manual for studying the Bible with Thai Buddhists.

David S. Lim is from the Philippines. He has served as academic dean at Asian Theological Seminary in the Philippines and Oxford Centre for Mission Studies in the UK. His PhD in New Testament Theology was earned from Fuller Theological Seminary. He now serves as the president of the Asian School of Development and Cross-Cultural Studies, president of China Ministries International-Philippines, board chair of Lausanne Philippines, and coordinator of the Asian House Church Movement. He has authored several books and articles on non-Western missiology, theological contextualization, and transformational development.

Sunil Sardar serves as the convener of Truthseekers International, which he founded in 2003. His goal and mission is to reconcile the low castes and outcastes of India in order to annihilate the caste system. He travels frequently throughout India to share with the people how Jesus is the Reconciler. He was ordained by East 91st Street Christian Church, served as President for the Tukdoji Maharaj Literary Convention, worked as an editor for a weekly Marathi newspaper named Ekmev Janka, and founded a church planting movement, Din Bandhu. He then served as the Secretary of Reconciliation for the Evangelical Fellowship of India, and eventually founded Truthseekers International. He has published several books, such as *Kabir* and *Sai*, and was head of a

Bible Translation project that recently published a bilingual New Testament in the language of the low castes and outcastes. His intimate work with these castes has given him a unique relationship with Indian Buddhists, who come entirely from those groups. He lives in New Delhi, India, but his wife and four children live in America, where most of them are pursuing their education.

Alex G. Smith was born and raised in Australia till age twenty-one. In Canada he graduated from Prairie Bible College and later the International Institute of Christian Communication in Kenya, Africa. In the USA he earned the DMiss and MA degrees at Fuller Theological Seminary and an MDiv from George Fox Evangelical Seminary. Veteran missionary to Thailand, he founded the Thailand Church Growth Committee, and co-founded SEANET (South, East, Southeast, and North Asia Network). He served as Adjunct Faculty at Multnomah University for eighteen years. Presently he is the International Trainer and Advocate in the Buddhist World for OMF International, under which he has worked for over fifty years. He has published numerous books and articles on ministry in the Buddhist world. His Asian church planting experiences deepened the conviction that multiplying contextualized local indigenous fellowships and training local lay pastors are priority strategies for mission. He resides with his American wife, Faith in the USA. They have three adult sons and four grandchildren.

G. P. V. Somaratna is from Sri Lanka. He has an MA in Missiology and an MA in Theology, as well as a PhD in South Asian history from the University of London. He served as head of the Department of History and Political Science, professor of modern history at the University of Colombo, Sri Lanka, and is now serving as senior research professor at Colombo Theological Seminary. He also served as adjunct professor at Trinity Theological College, Post Doctoral fellow at the Hebrew University of Jerusalem, and Global Research Institute of Fuller Theological Seminary. He has published numerous articles and books on the history of Sri Lanka and the impact of Christianity upon Sri Lankan Buddhism. He is widely regarded as one of Sri Lanka's leading scholars on Ceylonese history.

Steve Spaulding graduated from Fuller Theological Seminary's School of World Mission. He served as a regional missionary with Dawn Ministries in Southeast Asia from 1996 to 2006. He helped to found SEANET in 1999. At present he is the resident missiologist with One Challenge, based in Colorado Springs, Colorado. His vision for mission is to promote a version of the great commission, which he calls "obedient nations."

Mary Adams Trujillo is a researcher and scholar-practitioner of intercultural communication and conflict transformation. She currently teaches at North Park University in Chicago, Illinois, USA, where she also lives. She received a PhD in Communication Studies from Northwestern University in Evanston, IL. Her work incorporates applications of faith-based approaches to social justice issues. Mary's commitment to peace building is inspired by being a mother, a grandmother, and a great grandmother.

PART ONE

UNDERSTANDING FEAR, GUILT, AND SHAME CULTURES

O my God, I am ashamed and embarrassed to lift up my face to You, my God, because our iniquities have expanded over our heads and our wrongdoing has grown up to the heavens. Since the days of our fathers until this day, we have been in a great guilt. It is because of our iniquities that we, our kings, and our priests have been delivered—by the sword, by captivity, by spoil, and by being shamed—into the hand of the kings of the lands. This day is like that, too.
Ezra 9:6–7

For God has not given us the spirit of fear, but of power, and love, and self-control.
2 Timothy 1:7 (MEV)

Now the Lord is the Spirit, and where the Spirit of the Lord is, there is freedom.
2 Corinthians 3:17

1
Beauty for Ashes
CULTURE, CONFLICT, AND RECONCILIATION IN A BUDDHIST CONTEXT

Mary Adams Trujillo

Reconciliation is a word rich in personal, political, and spiritual meaning for both Christians and Buddhists, signifying fulfillment of the deepest human longing for wholeness and peace. The English word "reconcile" comes from a Latin root that refers to unity, restoring to harmony, settling, or making something consistent or compatible.

For Buddhists, the notion of reconciliation, or *patisaraniyakamma*, speaks of return to a previous state of friendly, trusting, and harmonious relationship. These relative similarities in meaning belie deep contextual incongruities, however. For the follower of Jesus, reconciliation is more than a word or an idea. Reconciliation speaks to God's drawing of all humanity to Godself through Jesus, signifying the ultimate relational process for personal and social healing. Christians believe that humanity's relationship with God has been broken due to human sin. Therefore human to human relationships are also broken. Buddhists do not believe in God, and therefore ascribe broken human relationships to ignorance, material attachments, or sensual cravings. The diverse meanings and implications of "reconciliation" point toward the personal, social, spiritual, and theological dimensions of analysis that must occur as Christian missiologists consider the meaning of "reconciliation" within Buddhist and other contexts.

THE MULTI-LEVEL PROCESS OF RECONCILIATION

What is required for reconciliation? How and where can reconciliation take place given the theological differences between those practicing Christianity and Buddhism? Must followers of Jesus or Buddha compromise the integrity of their beliefs in order to be reconciled with each other? Paradoxically, it is culture, and the daily living out of social conflicts over values, including religious beliefs, that enables a set of practical intersections where forms of reconciliation may occur.

Inherent in the nature of intercultural conflict is the capacity to prompt reconciliation in either of the aforementioned definitions. Culture is the substance, while the experience of conflict serves as the fire or catalyst to ignite change between individuals and groups. From the ashes of intercultural conflict emerge profound possibilities for reconciliation at deep personal, social, and spiritual levels.

In practice, reconciliation is an ambiguous, nonlinear, multidimensional, and multi-layered quest for transformation of the structures and processes common to human societies. Reconciliation is humanity seeking a spiritual home. One type of reconciliation may reduce ideological differences to an agreed upon common denominator for purposes of "getting along." Another level of reconciliation aspires to engage difference in order to embrace that which is common to humanity. Second Corinthians refers to a ministry of reconciliation, through which believers are to represent God's love and forgiveness so that others might also be reconciled. Boesak and DeYoung assert that the Apostle Paul's use of the word *katallasso*, "to change, exchange, or effect a change" defines reconciliation as a willingness to exchange places with "the other" (2012, 12). This type of reconciliation enacts and embodies the love of Christ through conscious and intentional identification with the sociopolitical struggles of "the other."

In so doing, new relationships and supporting frameworks for peace and justice are created.

This paper will discuss reconciliation as an integrated holistic process that occurs in three nested stages. The first or outer stage will acknowledge and describe differing cultural patterns and values. The second stage looks to identify extant intracultural elements that address conflict processes. The third or core stage of this inquiry connects culture and conflict to the intangible essence that releases the potential of reconciliation for the Christian missiologist. The author writes as a western Christian academic whose perspectives often include the theoretical. We will begin by defining culture and conflict. Next, the interrelationship of culture and conflict as embodied in values and language will be exemplified. Finally, a model of social justice praxis that affirms mutual values, and that embodies and facilitates reconciliation will be presented.

CULTURE AND CONFLICT EXEMPLIFIED BY VALUES

As spiritual and moral principles that "live" and are enacted by and within people, culture is also an organic entity with an inherent will and mechanisms to survive. Marsella has defined culture as

> Shared learned behavior and meanings acquired in life . . . passed on from one generation to another for purposes of promoting (individual and social) adaptation, growth, and survival. These behaviors and meanings are dynamic and responsive to change and modification in response to individual, societal, and environmental demands and pressures. Culture is represented externally in artifacts, roles, settings, institutions and internally in values, beliefs, expectations, consciousness, in (ways of knowing . . .

and worldviews, including cognitive/affective/sensory styles). Cultures can be temporary, situational, or enduring. (2010, 19)

Paradoxically, culture exerts a pull that is felt, but remains largely invisible to its members. Therefore, intercultural conflict exposes and challenges people's unexamined and often invisible assumptions, expectations, and practices. Conflict occurs as differing individuals or groups interact and perceive that their differences pose a significant threat to needs, values, or resources (Ting-Toomey 1999, 194). Inevitable in all human interactions, conflict has the potential to destroy or create. Whether between individuals or groups, between children, adults, or nations, conflict essentially has virtually the same root causes and manifestations across the developmental spectrum.

Across time and culture, children fight over toys, adults fight over money, nations fight over resources. Children may hit, adults may quarrel, and nations go to war. Across groups, conflicts are generally escalated or exacerbated by an increase in expressed strong emotion like anger or rage, broken relationships, insufficient or inappropriate conflict resolving practices, and the presence of third parties who act as provocateurs.

Conversely, conflict de-escalates when parties express compassion and empathy, have genuine friendships before the conflict, attend to the face needs of the other, and make use of third parties respected by both sides who can act as mediators or cultural interpreters. Further, the restraint or expression of emotion, the direct or indirectness of the messages, and the degree to which verbal and nonverbal cues are read are significant elements of intercultural conflict (Hammer 2002).

In the light of Scripture, "As far as it depends on you, live at peace with everyone" (Rom 12:18 NIV), Christians do not need to fear conflict as such. Conflict, whether within or between cultures, is usually experienced very personally and often produces feelings of guilt, shame, or fear in one or both parties (Georges 2014).

While guilt, shame, and fear may be perceived as negative outcomes, they can also serve as necessary precursors for and essential instruments of personal, social, or spiritual reconciliation. Indeed, Peter Phan, who is no stranger to intercultural conflict, identifies reconciliation as both a process with strategies to facilitate resolution of conflict between groups and "an eschatological gift bestowed by God, a transcendent blessing" (Phan 2006, 90).

Essential to understanding any given culture is knowledge of its values, the core of its system. Values are a set of rules that govern and reflect a culture's relationships, aspirations, and practices formed in response to peoples' histories, religious influences, and even environmental conditions. Cultural values are embedded in beliefs, attitudes, and knowledge, with a barely discernible distinction between deeply held and felt concepts thought to be true and "actual" thoughts, memories, and interpretations of events. Cultural behavior, informed by these "rules" maintains built-in resistance to anything that threatens survival. People groups form and generate beliefs, feelings, and a predisposition to act in certain ways that are consistent with worldview, or orientation to God, humanity, nature, questions of existence, the universe, life, suffering, death, and other philosophical issues. Religion and history are major sources of worldview.

QUESTIONS AND RESPONSES THAT DEVELOP VALUES

Anthropologists Kluckhohn and Strodtbeck (1961) have crafted a useful model for making comparisons of cultural values across groups by suggesting that all societies develop values based on responses to five essential questions. Although the questions are presumed to be universal, the responses, or value-based behaviors and cognitions, are culturally specific. The first question is what is the nature of humanity? Responses are placed on a continuum ranging from good to evil. The second question, "What is the relationship of humans to nature?" (including the supernatural), elicits a range of responses from "dominate" to "in harmony with" to "be dominated by." Third, what is the orientation for time? Responses are past, present, or future. Fourth, how should humans relate to each other? Responses determine whether hierarchically, collaterally, or according to individual merit. The final question assesses the primary motivation for activity or behavior. Responses are to express one's self or "being"; to grow, or "being-in-becoming"; or achieving, or "doing."

Georges (2014) has further delineated cultural values according to three "moral emotions" and responses to sin. These moral emotions often function as gatekeepers to maintain the culture's form, identity, and indeed, its survival. Georges names these as fear/power, guilt/innocence, and shame/honor. Fear/power cultures refer to animistic contexts, typically tribal, where people afraid of evil and harm pursue power over the spirit world through magical rituals. Guilt/innocence cultures are individualistic societies, mostly western, where people who break the laws are guilty and seek justice or forgiveness to rectify a wrong. Shame/honor cultures describe collectivistic societies, common in the East, where people are shamed for not fulfilling group expectations and who seek to restore their honor before the community. Shame is a negative evaluation from others, while guilt is a negative evaluation of self, although the exact meaning and function are contextually derived. Although emotions are common to all people, the ways in which they are perceived and expressed is highly informed by culture. In western cultures, acceptance of guilt suggests that there is some corrective or reparative action that should occur. Shame is associated with fear of having one's actions exposed as deficient. Because of the interdependent nature of collectivist cultures, and the value placed on relationships, shame because of others' actions can be experienced as one's own shame.

In contrast, individualistic cultures allow for emotion to be separated and isolated from experience, leading to compartmentalized understandings. Personal and social power are highly valued. The self is seen as a rational, powerful, independent actor, with choices and actions made according to personal goals and resources. Fear, especially of the non-rational, such as ghosts and spirits, is considered a weakness.

Across all cultures, there seem to be gender based display rules that regulate expression of behavior and emotion. For example, men may not be permitted to publicly express fear or sadness. Women, may not be allowed to publicly display their emotions in the same way as men, so they may/must rename or express these feelings in a way that is culturally acceptable. These renamed feelings may be experienced as or accompanied by shame or guilt. Of particular significance here is that these moral emotions serve an essential role in the process of reconciling intercultural conflict which then opens up a path for personal, social, and spiritual reconciliation. The following example illustrates opposing views of shame.

> During the opening ceremony of the 1988 Seoul Olympics, American athletes embarrassed the Koreans: the American athletes suddenly broke formation as they entered the stadium. They soon shouted, screamed, and pranced around in small groups as if they were in an American rodeo. The hosts were so shocked with shame as they watched the errant behavior helplessly and in total disgust. Although the hyperactive Americans finally settled down for the festive but solemn ceremony to proceed, the damage had been done. In Korea, as in other East Asian countries, the shame emotion maintains the traditions and governs the behavior of its citizens. The society is organized around interdependence and hierarchical structure. Therefore, avoiding the risk of triggering shame in others and in oneself is a constant

preoccupation of Koreans. Saving face, known as Che Myun among Koreans, is the order of the day; losing face is the disorder that disturbs the Korean psyche beyond the realm of imaginations in western standards. (Rue 1994, 23)

If viewed from the perspective of the US athletes, the conflict would not have been apparent. In their minds, they were justifiably proud of their accomplishments and demonstrated the behaviors that flow from cultural values that encourage and permit individualism, spontaneity, and iconoclasm. They likely felt that they had a "right" or were entitled to express their emotions if they chose. Rue points out that in the US, this "penchant for disinhibition, spontaneity, and independence is so highly valued that social missteps and cultural naiveté are often tolerated and forgiven" (ibid). Because US culture often focuses on shame as an emotional state, as opposed to a means of social control, individuals in the US may find themselves "feeling" ashamed of being ashamed. As Georges and others have pointed out, people from honor cultures, like the US may conflate shame and guilt and may focus on "defending" their honor by declaring their ignorance or lack of malicious intent. Essential to understanding fear/power, guilt/innocence, and shame/honor is to see these moral emotions as interrelated and value driven, with meanings mediated whether the self is seen as interdependent or independent. Thus, the depth of the feeling or the power of shame for collectivists is virtually incomprehensible for westerners. Self-esteem is enhanced by self-effacement, ideals which stand in direct conflict with individualist values. However, it is important to note that what are negative "moral emotions" in individualist cultures, serve as socially constructive, albeit unpleasant, in collectivist cultures. Collectivist cultures implicitly understand that shame or failure produces greater adherence to group standards and values.

CONFLICT AS DIMENSIONAL PROCESS

Each of these cultural variables has potential for "causing" conflict, and this is not necessarily bad. It is important to note that although conflict involves emotions, conflict itself is not an emotional state. Conflict is a process. As such, the self-reflection encouraged in Psalm 139 redirects emotions of guilt, shame, and fear from personal or cultural concerns toward a larger missional purpose. The Christian practitioner, whether individualist or collectivist, enters conflict with a posture of deference to God.

> Search me, O God and know my heart; test me and know my anxious thoughts . . . See if there is any offensive way in me, and lead me in the way everlasting." (Psalm 139:23–24 RSV)

This orientation is a marked difference between Christianity and Buddhism. While Buddhism encourages and supports harmonious relationships and critical self analysis, Christianity mandates these practices in the context of relationship with a holy God. In this way, guilt, shame, and fear are not stand alone emotions but rather potential points where the Spirit of God may enter, bringing light and healing to situations. Through the fire of conflict, the Holy Spirit may reveal experiences, practices, and beliefs that lead to transformative outcomes. Paradoxically, Buddhism requires the enlightened self to motivate itself toward a deeper level of enlightenment.

Further, Hofstede, who defines culture as "the collective programming of the mind that distinguishes the members of one group or category of people from others" infers the significance of guilt/shame/fear in the preservation of face in maintaining Asian cultural traditions (2011, 1). Face refers to "an individual's claimed sense of favorable image in the context of social and relational networks" (Ting-Toomey 2014, 373). Hofstede's six identified value dimensions are relevant for understanding how conflict emerges in intercultural relations; three will be mentioned here. These include power distance, or the degree to which inequalities in power are socially accepted. High power distance cultures emphasize status, reinforcing honor and shame on multiple levels, not just economically. Cultures with low power distance are more or less egalitarian, but may also exhibit distinctions based on class, gender, social status, and so forth to create and maintain hierarchies that engender honor or shame.

Hofstede's dimension of uncertainty avoidance is a culture's tolerance for ambiguity. Cultures that avoid uncertainty are likely to have strongly enforced notions of hierarchy, strict roles, and few opportunities for social mobility. Within these cultures, the honor/shame dialectic is clearly observable to those outside the norm. The need for absolutes may also be manifested in the fear/power dynamic. The fear of evil spirits or the use of magic, for example, may be the result of superstitions, functioning as social norms in order to minimize individual and group vulnerability. A third dimension, individualism versus collectivism, identifies how culture manages individual and group identity concerns. If the function and purpose of culture is individual and social survival, as Marsella argues, then Hofstede's dimension of individualism versus collectivism illustrates and explains the root of many intercultural conflicts.

FOUR CONTEXTUAL MODELS

Ironically, even though religion is part of culture, cultural structures and practices may often conflict with religious beliefs. For purposes of illustration, comparison, and application, I present four generalized and hypothetical models of a Christian, US, Buddhist, and Thai context to show how beliefs, structures, and practices may contradict each other.

Christian Context

If there could exist a "pure" Christianity entirely separate from any particular national identity, several characteristics of humanity might be possible to observe. First, the nature of humanity would be considered fundamentally good, because humans are made in the image of God, as well as fundamentally evil because of the inherent sin nature. Humans would live in harmony with the created world, but in submission to God who is sovereign over all things. All dimensions of time would be reconciled because in God there is no past, present, or future. Humans would relate to each other as equals, again with Christ as the head of the church. Finally, motivation for behavior would be simultaneously to express and enact the will and love of God, while growing existentially, as Georges points out. Clearly, "pure" Christianity will not likely be found on this earth. Ethnocentrism, however, may blind missionaries to the fact that "their" Christianity is inherently culturally contextualized.

United States Context

In contrast, when Christian religious values are hypothetically overlaid onto a US culture, one sees clearly how religious beliefs and cultural practices may differ. The US, which mostly self defines as a "Christian nation," might look as follows: Human nature would fundamentally be believed to be "good" based on a prevailing social "truth bias." Beliefs of the dominant culture are maintained by social practices, including media reporting systems that ensure isolation from "unpleasant" realities. Second, humans dominate nature because they are afforded the right to, especially for purposes of economic gain. Recent concerns about climate change and other environmental issues have mitigated this philosophy to some extent. Indigenous populations in the US have maintained that people must live in harmony with the created world. The "fear" aspect in US culture is mostly a social fear, where people categorize and position designated groups to be objects of fear. Violence against the targeted groups is then considered legitimate and necessary in order to reduce a sense of fear and powerlessness. Examples of contemporary targeted groups in the US include African American males and Muslims. Third, humans should live in and for the future. Technology ensures this to be so. In theory according to the Declaration of Independence, all humans are legally equal. Individuals have the right, and are encouraged, to do what advances and promotes their individual well-being. An independent self-construal, the view of self as an independent actor, is the primary determinant of identity. Finally, motivation for behavior is to do and to achieve, with acquisition of wealth viewed as both evidence of worth and the result of one's own diligent effort. Students of culture are likely to find that each national culture modifies and adapts religious beliefs to fit its structures and practices.

Buddhist Context

Further, a generalized analysis of Buddhist religious contexts suggests that the primary value orientation is toward alleviation of human suffering and achievement of nirvana. Humans are assumed to be neither inherently good nor evil. Humans should exist in harmony with nature, because non-violence to sentient beings is valued. Individuals live in the present, except for a desire to achieve a future enlightened state. Karma and sangha, for example, suggests all humans are not equal on the journey; and that the motivation for all right action is to achieve an enlightened state that will end the cycle of birth and rebirth. A Buddhist ethical system would cast negative emotions and mental states that derive from guilt/honor, shame/innocence, and fear/power as results of attachment, desire, or ignorance. Buddhism would not automatically judge shame or guilt as negative, however.

Thai Context

When Buddhist religious values are hypothetically overlaid onto a culture, such as Thailand, one finds humans to be neither inherently good nor bad, but rather useful or not useful. However, humans are powerless against forces of nature and live at the mercy of natural forces or spirits. There is an accommodation for spirits in the daily lives of many Thai people. Relationships and even language is in the present moment, but always with an eye to future implications. Even within a collectivistic social structure, all humans are not equal, therefore group and individual status is important for determining behavioral guidelines and worth. As has been noted, the power dynamics related to fear and shame, may serve to build cultural cohesion and provide for acquisition of honor.

Differences between what is an interpersonal or intercultural conflict may not be immediately obvious because both may stem from and be complicated by personality, cultural system differences, and/or simple misunderstandings. These differences or misunderstandings are often filtered through lenses of ethnocentrism. Stereotypes form and are held in place by deeply felt fear, guilt, shame, prior unresolved conflicts, or historical antagonisms. For example, in attempting to share his or her Christian experience of the gospel with a resistant or offended Buddhist, both parties may feel that their deeply held values and beliefs are compromised. Both may feel deeply insulted or offended, but both have different "rules" for how that sense of offense is conveyed behaviorally. The US Christian is likely to vigorously pursue the discussion, highlighting points of difference to show the correctness of the belief. The Thai Buddhist, on the other hand, is likely to focus on maintaining the harmony of the relationship, and if necessary allowing the Christian to think there is agreement when in fact, there has been simply listening. Both parties may end up feeling equally frustrated or defeated.

INTERCULTURAL COMPETENCE

For people who have as their mission the sharing of the gospel with a goal of having the message received and acted upon, intercultural communication competence is essential. One must have knowledge, skills, and attitudes to bridge cultural divides and manage the conflict that inevitably occurs between culturally different groups. While earnest desire, sincerity, and biblical knowledge are necessary qualities, they are not sufficient to assure intercultural competence.

Intercultural competence in Buddhist contexts requires knowledge of the core structures of Buddhism, how these beliefs are practiced in the local cultures, local values, traditions, histories, politics, and worldviews. Proficiency in the local language and dialects is a given. Further, even if one has a body of knowledge, the successful missiologist must also have interpersonal communication skills such as listening, speaking, and nonverbal and verbal interpretation to effectively interact with members of cultural groups different from one's own. Further, one should be aware of one's predominant communication and conflict styles and how those fit into the local culture. The competent communicator must also recognize culturally specific display rules that explain what particular facial expressions or gestures might mean. A good heart or intention is not enough to counteract deeply held ethnocentrisms.

Just as sharing one's faith is most effective in the context of relationship, having egalitarian relationships with members of host cultures ensures opportunities to practice intercultural conflict resolution. An additional benefit of relationship comes in the form of learning to be a good and patient listener. Listening provides a practical opportunity to decode cultural values and meaning through attention to language use.

LEARN FROM CULTURAL WISDOM

Stories and proverbs, so easily shared in relationships provide relatively easy ways to understand how others think, feel, and believe. Both practices are widely used and accepted by Christians and Buddhists. Proverbs are "nuggets" of cultural wisdom. Listening for these expressions, and then using them appropriately in conversation is a way of "hearing" and sharing cultural values. Examining these stories and proverbs allow listeners to frame questions and deduce answers for how to relate to "the other." Following are examples of Thai proverbs with corresponding biblical or similar western meanings (Srichampa 2005).

Pid tong lang pra. "Put your gold leaf on the Buddha's back." The meaning of this is that acts of generosity, particularly alms given to the poor, should be done in secret. A corresponding biblical verse is found in Matthew 6:3, "But when you give to the needy, do not let your left hand know what your right hand is doing." For Thai society, this would be consistent with not making oneself obvious or standing out from the crowd.

Maa khee mai meekhrai yohk haang. "Self praise is no recommendation." From a collectivist, interdependent construal, one's own opinion of oneself is not as important as the regard of others. Biblically, "For by the grace given me I say to every one of you: Do not think of yourself more highly than you ought, but rather think of yourself with sober judgment, in accordance with the measure of faith God has given you" (Rom 12:3).

Gam dar khrai gaaw gam nan yaawm sa naawng. "One reaps what one sows." Galatians 6:7–8: "Do not be deceived; God is not mocked: for whatever a man sows, he also will reap."

Hen saeht faang nai dtaa phuu euun dtaae mai hen thaawn soong nai dtaa dtuaa aehng. "Find fault in others while ignoring one's own faults." Luke 6:41–42, "Why do you look at the speck of sawdust in your brother's eye, and pay no attention to the plank in your own?"

Gin bouun ron tong. "Eating betel nut burns the stomach." Conscience makes cowards of us all; a guilty conscience needs no accusing.

The next story, told in retrospect, shows differences in how relationships are culturally perceived and constructed, as well as what is missed when relationship does not exist. In the telling of his story, Suwichit Sean Chaidaroon shares invaluable cultural information for western listeners. He illustrates how the inherently ethnocentric and value driven nature of culture impacts the processes and practices for resolving conflict between groups.

> I first came to America in 1999. As a Thai student who had never been out of the country before, I was excited to meet with people from other countries . . . When I was young, my parents taught me that *kreng jai*, or considerate, is the best strategy when with people that I first meet, or even with people I know very well. If you show your consideration to others, they will reciprocate in the same manner. So, as part of being *kreng jai*, I try not to speak up very often in hopes that other people I meet in America would consider that I am nice and sincere to them and that they would be nice in return and grant me a favor when I need [one] . . . One day, my American classmate asked me to join the departmental soccer team . . . so they could join the University's tournament. Even though this activity did not require a great skill and all my friends were studious students who barely knew how to play soccer, I really felt uncomfortable to join the team, as I never played this kind of game before. At the same time, I did not want to refuse his wish because I was afraid it would hurt his feeling. So, I said to my friend, "I will try my best to show up at the game."

> The day after the game, my friend came to talk to me again and he seemed very upset. He asked why I did not go to the game as promised. I was speechless as I thought he should have known that I was reluctant to accept his invitation in the first place . . . I am certain that if I had said the same thing to Thai people, they would have known right away that I am refusing to play in the game. (Chaidaroon 2003, 294)

For Chaidaroon, reticence and politeness were cultural values that served him well in Thailand, but led to intercultural conflict with his colleagues in the US. However, as Chaidaroon tells his story, giving context to the behavior, even the most culturally ignorant person is likely to understand why Chaidaroon acted as he did. As Chaidaroon reveals his interior motivation and desire to be liked, possibilities are created for dialogue and relationship at a deeper level. He is telling the listener indirectly that pleasantness is instrumental and that there is an expectation of reciprocity. Will the listener's ethnocentric filter hear pleasantness as only an expression of emotion? The story also shows the collectivist value on interdependence and how persons are not likely to see their needs, relationships, and actions as separate from others. Differences between guilt and shame may feel virtually indistinguishable.

Again, because of the interdependent nature of collectivist cultures, and the value placed on relationships, shame because of others' actions can be experienced as one's own shame. There are multiple implications for intercultural conflict, missiology, and reconciliation as the following painful example of presumably well-intentioned but ethnocentric behavior, illustrates. In the telling of the story, Rev. Tongpan Phrommedda teaches through story and proverb:

When we went out on our visitation to the villagers, the missionaries would give free medicine to lepers but for others who were feverish or sick they had to pay for it. One time when the missionary got home, he brought the money in a sack to the maid and told her, "Iron this money." The maid looked at the missionary confused and asked why.

"But, acharn, (Thai honorific meaning Reverend or professor) why?" And the missionary said, "To kill the germs."

Now if the missionary had just said this to his wife and this had stayed in the family, it would not have been a problem. But the maid went to her home village that night and told everyone the foreigner believed that our money was dirty so she had to iron it to kill the germs. Everyone who heard was infuriated. We have a saying, *"nok me hu, nu me beek"* (birds have ears and mice have wings.)

The word spread everywhere. (de Neui n.d., 54)

Both stories illustrate elements of intercultural conflict: differing communication styles, value orientations, power positions, conflict styles and expectations, and self-construal; as well as the use of local knowledge. Thus, to the Christian missiologist, "Let him who has ears to hear . . ."

The desired outcome for Chaidaroon was to allow for mutual face-saving and relational maintenance, not necessarily to gain something substantive immediately. Therefore, Chaidaroon as a member of a collectivist culture, (with an interdependent sense of self) will likely frame conflict in terms of social relationships, and will typically negotiate face related issues such as honor or shame, prestige or humility before issues are addressed. Communication styles in many, but not all collectivist cultures favor indirect speech to preserve harmony. This would mean the meanings of words are secondary to the context in which they occur. Communication partners in these instances read and decode nonverbal behaviors as individualist cultures decode spoken language. In the above examples, one can also recognize the dynamics of shame and guilt as both responses to and motivators of behavior. Again, the interdependent self-construal sees itself as relational, connected, and social network driven.

Members of individualist cultures, like the US graduate students and the missionary, typically view conflict in terms of its potential outcomes. The goal is to win, because winning affirms a powerful, honorable independent self-construal. An independent self-construal perceives itself as individual, separate, and internally attribute driven. The individualist views the conflict partner as an opponent and tries to preserve his or her own face. This is accomplished by offering clearly articulated, directly spoken, rational arguments.

The missionary story in particular illustrates how the conflict styles, values, power positions, and competencies intersect. The intention of providing free medicine to lepers is noble and seemingly affirms the worth of all people and should not necessarily be a cause for conflict as it would have been culturally consistent with doing good deeds for others. The primary cause for conflict was the expressed incompatibility of independent and interdependent self-construal. The missionary's independent/individualist concern was protection from sickness, which could be a western version of the fear/power dynamic. The way he communicated his desired outcome prioritized his need over the face of the community as represented by the maid. Presumably, his intention was not to offend, but to protect himself. Community "moral emotions" of shame and guilt were clearly evident, as well as the ease with which shame was bestowed by the missionary. Additionally, the collectivist nature of the community is also evident in how the community, not just the maid, received the news, and unified against the outsider. Differences in power distance were evidenced in the way that the maid addressed the missionary, the way the missionary addressed the maid, and even in the way that the Reverend told the story. The proverb that the storyteller points to, *"nok me hu, nu me beek"* (birds have ears and mice have wings), would have been important information for the missionary to know and understand beforehand.

CONFLICT, TRANSFORMATION, AND RECONCILIATION

That the human story is replete with accounts of personal and social alienation and estrangement as well as stories of relationship, community, and transcendent love speaks to the design by one Creator. Just as every cultural history documents wars and strife, every cultural history can also claim love and peace. The desire for peace and human well-being is universal, although language and underlying methodologies may differ.

Opposing theologies do not restrict harmonious relationships between persons. Thus, Buddhists and Christians can agree that the lived experience of peace is a desired outcome, even though only the Buddhist will believe that one cannot find ultimate peace except through death and karmic reincarnation. While Christians will not agree that the goal of life is to reach nirvana, Christianity does affirm that personal acceptance of the death and resurrection of Jesus Christ reunifies the believer with God. Buddhists believe that inharmonious relationships result from human striving; Christians believe that broken human relationships result from humanity's broken relationship with God. Seen in light of what humanity has in common, culture is simply the collective social creation of particular peoples, or the "world." Cultural divides, even religious ones, are not insurmountable. These contested spaces offer opportunities for self-examination as well as for repentance.

The Christian missiologist has Jesus as a model for working through the thorny and most often painful issues and situations of culture in order to achieve a deeper relationship with God. The Christian relies on the emergence of God's Spirit in seemingly irreconcilable conflicts. When human emotions and reasoning alone do not produce desired results, the practitioner learns to seek out and rely on an eternal, omnipresent, omnipotent, loving God who cares so deeply for humanity that God sent God's beloved Son as an emissary to the "world." In this sense, the missiologist is also to be an emissary, for

> He, himself is our peace, who has made the two groups one and destroyed the barrier, the dividing wall of hostility by setting aside the flesh with its commands and regulations. His purpose was to create in himself one new humanity out of the two, thus making peace and in one body to reconcile both of them to God through the cross, by which he put to death their hostility. (Eph 2:14–17 NIV)

Without question, the fundamental theological differences between Christianity and Buddhism generate intense cognitive, emotional, social, and spiritual conflicts within individuals and between groups. Yet Phan declares that conflict is a gift (Phan 2006, 90). The greatest gift of the process of conflict, and especially intercultural conflict, is the breaking up of status quo and the opening up of possibilities. Both parties have access to spiritual practices, but for the Christian practitioner, the Holy Spirit enters into and transforms broken places and relationships. The result of a Holy Spirit-led reconciliation process is a working out of God's will. The end, which is not really an end, but a beginning, is the peace that "passes all understanding," the shalom that enables all to partake of the love of God. God does not guarantee that the conflict resolution will be painless; he only guarantees that he is our peace.

As noted, conflicts can generate mistrust and hostility as well as, in their overcoming, bring forgiveness and reconciliation.

Thus, while recognizing that reconciliation, in the ultimate sense, is a work of grace through the Holy Spirit, the Christian missiologist in the Buddhist context can still look for elements that bridge interests and which facilitate improvements in intercultural communication. Casting differences aside for the moment, all religion offers its adherents a framework for right living, offering revelations of truth so that they can live lives of meaning and purpose. The broad strokes of all religious systems deal with the sacred and profane, life and death, right and wrong, good and evil. A key for reconciliation efforts among people groups is to find how specific values and beliefs are encoded in everyday life and then use those elements to bridge minor differences.

Bridging minor differences makes a path where discussion of higher order differences like doctrine may occur. For example, while believing that earthly life may be filled with suffering and the goal of life is to become free from the cycles of suffering, a Buddhist is still more likely to prefer a safe, mutually respectful relationship with their Christian neighbor to one filled with hostility or fear. Although a Christian's perspective may be that salvation through Jesus Christ is required in order to be reunified with God, that same individual is also likely to prefer a harmonious and respectful relationship with a Buddhist neighbor to a contentious, hostile one. Most community members will appreciate social agreement that provides at least a superficial basis for developing interpersonal relationships through which conflict can be diffused. For the Christian, the bridge that is Christ enables and mandates believers to, "live in peace with everyone" (Rom 12:18).

However, neither culture, conflict, nor reconciliation can be examined apart from political considerations or power relations. For Christians who are a political and numerical minority in Buddhist countries, effectiveness alone dictates attention to local structures, practices, and relationships. Second, many Christians who come as missionaries for example, come from Western, Eurocentric environments and bring a certain ethnocentrism with them. This ethnocentrism may cause them to see local people as an "other" needing to be converted, but whose local customs "get in the way." Unexamined and unchallenged ethnocentrism blinds missionaries, in particular, to their own faults or customs that actually "get in the way" of being ambassadors for Christ. Indeed, it is in these spaces of intercultural conflict that the Christian missiologist must question and possibly lay down notions of what is "true" or "right," what is cultural, and even what is biblical.

As evidenced in the story of the missionary, ethnocentrism, which is a form of pride, also hinders local people from receiving Jesus. Prayerful reflection on intercultural conflict can transform a dispute from ethnocentric to Christocentric. Hattam sees reconciliation as a healing practice and as a metaphorical space to articulate new cross-cultural discourses (2004, 2). In this social justice dimension of reconciliation, injustice is confronted, traumatic events are healed, and sentiments of guilt, anxiety, and resentment are acknowledged.

RESOURCES FOR RECONCILIATION

Hattam suggests that what has come to be known as socially-engaged Buddhism is a resource for teaching and learning about reconciliation. Recognizing that political involvement requires careful navigation even in one's own country, a theology that includes social justice is a way to bridge the gap between words and actions. In Buddhist context cultures, the task of reconciliation can move beyond the saving of individual souls and building of churches by engaging with the issues of the local community. Salvation, in collectivist cultures must include a broad vision for collective healing of the local community, as well as for the individual. These efforts must include social justice. Care for the "least of these" is not only at the heart of Jesus' message, but has the effect of enlarging territory in transformative ways. For example, women and girls in virtually all cultures, and even more so in high guilt/shame/fear cultures are disparately impacted by educational and economic inequities, violence, environmental degradation, and social limitations. Standing in support of issues that affect women and girls will automatically elevate the community, although not necessarily the prestige or safety of the activist.

Some of the emerging models of socially-engaged Buddhism, although engaging social justice with different end goals, offer opportunities for missionaries to hear and align themselves with the struggles, interests, and deepest needs of local women, poor, or otherwise marginalized people. For Buddhists, these models of social engagement are framed in terms of universal responsibility and practical spirituality and are represented by the Dalai Lama, Thich Nhat Hanh, and Sulak Sivaraksa among others. These individuals incorporate Buddhist sensibilities and practices into an understanding of the world as a place of injustice. Practices include cultivating mindfulness or *metta*, which is loving kindness, toward opponents.

As has been pointed out previously, if Christianity is liberated from its cultural constraints, which can be approximated when practitioners understand the dynamics, structures, and functions of culture, the potential for the unleashed power of God is unimaginable. Literally, as it is written, "What no eye has seen, what no ear has heard, and what no human mind has conceived—the things God has prepared for those who love Him" (1 Cor 2:9).

It is in the places of deepest social conflict that guilt, shame, or fear reside. These are the liminal spaces where humans need allies and the unconditional love that only the gospel of Jesus Christ provides. It is in places of deepest conflict and broken relationships that the ministry of the Holy Spirit brings reconciliation, transformation, and peace. In this way, conflict becomes not just a difference of opinion, but a catalyst for personal and social change. Reconciliation becomes more than a word with many meanings; it becomes the raison d'être for the Christian in a Buddhist context.

Christian missiology, as a pedagogy of reconciliation, has a legitimate role in dismantling systems of oppression and bringing forth social transformation. All forms of stigma, whether stemming from violations of human dignity, denial of basic economic needs, issues of health, education, or social violence create conditions where guilt, shame, and fear flourish. Persons in these spaces need allies and the unconditional love that only the gospel of Jesus Christ can provide. Persons experiencing these conditions also need the resources, strategies, and capacities that denominations and institutional churches can provide. In finding mutually respectful ways to work together on issues identified as important by local people, Christians and Buddhists engage conflict, learning from and with each other. Admittedly, this learning by doing is not an easy, painless process. However, engaging conflict by breaking down human boundaries allows the Holy Spirit to bring reconciliation, transformation, and peace. Quoting John Paul Lederach, Peter Phan observes that

> The challenge posed by reconciliation is to open up the social space that permits and encourages individuals and societies as a collective to acknowledge the past, mourn the losses, validate the pain experienced, confess the wrongs, and reach toward the next steps of restoring the broken relationship. (Phan, 92)

BEAUTY FOR ASHES

A story is told that before Buddha died and passed into nirvana, he instructed his followers to place the ashes from his cremation beneath a stupa that would come to symbolize his attainment of the Enlightened Mind. Today, ashes are still culturally significant in Buddhist funeral traditions, signifying veneration of the deceased. In the Hebrew Bible, ashes signified penance, mourning, grief, or humiliation. Yet Isaiah, the prophet chose mourning to speak metaphorically and literally of one who would come to "grant to those who mourn in Zion, Giving them a crown of beauty instead of ashes. The oil of joy instead of mourning" Isaiah 61:3 (NIV).

Acknowledging that there are theological and cultural differences in these examples, ashes represent the paradoxical emergence of hope and joy from seemingly irreconcilable conflicts. Conflict has the capacity to destroy relationships between people and people groups. Conflict also offers the gift of creating a metaphorical or actual space where people can examine their differences and thoughtfully seek methods to reconcile difference at multiple levels. Buddhists will call this thoughtful examination mindfulness. Christians will call this process prayer. Through both, mourning is juxtaposed against veneration, restoration comes through destruction. Specifically for the Christians who live and work in Buddhist contexts, the confusion and chaos of intercultural conflicts brings the opportunity, indeed the necessity, to see and hear God differently, with confidence that the Spirit of God leads the believer into all truth.

Conflict is a humbling, although not inherently humiliating, process requiring trust in God to lead the believer to unknown realms of relationship. Reconciliation requires willingness to lay preconceptions, often concealed as ethnocentrism, onto a holy fire. As disputants are reconciled to each other, even in a social sense, the believer who seeks God in this conflict, moves closer toward reconciliation with God. In this way, the missiologist embodies this message: crucifixion comes before resurrection, resurrection requires crucifixion. Because of this ministry of reconciliation, the believer is reconciled with Christ, who suffering through painful and difficult processes of intercultural conflict, emerged from and triumphed over guilt, shame, and fear. With Christ as a model, and from these ashes, every element necessary for conflict resolution, forgiveness, transformation, and reconciliation has arisen.

REFERENCES

Boesak, Allan, Aubrey DeYoung, and Paul Curtiss. 2012. *Radical reconciliation: Beyond political pietism and Christian quietism.* Maryknoll, NY: Orbis Books.

Chaidaroon, Suwichit Sean. 2003. "When shyness is not incompetence: A case of Thai communication competence." *Intercultural Communication Studies* XII (44): 294–306.

de Neui, Paul. n.d. Unpublished manuscript. *Voices from Asia: Communicating contextualization through story*: 50–56.

Georges, Jayson. 2014. *The 3D gospel: Ministering in guilt, shame, and fear cultures.* Timē Press.

Hammer, Mitchell R. 2002. *The intercultural conflict style inventory: Increasing competence across the cultural divide.* Ocean Pines, MD: Hammer Consulting.

Hills, M. D. 2002. "Kluckhohn and Strodtbeck's values orientation theory." *Online Readings in Psychology and Culture* 4(4). http://dx.doi.org/10.9707/2307-0919.1040.

Hofstede, G. 2011. "Dimensionalizing cultures: The Hofstede model in context." *Online Readings in Psychology and Culture* 2(1). http://dx.doi.org/10.9707/2307-0919.1014.

Marsella, Anthony J. 2010. "Ethnocultural aspects of PTSD: An overview of concepts, issues, and treatments." In *Traumatology* 16 (4): 17–26 DOI: 10, 1177/1534765610388062.

Phan, Peter. 2006. *Global healing and reconciliation: The gift and task of religion, a Buddhist-Christian perspective.* Buddhist Christian Studies 26: 89–108.

Rue, David S. 1992. "Shame and confusion among Korean American youths." In *Korean Americans: Conflict and harmony*, edited by Ho-Youn Kwon. Chicago, IL: North Park College and Theological Seminary.

Srichampa, Sophana. 2005. *Thai and Vietnamese proverbs and common expressions: The influence of Buddhist and local beliefs*. Paper presented at the International Conference on Cultural and Religious Mosaic of South and Southeast Asia: Conflict and Consensus through the Ages, January 27–30 in New Delhi, India.

Ting-Toomey, Stella. 1999. "Constructive intercultural conflict management." In *Communicating across cultures*. New York: The Guilford Press.

Trujillo, Mary Adams. 2000. "Even the white ants confer before they scatter: Use of the proverbs in West African peacemaking traditions." *Journal of Intergroup Relations*, Vol XXVII, 1:15–25.

Van Ginkel, Eric. 2004. "The mediator as face giver." *Negotiation Journal* (October): 475–87.

Wong, Ying, and Jeanne Tsai. 2007. "Cultural models of shame and guilt: The self-conscious emotions." *Theory and Research*: 209–23.

Zhang, Qin, Stella Ting-Toomey, and John G. Oetzel. 2014. "Linking emotion to the conflict face-negotiation theory: A U.S.-China investigation of the mediating effects of anger, compassion, and guilt in interpersonal conflict." *Human Communication Research* 40: 373–95.

2
Three Distinct Cultural Views of Reality and Its Relation to Our Missional Calling

Steve Spaulding

When we speak of a conversation, we're obviously talking about communication. And, if it's communication among cultures, then allow me to illustrate this description of a humorous video. A German youth is being introduced—the first day on the job—to a post at a German Coast Guard station. When the older boss leaves him with his wall full of screens and instruments, suddenly a distress call comes from some nearby ship in the area: "May-Day . . . May-Day; we are sinking!" He responds with clarity, "This is the German Coast Guard . . . What . . . are you *s(th)inking* about?" (Mantrat 2006).

In recent decades, we've become more aware of multiple ways that communication happens, and in the case of human interaction, the latest statistic that less than ten percent of our communication activity is the words that come from our lips (Eastman n.d.). Everything else is body language, other actions or levels of interaction, visual interference, outside influences, or technologies of the ones communicating. We must realize that communication itself is a complex activity and has many other features besides the actual content of our message.

We must also acknowledge that so often we oversimplify the communication of the most important message we sense we are conveying. We're not realizing that it's not just verbal communication that needs clarity. The worldview and cultural assumptions behind what we're saying are at least as important as the mere content of the words we're communicating.

BACKGROUND AND EXPLANATION OF THE THREE

When we deal with guilt, shame, and fear cultural paradigms or perspectives of reality, we may first ask, "Where did these concepts come from?" There are two answers to this. First, these cultural distinctions really arose over the last half-century. In the wake of what seemed, to westerners, bizarre activities of the Japanese during WWII, anthropologist Ruth Benedict popularized the term "shame culture" in her 1956 publication, *The Chrysanthemum and the Sword*. Even before this, Eugene Nida stated, "We have to reckon with three different types of reactions to transgressions of religiously sanctioned codes: fear, shame and guilt" (1954, 150). Nida's and Benedict's points of clear cultural differentiation do not seem to have been followed by most mission practitioners for another fifty years! In the past decade, however, this has changed (Georges 2014; Mischke 2015; Tennent 2007; Wu 2012). In my own organization, among others, discussion of this phenomenon is included as part of the preparatory sessions for out-going missionaries. Today, in the West—or specifically in the USA—there have been repeated observations that while our western roots are clearly more the guilt realm than in the shame or fear realms, for various reasons the shame factor has risen to prominence. A broad generalization of our culture's views of reality, especially as it has to do with being right or wrong, has eroded into much more of a set of values which sees shame as a major factor in our socialization and the way we deal with our everyday world (Crouch 2015).

The second answer predates even the proliferation of independent nomenclature in Benedict's anthropology or Nida's missiology. We can trace a general understanding of these three realities of guilt, shame, and fear from the very beginning of and throughout the biblical text. We will deal with this below.

Before pursuing that source, it is first necessary to define these three cultural perspectives. Christ-followers ground these views of reality in the origin of sin found in Genesis 3. If a culture tends to have one of these three perspectives over the rest, i.e. guilt, shame, or fear, the development of these views has had much to do with the fact that humanity is fallen. According to the Scriptures, when that first act of disobedience was committed, the bite of that forbidden fruit was taken, at that moment these three elements of guilt, shame, and fear arose. That is not to say that all elements of these three approaches are the simple result of human sin. Some have to do with the way cultures evolved with unique approaches, strengths, and weaknesses in social and lifestyle choices.

Guilt cultures include societal groupings in which "being right versus being wrong" and justice are, in some ways, among the highest ideals. Many western contexts hold to this cultural framework. All three groups, guilt, shame, and fear, have overriding metaphors that describe their particular societal commitments, especially in the moral and social realms. In the case of guilt cultures, a dominant institutional metaphor is the courtroom. If something in a western culture goes wrong, the question is, "Who did it?" The validity or error of the actions of the accused comes under judgment. This happened with Adam and Eve. Both knew God's limits and together they broke those boundaries as can be seen in the temptation and their mutual submission to it.

Shame cultures are societies in which there is still a conscience which does in fact tell people when they are doing wrong. But often within them, there is much more social cohesion which defines the place of individuals within the larger group. That group could be an immediate or extended family, a village, tribe, or even the larger ethnic or national identity. Shame cultures do not embrace the radical individualism that most guilt cultures do. They are more corporate in their dealings with life, have a much stronger sense of collective identity and, as a result, all relationships are understood within a hierarchy of some sort of patron/client. That is partly why they are called shame cultures because the positive corollary to shame is honor and this only occurs in the social context. Those who live in guilt cultures are almost completely blind, or reactive to, true honor in their relations, whether in the home or in larger institutions like government. Since the Bible was written within contexts that were much more shame oriented, those in guilt cultures tend to have a harder time appreciating or applying key biblical texts. They lack a fundamental appreciation for true honor having never personally experienced the removal of shame. Scripture gives much more space to and verbal treatment of "shame" themes than "guilt" themes. See the biblical roots study below to verify this. A governing metaphor in a shame-oriented society is the community, a village; a more relational and corporate model. Geographically, in terms of our global village, these cultures tend to come from the major Asian religious bodies (Muslim, Hindu, and Buddhist).

Fear cultures are, in some ways, the easiest to identify. They are characterized by the tangible impact felt from the unseen realms of spirits, angels, demons, and other cosmic forces. As societies they are animistic, usually the smaller tribal groups within larger societies or countries. The global mission community has done a commendable job in seeking to reach tribes by addressing what Dr. Paul Hiebert entitled "the excluded middle" (1982, 35–47). European cultures that embraced the Enlightenment worldview usually fail to recognize the world of the unseen, but during biblical times this perspective was dominant. The metaphor for this group, if there is one, is a combative or military one between powers. When the good news of the gospel comes to these people, the biggest question in the minds of many has to do with fear of recrimination and freedom from spiritual forces believed to govern birth, death, and every aspect of life in between and beyond—generationally.

These are the three primary cultural paradigms, guilt, shame, and fear, but as experts are quick to point out, there is no society that is singularly attached to just one of these paradigms. Each is always a mixture, but in most cases there is one dominant characteristic. Jayson Georges has developed a "Culture Test" that assists in determining percentages of dominant characteristics plotted out on a triangular grid. He points out that while whole societies tend to fit into one side or one dominant angle of the triangle, individuals within these groups will vary in terms of how much of their worldview is dominated by one or another of these intersecting views (Georges 2014). For example, the rural North American farmer may be more corporate in his identity and therefore live in more of a balance between the guilt culture of the West and the shame cultures of the East while the New York lawyer would tend to be more immersed in the guilt culture with few signs of participation in the cultures of shame or fear.

A VISIT TO BIBLICAL ROOTS

A shocking discovery for many western theologians is that western guilt-orientation is far less common in Scripture than that of honor and shame. Cultures into which the Bible was originally written were far more shame oriented, with some basic assumptions of fear cultures as well, than the European legal or law-oriented guilt cultural paradigm. "To the surprise of many people—the word 'guilt' or 'guilty' occurs only twenty-seven times [in Scripture], while the word 'shame' or 'shamed' occurs 225 times in the Old and New Testaments" (Francis 1992, 6).

Most biblical writers point out that the story of the fall of humanity found in the first chapters of Scripture has elements of guilt, shame, and fear as integral parts of the narrative. While the scene does incorporate guilt, the dominant theme is humanity's status of honor before the Fall and the shame and fear that dominated their actions and God's reactions, after their misdeed.

Given that Scripture as a whole has almost a ten-fold higher use of the shame theme than it does of guilt, it is clear that much western theology ignores a major part of our relation to God and to one another. When studies are made of the primary western theological treatises, the treatment of shame versus guilt in those texts is almost inverse to the way these themes are treated in Scripture. Werner Mischke, in his book, *The Global Gospel: Achieving Missional Impact in our Multicultural World*, tracks this blind spot especially in contemporary theological dictionaries, pointing to a profound lack of coverage on this dominant theme in Scripture (2015).

For each of the categories of fear, guilt, and shame there is an inverse positive term for post-Fall categorizations: innocence in relation to guilt, honor in relation to shame, and power or deliverance in relation to fear. These terms point to the pre-Fall condition of humanity, but also to God's clear intentions for this lost planet within all of subsequent history.

A review of the stories of Old Testament heroes readily reveals what Mischke calls an "honor-status reversal" motif (2015, chapter 10). This is the idea that God, in dealing with his creatures, allows them in some way to be humiliated or shamed. He then allows his grace and power to manifest in ways that truly honor Godself and also brings exaltation or a return to a better future. The story of Christ portrays this perfectly in the Gospels and in Paul's descriptions (Phil 2). Furthermore shame is a significant theme in the prayers and songs of Elizabeth, Mary, and others in the announcement and event of Jesus' birth. His crucifixion is a story of shame at its absolute worst in his context. Jesus' resurrection and glorification speaks to his exaltation to the Father's right hand (Ps 110:1) and his impending victory over his enemies. Mischke points out that this reversal is not just a storyline of the heroes of Scripture and for Christ, but is a theme of our spirituality; running through the Beatitudes, the parable of the prodigal son, Paul's Books of Romans and 1 Corinthians, and even running through the final book of the Bible, Revelations.

Roland Muller pointed out that his frustration as a missionary to peoples in the Middle East was primarily overcome when he seriously studied the *many* implications of how his audience was processing Scripture and interpreting categories that he had simply never thought of. My own pilgrimage, after I read and began digesting the bulk of what Muller was saying, was punctuated by the daily reading of Scripture I was doing at the time. Here is one passage that moved me toward a more holistic gospel than the one in which I'd been professionally trained by those good guilt-culture institutions:

> You see, at just the right time, when we were still powerless, Christ died for the ungodly . . . But God demonstrates his own love for us in this: While we were still sinners, Christ died for us. Since we have now been *justified* by his blood, how much more shall we be saved from God's wrath through him! For if, when we were God's enemies, we were *reconciled* to him through the death of his Son, how much more, having been reconciled, shall we be saved through his life! (Rom 5:6, 8–10 NIV; emphasis added)

Here Paul mentions three distinct ways that Christ's death brought about different aspects or arenas of the good news. First, it was clearly designed for the fear cultures, who need power over the forces of darkness that hold them captive. Second, the guilty sinners need justification, as in the courtroom metaphor, to be declared righteous. And finally, the enemies of God, those who have a broken relationship (vertically and horizontally) need reconciliation to abolish shame and re-establish honor. In each case, it's the death of Christ that accomplishes this, but there are three kinds of "we" here. Whether we're powerless, guilty sinners, or shamed enemies of God, we all can be brought back into proper relationship with Him, powerfully delivered from the powers of darkness, declared righteous, and washed clean of our animosity and dishonor.

HOPE FOR THE FUTURE

I recall one of my first visits to Thailand in which missionary Alan Johnson described to me what would happen (and had happened) when a Thai pastor was involved in some adulterous affair in his church. The greater disturbance would not come from the congregation once they heard and confirmed this news. But if the pastor's indiscretion were ever announced in the church service, this would have enormous implications. The pastor would basically disappear from ministry activity for a season, but then would reappear in another setting to do his ministry once again, with no mention of the previous offense. No reconciliation or restoration officially would likely be done, a typical reaction within a truly shame-oriented culture. In that context, losing face is a much bigger factor than even the wrongful act itself.

These things must be dealt with sensitively by people who understand that these three different approaches to reality each have redemptive qualities. God has provided us with multiple biblical examples of when, why, and how they need to be properly overcome or faced with solid, constructive outcomes.

I see a future opening up to us, in part, because of this new way of communicating the good news among very distinct cultures. One can be an optimist about this chaotic age in which we now live. Given all of the terror threats and significant changes, many people in the West seem to be fraught with fear about our future. In terms of optimism, I stand upon just a few things, which have caused me to hold on to a bright future. They are, first, the only prayer our anointed one left in our hands to pray, "thy Kingdom come, thy will be done, on earth as it is in heaven." Secondly, the

Old Testament verse most often quoted in the New Testament is, "The Lord said to my Lord, 'Sit at my right hand until I make your enemies a footstool for your feet'" (Ps 110:1). This is kingdom language and it is also eschatological language. When quoted in Hebrews 10, the writer clearly declares that Christ is now waiting for this to become a reality (Heb 10:13). He will not come back until his enemies have been made a footstool for his feet. In 1 Corinthians 15, Paul quotes it and reminds us that "the last enemy to be destroyed is death" (1 Cor 15:26). This is clearly an indication of the second coming, for therein will be the general resurrection.

Also, an optimistic view is based on several elements of our age, which we believe are dovetailing or synergizing for an unprecedented harvest for the ultimate rulership of God. First, there are the clear and rapidly developing technical advances of our global civilization. There are people involved in the Bible translation business. Their technical developments are cutting the time of translating the entire Bible into a brand new language into a fraction of the years it used to take to do the very same process, even just two decades ago! This simply points to the fact that radically different cultures, along the lines of these distinct paradigms, are coming into more rapid contact with the rest of the global body of Christ more quickly, and there is a growing, mutual education of the depth and breadth of the teachings of God in our different, cultural circles.

Another fact of globalization and urbanization is the fact that ethnic groups, which used to be seen as very hard to get to or to evangelize are populating most of the world's largest urban agglomerates. Mass migration means that the nations have come to our back door, almost regardless of where we live on this shrinking planet. There are many elements of this migratory reality which essentially magnifies and forces us to learn better about these three distinct paradigms of reality: guilt, shame, and fear. Almost daily we are contacting people of radically different views of reality. This forces us to be better prepared to communicate

God's truth, in different perspectives, almost routinely, and not as "career missionaries" relocating to some remote corner of the world to do this work.

We also know that the church is much more unified than it has been in a long time. Some optimism has to do with the fact that Jesus is, in fact, not going to return for a harem, but for one bride, and the largest elements of Christianity, the three major blocks of the church, are showing unprecedented signs of organic unity, on levels which would have been, and were practically, unthinkable just a generation ago. But also, the church is also much more global than it has ever been before. Mission is now from everywhere to everywhere, and that means it's not just a graduation from the "three selfs" of Henry Venn over a century ago, but also a fourth "self" in "self-theologizing." This means that all cultures, as they embrace Christ, are able, with the many outsiders cheering them, capable of exploring a theology which is part of their own self-awareness. This is an understanding of their own fear, shame, or guilt-based longings and interpretation of our common text, and with the help of the rest of the body and bride of Christ, able to move forward into God's grand dreams for each nation or people group.

When the great exploration of what are now called insider movements came along, Ralph Winter wrote:

> The idea of "radical contextualization" is an incredibly new frontier. It's not just how many minority peoples are left. It's how many large blocs are still untouched or unchosen. It's how many peoples that are supposedly already "reached" are not really reached. Well, is it possible that within these large blocs of humanity we have achieved (with trumpets blaring) only a *form* of Christianity that ranges from sturdy and valid but foreign, to maybe superficial or phony? . . .

We may need to go beyond mere radical contextualization. The biblical faith has gone beyond Judaism. The NT has shown us how that can and must be done for the sake of the Gentiles. We have now also long seen how our biblical faith has been able to go beyond Roman Catholicism. To go beyond Judaism did not invalidate the faith of those believing Jews who remained Jews. To go beyond Roman Catholicism does not invalidate the faith of those believing Catholics who have stayed behind.

Is it time to allow for the possibility that some people around the world will choose to go *beyond Christianity* as we know it? . . . We have seen our gospel work fairly well—to draw people into evangelicalism, a westernized evangelical movement. But by and large this has happened only if they belonged to a minority or an oppressed group—like tribal peoples, or Koreans under the Japanese. . . The future is correspondingly bleak for the further extension of our faith into the vast blocs of Chinese, Hindus, Muslims and Buddhists *unless we are willing to allow our faith to leave behind the cultural clothing of the Christian movement itself.* Do we preach Christ or Christianity? (2015, 330–32; author's emphasis)

I include this extensive interview because in this article Dr. Winter was speaking of a third reformation. And I believe that's the wave on which we're currently standing. It will take the synergy of several key global movements on top of the wonderful things that our globalizing, techno-advancing world is already doing. It will include insider movements, in which we see our faith no longer asking people to leave their religio-cultural trappings in order to follow passionately after Christ. It will also be proclaiming the good news in terms of proclaiming a gospel that is authentic good news for all hearers. It will also be other developments like business as mission which ennobles the rank and file follower of Christ to be the cross-cultural missionary he or she already is, and from which they will be able to plant a completely different kind and style of church than those entities which were routinely reduced to a building and a budget instead of a people of God on fire for God anywhere and everywhere. Finally, I see a task that runs much deeper than our mere populating of heaven with our escape rafts, but rather a set of nations or peoples which have been so discipled that they are, as nations, fully obedient to Christ, as he himself said, and inferred elsewhere, over two thousand years ago (Matt 28:18–20; Rev 21:24–26; Gen 49:10; Rom 16:25–26).

As the missional body of Christ learns through the arduous work of understanding our cultural paradigms of evil, and then interprets Scripture to be speaking to *all* of these views of reality, we may find an unprecedented level of response to what is then, truly good news! If the primary source of daily worry or cultural uncertainty is not guilt but shame or fear of the unseen, which are all, clearly biblical frameworks for the redemptive work of Christ, then will we not see an unrivaled response to the more comprehensive, redeeming work of our Lord?

References

Benedict, Ruth. 1954. *The chrysanthemum and the sword*. New York: Meridian Books.

Brown, Brene. 2012. *TED talks*. https://www.ted.com/talks/brene_brown_listening_to_shame?language=en.

Crouch, Andy. 2015. "The good news about social media: Social media is leaving us more ashamed than ever—and more ready to hear the gospel." *Christianity Today*, March, 32–41.

Eastman, Blake. n.d. "How much of communication is really nonverbal?" http://www.nonverbalgroup.com/2011/08/how-much-of-communication-is-really-nonverbal.

Francis, Glen. 1992. "The gospel for sin/shame-based society." *Taiwan Mission Quarterly 2*, no. 2 (October): 5-16.

Georges, Jayson. 2014. *The 3D gospel: ministry in guilt, shame, and fear cultures.* Timē Press.

Hiebert, Paul. 1982. "The flaw of the excluded middle," *Missiology*, 10, no. 1 (January): 35-47.

Mantrat. 2006. "German coastguard sinking—Learn English commercial." https://www.youtube.com/watch?v=gmOTpIVxji8.

Mischke, Werner. 2015. *The global gospel: Achieving missional impact in our multicultural world.* Scottsdale, AZ: Mission ONE.

Muller, Roland. 2000. *Honor and shame: Unlocking the door.* Philadelphia, PA: Xlibris Corporation.

Tennent, Timothy. 2007. *Theology in the context of world Christianity: How the global church is influencing the way we think about and discuss theology.* Grand Rapids, MI: Zondervan.

Winter, Ralph. 2015. "A third reformation? Movements of the Holy Spirit beyond Christendom." In *Understanding insider movements: Disciples of Jesus within diverse religious communities*, edited by Harley Talman and John Jay Travis. Pasadena, CA: William Carey Library.

Wu, Jackson. 2012. *Saving God's face: A Chinese contextualization of salvation through honor and shame.* Pasadena, CA: William Carey Library.

3
"They Don't Feel Guilty!?!"
BIBLICAL ETHICS AND MORALITY IN HONOR-SHAME CULTURES

Jayson Georges

> *"Without a sense of honor in men,*
> *all society and civilization would instantly break*
> *down and become impossible."*
> *~Ku Hung Ming, Chinese scholar*

Western ethics dismisses the cultural values of honor and shame as morally inferior. Contemporary philosopher Margaret Visser notes, "The civilizations of the West have striven hard and consciously for two thousand years and more to liberate themselves from the thrall of honour and shame . . . We accepted in their place a moral system where guilt and forgiveness are supposed to replace honour and shame" (2005, 41). Western missionaries and theologians follow this pattern, often unknowingly, when communicating a guilt-based moral paradigm that is foreign to "honor-shame cultures."

However, Christians in majority world contexts need not pivot from shame-based morality to a guilt-based morality. The Christian life can be lived within the framework of honor-shame values. Indeed, Christians can follow Jesus, embody kingdom truth, and live morally within an honor-shame context by transforming their honor code in light of God's true honor. To develop a biblical morality for honor-shame cultures, we draw from anthropology, philosophy, neurology, and theology. This paper will examine Paul's strategy for moral change in 1 Corinthians as a case study of honor-centric ethics, then conclude with practical implications for ministry.

Our objective is not to replace guilt with shame in Christian morality, but to put them on equal ground. We seek to balance the scale, not tip it. But considering how heavily weighted western thought is in favor of guilt-based morality, reaching a biblical equilibrium requires significant pushing on one end and pulling on the other.

DAVID'S SHAMEFUL SIN

Why was it wrong for David to sleep with Bathsheba? The story concludes, "But the thing David had done displeased the Lord" (2 Sam 11:27b). But exactly how did it displease God? On what basis was David's action sinful? This questioning is more than philosophical pedantry, but an inquiry into the foundations of morality and ethics. Asking "why was it wrong?" offers a portal into the broader conversation of how cultures define right and wrong. The story of David's adultery points toward a biblical morality for honor-shame cultures.

The typical western reading of David's adultery interprets it as a violation of the law—David sinned by breaking God's rules. The ESV Study Bible illustrates this legal perception of David's wrongdoing in its study note on 2 Sam 12:1–31:

> David started by breaking the tenth commandment (coveting, Ex 20:17), then the seventh (adultery, Ex 20:14), and then the sixth (murder, Ex 20:13), while the Lord silently watched his behavior. Here at last the Lord calls him to account for standing above the law . . . . Nathan apparently asks David to intervene in a legal matter. (The ESV Study Bible 2008)

Curiously, the text of 2 Samuel never mentions the Ten Commandments nor implies any legal violation. Nathan assumes the moral logic of honor and shame and frames David's behavior as fundamentally shameful. As a prophet of God, Nathan's divine oracles offer a portal into God's view of the situation.

Nathan's parable (2 Sam 12:1–6) introduces a rich man with many flocks and a poor man with one sheep. These descriptions introduce the social status of the two people, not simply their material wealth. A rich person with very many flocks would have functioned as a revered patron providing for the needs of others, a person commanding significant honor.

"Now a traveler came to the rich man, but the rich man refrained from taking one of his own sheep or cattle to prepare a meal for the traveler who had come to him" (v. 4). The rich man was inhospitable and ungenerous—a cardinal sin within collectivistic societies. The thought of a rich person not butchering a sheep or goat for a distant traveler is a disgrace. David immediately abhors such a shameless violation of social customs, implicitly affirming the honor-shame logic of Nathan's parable.

Nathan's critique follows the common prophetic pattern wherein God compares sinful Israel to shameful members of society (e.g., adulterers and harlots, cf. Jer 3; Ezek 16; Hos 1–3), not guilty felons or delinquents per se.

David's own shame was notable, but more significant was how David shamed God. Twice the story states David action's "despised" God (v. 9, 10). Nathan then says David "utterly scorned" the Lord (v. 14). David's actions were wrong because they failed to honor YHWH as God. David's actions disgraced and scorned God (cf. Rom 2:23).

Nathan asks rhetorically, "Why have you *despised* the word of the Lord, to do what is evil in the eyes of the Lord?" (v. 9). Here "the word of the Lord" does not refer to the Bible, the law, or to legal commandments, as modern literates might assume. Rather, the preceding verses indicate "word of the Lord" is the historic promise God made to David in 2 Samuel 7:4ff—the covenantal relationship God initiated with David to make him a great king with a royal dynasty, the oath God pledged to fulfill (cf. Rom 9:6).

God offered to be David's patron who would save and exalt David (2 Sam 7:9–16), in exchange for praise and loyalty from David (2 Sam 7:18–29). Thus, 2 Samuel 12:7–8 lists God's benefactions to prove he was indeed faithful to honor David with power, salvation from Saul, wives, and rulership. In fact, God would have added more if that were too little. In other words, God was not some tight-fisted, rich person who shamefully refused to share with others (à la David!), but a generous patron. David's actions despised God's covenantal promises and suggested God was incapable of keeping his word. David is a disloyal client to the generous patron, an insult of grave proportions.

In verse 10, we again read, "you have despised the Lord." The language intensifies in verse 14—"By doing this you have shown *utter contempt* for the Lord" (emphasis added). David's actions "*utterly scorned*" God (NRSV). David's sin was foremost against God and his honor. David despised God's name by dismissing God's promise. David broke covenant with God, bringing shame upon both parties.

The next verses (2 Sam 12:11–14) predict the disgraceful consequences of David's shameful behavior—his own disloyal sons would lead a mutiny and neighbors would sleep with David's wives in broad daylight (cf. 2 Sam 16:22). God uses David's family, typically the source of one's honor, to bring about his shame. David will face public shame because he was a shameful person who despised God. This story illustrates how honor-shame cultures, such as those of the Bible, define ethics and point Christians toward a biblical morality for honor-shame cultures.

COMPARING GUILT-BASED AND SHAME-BASED MORALITY

In the 20th century, the labels "guilt" and "shame" became conventional designations for comparing tacit systems of social control. To help western militaries understand the Japanese mindset during World War II, anthropologist Ruth Benedict popularized the notion of "shame-based" and "guilt-based" cultures (Benedict 1946). This etic binary, though plagued with inherent challenges, has proven to be helpful for contrasting ethical approaches in western and majority world cultures (cf. Creighton 1990). Noting the basic features and assumptions of each moral system does not suggest either/or essentialistic categories. Rather, guilt and shame are endpoints on a broad spectrum.

In Buddhist contexts, shame is the primary, though not exclusive, moral emotional governing social behavior. According to 215 respondents from www.TheCultureTest.com, countries with a Buddhist majority are 16% guilt-oriented, 57% shame-oriented, and 27% fear-oriented. This tentative data suggests a key role for honor and shame in practicing Christian missiology in Buddhist contexts.

Guilt-based morality bases notions of right and wrong on laws and rules. The law ensures individual rights and one's personal freedom. The legal system defines the range of acceptable behaviors. Maturity is measured by the degree to which one independently observes such laws. A law-abiding citizen does right, regardless of social pressure or context. People are socialized to feel guilty for transgressing a pre-defined wrong. A guilty conscience fears the threat of punishment or retribution for committing negative acts.

In shame-based cultures, the stigma of social disapproval and rejection shapes behavior. Shame is triggered by the threat of being exposed for failures or flaws. The external sanction of public opinion ensures conformity (Cunningham 2013, 54). Shame is not simply the painful fear of exclusion; it is also a healthy sense of modesty and social regard. Shame can function as a healthy warning system. However, the difference between guilt and shame cultures goes beyond people's subjective response to sin. The two systems hold contrasting values and philosophical foundations. The emotions of guilt and shame each function within a unique socio-cultural-moral ecosystem, each with particular beliefs and behaviors deemed right. Thus, the very definition of wrongdoing differs in the two cultural systems. People experience sin differently because cultures perceive sin differently.

The European Enlightenment dissected a world governed by rules and patterns. Scientists studied the laws of nature, while philosophers examined the laws of morality (Richards and O'Brien 2012, 157–61). In 1785, philosopher Immanuel Kant wrote *Grounding for the Metaphysics of Morality* to explain how people should morally act. Kant based morality on his famous "categorical imperative"—an unconditional requirement that must always be obeyed, a sort of universal law of right and wrong for all circumstances. This notion that rules apply 100 percent of the time to 100 percent of the people remains common in western Christianity. Consequently, biblical morality becomes "discerning God's moral standard." The discipline of ethics is the study of the specific instructions from God (The ESV Study Bible 2008, 2536). This *a*relational and *a*communal approach to ethics echoes enlightenment thinking.

In guilt-based moral systems, justice reigns supreme. English speakers claim axiomatically, "Justice must be served," referring to a universal moral law to which all humans must submit. According to such a moral logic, even the Creator must observe its dictates to remain "just and holy," since "only an unrighteous judge lets a crime go unpunished." In such a view, immorality violates universal moral laws and punishment absolves guilt.

Shame-based cultures employ a different moral logic. Being collectivistic, they base notions of right and wrong on communal relationships and roles. Honor-shame cultures define morality relationally and concretely, not legally or abstractly. In short, what is best for the relationship is morally right; what brings shame is wrong.

Social reality is defined and governed by relationships, not rules. Because behavior is guided by sensitivity to dynamic social roles (and not a fixed inner autonomy), acceptable behavior depends upon the context. Much to the vexation of westerners, an honor-based ethic allows two contradictory actions to be simultaneously right. This is exactly what we find in Romans 14:5–6, "The one who eats, eats in honor of the Lord, since he gives thanks to God, while the one who abstains, abstains in honor of the Lord and gives thanks to God" (ESV). Also, an action can be wrong in one context (Rev 2:20) yet permissible in another (1 Cor 8:8).

These dynamics are evident in Japanese morality, which "tends to judge the value of an act in a situational context based on its impact on significant relationships" (Creighton 1990, 297). Japanese ethics is shaped by *giri* (duty, obligation), a code of behavior that varies depending on the circumstances and depending on those involved. So they apologize not for legal violations but for *machigai*, which literally means "misplacement in context" (Creighton 1990, 297).

This "situational" ethic is not just pragmatic face-saving, but the morally right thing to do. Sin could be viewed as not functioning properly in a relationship or community. Honor and shame carry essential moral meaning. For the Confucian philosopher Ruiping Fan, "honor, disgrace, and shame are relational moral concepts" (Fan 2010, 145). When the Levites despise and dishonor God with their defective sacrifices, God asks of them, "Is that not wrong [ESV, evil]?" (Mal 1:6–8). Shaming is a moral evil. Honor and shame are not simply negative emotions or social sanctions (as per psychology or anthropology), but moral values promoting social good and virtue.

This contextual ethic in honor-shame cultures can cause westerners to condemn others as "immoral" or "morally loose." This leads to presumptuous and ethnocentric descriptions, such as "Shame cultures don't believe in sin," or "They don't have a conscience." Ghanaian theologian Kwame Bediako comments,

> Some suggest that ours [Ghanaian] is a 'shame culture' and not a 'guilt culture', on the grounds that public acceptance determines morality, and consequently a 'sense of sin' is said to be absent.

> However, in our [African] tradition, the essence of sin is in its being an antisocial act. This makes sin basically injury to the interests of another person and damage to the collective life of the group. (Bediako 2004, 26)

In this framework, sin fails to fulfill relational obligations; it breaks covenant with both humans and God. As seen in 2 Samuel 12, shame is more than an emotional response to sin; it is also a public and objective basis for sin itself.

Western theologians and missionaries have regrettably viewed shame as bad and guilt as good. To make way for a biblical morality for honor-shame cultures we must examine these two misleading assumption.

FOUR SHORTCOMINGS OF GUILT-BASED MORALITY

A guilt-based ethical approach can have limited moral effectiveness. This is a consequence of four shortcomings. These limitations do not invalidate such an ethical approach as being "unbiblical" as a whole; all perspectives have limitations.

First, guilt-based morality often presents retributive punishment as the just solution (and deterrent) for wrongdoing. However, the western legal system's punitive approach to wrongdoing "deepens society wounds and conflicts rather than contributes to healing or peace" (Zehr 2015, 2). An obligation to dispense punishment as demanded by justice dis-integrates communities and relationships, and such alienation increases recidivism by exacerbating shame (Braithwaite 1989). "Our application of justice norms have justified shocking cruelty and continue to do so" (Demetriou 2015b). Solitary confinement and the death penalty are but two examples of such horrendously violent, yet legalized ostracism (Goode 2015; Oppenheimer 2015). Research has demonstrated that such punitive responses to wrongdoing actually compounds human brokenness by increasing shame and disconnection (Hari 2015).

Second, the individualism inherent in guilt cultures can lead to immorality. When recently teaching a class in Chad, Africa, I noted the "individualistic" and "collectivistic" tendencies of various cultures. As an example, I explained how young Americans make significant decisions (i.e., university, spouse, career, etc.) independently of family. One Chadian then surmised, "Well then there must be all kinds of immorality and debauchery in America! For without family, how can people know how to choose the right behavior?"

For this Chadian Christian leader, defining ethics apart from community was simply inconceivable. How could individuals possibly know right from wrong by themselves when the heart is full of sin and deceit? The focus on individual rights and law-observance gives little weight to relationships or community, the very definition of sin for group-oriented contexts. From an honor-shame perspective, the individualistic values of self-reliance, absolute honestly, and equality can be the antisocial vices of stinginess, humiliation, and disrespect. The individualistic values of guilt cultures are not always Christian virtues.

Third, rules and laws rarely induce moral change. From 2002–2010, the United States spent $904 million in Afghanistan funding the "rule of law and justice" to "develop effective justice sector institutions" (Sun Wyler and Katzman 2010). The current situation in Afghanistan suggests this legal approach has not positively influenced society in that country. This is reflected in the New York Times headline, "In Spite of the Law, Afghan 'Honor Killings' of Women Continue" (Nordland 2014). Laws reflect values, but are incapable of changing values (Freeman 2015). Laws can define right behavior but do not produce right behavior. Certainly, Christians can agree on this point (Rom 3:20). Being weakened by human flesh, the law is powerless to save from sin and death (Rom 8:23). After all, regulations "lack any value in restraining sensual indulgence" (Col 2:23).

Four, Dietrich Bonhoeffer critiqued the internal conscience and guilt as idolatrous in his *Ethics*. To summarize Bonhoeffer, the human conscience is "concerned not with man's relation to God and to other men, but with man's relation to himself" (1995, 28–29). Conscience pretends to be the voice of God defining morality. When our internal conscience becomes the new origin of good and evil, "man has become judge over God and men, just as he is judge over himself" (ibid). Moreover, since rules and laws are always defined as either "permitted" or "forbidden" (with no positive commandment), Bonhoeffer notes how for the conscience, what is "permitted is identical with good, and conscience does not register the fact, that even in this, man is in a state of disunion with his origin (God). It follows from this also that conscience does not, like shame, embrace the whole of life; it reacts only to certain definite actions" (ibid).

Bonhoeffer likely lost faith in the moral role of the conscience as he witnessed the Nazi regime hijack the German Protestant Church with minimal resistance. Perhaps, the internal conscience should not be equated with "God's law on our hearts," but a duplicitous and corrupt voice needing to be checked by the community (cf. Prov 16:2; Titus 1:15).

These four limitations do not invalidate guilt-based morality. Yet, they do call for a balanced evaluation. Guilt can be good, but it may not always be the best way to frame morality. A shame-based morality can address these gaps. But unfortunately, honor and shame are often dismissed as inferior moral values in guilt-oriented societies.

FALSE STEREOTYPES OF SHAME-BASED MORALITY

People educated in western contexts inherit a long tradition of viewing honor-shame cultures as morally degenerate and socially inferior. This is a vestige of social Darwinism trumpeted as "progressivism" (Creighton 1990). In this western tradition, the experience of shame governs morality only in pre-civilized contexts, which have yet to graduate up to more rational models based on individual moral autonomy. The field of psychology generally views the private emotions of guilt as helpful and shame as hurtful (Tangney and Dearing 2002). This biased perspective bleeds into anthropological evaluations of public social sanctions. Upon reviewing the literature on shame, David Augsburger states, "The negative definition and evaluation of shame is also virtually unanimous among western theologians and missionaries" (Augsburger 1986, 114).

The positive counterpart of shame—that is, honor—bears an equally poor reputation. Western culture associates honor with immaturity, pride, selfishness, and even blasphemy. For example, C.S. Lewis, in his sermon "The Weight of Glory," observes the honorific aspects of biblical salvation, then personally acknowledges, "All this makes no immediate appeal to me at all, and in that respect I fancy I am a typical modern. Glory suggests two ideas to me, of which one seems wicked and the other ridiculous" (Lewis 2001). Popular discourse associates honor with its repulsive aspects (i.e., traditionalism, oppression, and violence) and overlooks the positive dimensions (i.e., community, generosity, or hospitality). Westerners hold a deep philosophical aversion to honor. We are "face-blind" and "face-adverse" (Flanders 2011)—a rather dangerous cocktail.

The western repulsion to honor and shame then assumes that guilt-based cultures are best suited for reflecting the values and reality of God's kingdom. Jonathon Sacks, former chief rabbi of England, reflects this sentiment when distinguishing "between shame cultures, like ancient Greece, and guilt cultures like Judaism and Christianity" (2014). Claiming Christianity is a "guilt culture" ignores the moral vision of first-century Christianity and taints our missiological approaches with cultural biases.

Even more revealing is the implicit bias toward a law-based morality coded into western thought and theology. Examples of such a bias include: prioritizing legal conceptual metaphors in theological discourse as the most epistemologically plausible (Ott 2013), defining justice as primarily retributive (Marshall 2001), viewing sin in terms of guilt and then shame as a byproduct or subset of that guilt, and making prejudiced dichotomies such as "guilt is objective; shame is subjective" or "guilt is before God; shame is before humanity."

There has been a regrettable absence of reflection upon honor in nineteenth and twentieth century philosophical discourse (Sessions 2010). Western scholarship excused honor from the roundtable of moral discussion and wrote its obituary. This demise of honor and shame as moral values affects western missiology (Mischke 2015), wherein honor-shame cultures become inferior vessels not worthy of housing Christian truth and righteousness. But change is in the air.

A stream of twenty-first century honor apologists, both academic and popular, are rehabilitating honor in philosophical discourse (Sessions 2010; Oprisko 2012; Deonna, Rodogno, and Teroni 2011; Cunningham 2013; Olsthoorn 2015; Bagby 2009; Jacquet 2015; Appiah 2010; Demetriou 2015a; Fan 2010). Titles like *Modern Honor*, *Honor For Us* and *The Honor Code: How Moral Revolutions Happen* indicate an increasingly positive view of honor among philosophers. Current discussions are suggesting honor and shame can be redemptive moral values. Even though "[h]onor is purportedly archaic, primitive, violent, patriarchal, vain, superficial, discriminatory, conformist, and even silly" in traditional western discourse, philosophers are noting "[w]e can ignore or banish honor only at our peril. . . . We need a sense of honor, one duly cleansed of the undeniable ills of honor's past" (Cunningham 2013, 3).

BIOLOGICAL ROOTS FOR HONOR AND SHAME

C.S. Lewis identified glory as an essential component of being human. The pursuit of honor is not some cultural abnormality or byproduct of sin.

> Glory, as Christianity teaches me to hope for it, turns out to satisfy my original desire and indeed to reveal an element in that desire which I had not noticed . . . Apparently, then, our lifelong nostalgia, our longing to be reunited with something in the universe from which we now feel cut off, to be on the inside of some door which we have always seen from the outside is no mere neurotic fancy, but the truest index of our real situation. And to be at last summoned inside would be both glory and honour beyond our merits and also the healing of that old ache. (Lewis 2001, 8)

Recent scientific research has connected this yearning for honor to biological realities. The pursuit of honor and avoidance of shame appears hardwired into the human brain for a biological purpose. With the discovery of mirror neurons, scientists see that all humans "have an inborn desire to be treated well because we are psychologically programmed to believe that our lives are dependent on it" (Hicks 2011, 6). Conversely, our bodies instinctively avoid shame. The limbic system within our brain senses social threats (i.e. shame) the same way as physical threats. Both types of imminent danger trigger the same self-preservation instincts. Physical pain and social pain share a common neural basis and the same computational mechanisms of the brain (Eisenberger and Lieberman 2004; Williams, Forgas, and von Hippel 2005).

Christian neuropsychiatrist Curt Thompson notes how shame disrupts and dis-integrates connections and communication between various parts of the human brain. Shame leads "to either rigid or chaotic states of mind and behavior, lived out intra- and interpersonally" (Thompson 2015, 46). Morality must account for these core neurological features of the human experience, lest it not correspond to physical reality.

Secularists interpret the biological proclivities toward honor and aversion from shame as part of our "evolutionary roots." Christians however explain this same reality theologically—people were created in the image of the honor-seeking God. Honor is an intrinsic aspect of our humanness.

God crowned humankind with glory and honor and made them rulers with everything under their feet (Ps 8). God's original creation was defined by an absence of shame—"Adam and his wife were both naked, and they felt no shame" (Gen 2:25). The realities of honor and shame in humans date back to creation. In fact, our experiences of shame testify to the ontological reality of human honor (Lichtenwalter 2014, 124). Shame bears prophetic witness to the honorable state God originally bestowed. Shame is "a voice from our true self" (Smedes 1993, 31).

These neurological and existential realities do not sanction every human pursuit of honor as morally good. After Genesis 3 the powers of sin and death pervert honor-shame dynamics in the human family. People lacking the glory of God idolatrously construct honor through false cultural systems (Jewett 1997, cf. Gen 11; Rom 1–2). Christian morality thus involves a transformation, or restoration, of honor.

REFORMING THE HONOR CODE

In *The Honor Code: How Moral Revolutions Happen*, Princeton philosophy professor Anthony Appiah suggests honor and shame are the best weapons for inducing profound social change for good (2010). He notes the historic practices of Chinese footbinding, gentlemen's dueling in England, and trans-Atlantic slave trading, though being illegal and morally wrong, ceased only when people viewed those actions as shameful and dishonorable. Confucius likewise stated, "Guide them by laws, keep them in line with punishments, and they will avoid wrongdoing but will have no sense of honor and shame. Lead them with virtue and regulate them by rites, and they will have a sense of shame and, moreover, set themselves right" (Analects 2:3). Social practices and morality are transformed when existing honor codes change. The catchy slogan "There is no honor in honor killings" is an example of this approach.

To change behavior, change what behavior is deemed honorable or shameful. Reform the honor code according to true honor. People's idea of what is honorable and shameful must be aligned with God's own code of honor. 1 Peter 4:14–15 is a straightforward example, "If you are insulted because of the name of Christ, you are blessed . . . if you suffer as a Christian, do not be ashamed, but praise God that you bear that name." Enduring persecution is honorable, not shameful.

This new honor is not a social construct, but grounded in the reality and experience of God. He alone is the essence, source, and standard of true honor. Morally acceptable behavior reflects God's honorable character. "And when God is the highest definition of that honor, we are faced with an impressive standard for honor. . . . This kind of honor is worthy of moral pursuit. It is a pivotal value that tends the heart toward the highest good—honoring God" (Lichtenwalter 2014, 121).

Christian discipleship bears witness to an alternative code of honor rooted in an alternative source of honor—God himself. The ministry of Jesus reveals God's true and eternal honor. The apostles instructed early Christians how to embody Christ's honor in a variety of contexts. God has given Christians great honor, so "[t]hey should not let it be besmirched. Rather, they should uphold this honor in the way they live" (Gosnell 2006). This involves esteeming the name and glory of God, conducting ourselves in an honorable manner (2 Tim 2:20–21; 1 Pet 2:12), and honoring others (Rom 12:10, 13:7; 1 Cor 12:23; 1 Pet 2:17). Living out God's honor code means upholding and displaying divine honor in all spheres and circumstances. We are to live in a manner worthy of God (Eph 4:1; Phil 1:27; Col 1:10; 1 Thess 2:12).

The problem with an unsanctified conscience is not foremost the absence of guilt, but the incorrect attribution of shame and honor. A redeemed honor code involves sensing shame before God for dishonoring him as disloyal children, for missing the target of God's glory (Rom 3:23). A believer's standard for righteousness is not an abstract moral code, but the honor of God. The conviction of the Holy Spirit changes from misplaced shame into well-placed shame (Harper 2013; Piper 2012). According to Hebrews 13:18, a "clear conscience" is not marked by legal innocence, but a "desire to live honorably in every way." Spiritual maturity is when one's emotional experiences of honor and shame accord with the divine realties of honor and shame (cf. Ezek 16:63; Mal 1:6, 2:2).

Contemporary research by cross-cultural sociologists corroborates the importance of shame in moral formation. Non-western cultures typically view shame as a helpful and appropriate response to failure (Wong and Tsai 2007, 216). Shame is a positive force causing people to try their best and to repair fractured relationships (ibid). Chinese philosopher Mencius said, "Man cannot live without shame. A sense of shame is the beginning of integrity" (Boutlier 2014).

The biblical honor code must not be reduced to a trite "ignoring culture and obeying God." Rather, biblical ethics requires believers to live out an honoring life in community. This dynamic is underappreciated in moral systems emphasizing individual rights and legal requirements. Biblical ethics involves conduct that is honorable before God and before people (especially or Christians living as a religious minority). For example, Jesus grew "in *charis* [i.e., favor, grace] with God and people" (Luke 2:52, cf. Prov 3:3–4) and Paul took pains "to do what is *kalos* [i.e., beautiful, proper, good], not only in the eyes of the Lord but also in the eyes of others" (2 Cor 8:21). In discussing Christians' response to funeral rites among Tai-Kadai Theravada Buddhist culture, one missionary emphasizes, "if Christians living in Southeast Asia are going to faithfully honor God, they will need to understand how to live honorably in their local community" (Whitsett 2014).

The dichotomy between God's honor and culture's honor gives a false either/or appearance to morality. A fresh classification with three types of honor offers a nuanced moral framework. Bad honor comes at the expense of others' shame (e.g., insults, violence, oppression, etc.). Good honor is a part of God's common grace for people who live wisely and respect others (Prov 12:8, 13:18, 15:33, 21:21, 22:4, 27:18). These virtues are consistent with God's honor standard. Eternal honor is ascribed only by God through Christ's atoning death (Ezek 16:14; John 5:44, 17:22; Rom 8:17; 2 Thes 1:12, 2:14). So Christians, being anchored in eternal honor, reject the bad honor and live out the patterns of good honor in this age. Thus, Christians live honorably before God and people.

THE HONOR-ETHICS OF I CORINTHIANS

This honor-shame approach to Christian morality integrates worship, ethics, theology, and community. Because honor and shame are innately social and cooperate realities, an honor-centric morality prioritizes relational harmony and communal edification, as seen in Pauline theology. "Paul's redefinition of honor thus gives prestige to such traits that promote social cohesion and mutual construction" (Barclay 2014, 313). "For [Paul], moral action is never a matter of an isolated actor choosing from among a variety of abstract ideas on the basis of how inherently "good" or "evil" each may be. Instead it is always a matter of choosing and doing what is good for the brother and what will upbuild the whole community of brethren" (Furnish 2009, 233). First Corinthians offers an apostolic case study of an honor-centric ethic.

The formation of God's covenant community is Paul's moral vision and ethical *telos*. So when certain Corinthians approach the issue of idol-meat as an individual right, Paul reframes it as a matter of community construction (1 Cor 8). Richard Hays notes

> The ethical norm, then, is not given in the form of a predetermined rule or set of rules for conduct; rather, the right action must be discerned on the basis of a Christological paradigm, with a view to the need of the community and the community's identity as God's covenant people. (1994, 37)

Here is Paul's dictum—"'All things are lawful,' but not all things are helpful. 'All things are lawful,' but not all things build up" (1 Cor 10:23 ESV). Paul affirms the plausibility of their claim, while noting the shortcomings of morality based on personal rights and lawfulness. A Christian may be right, but divisive and dishonoring. So our behavior should be informed by proper honor, "the parts that we think are less honorable we treat with special honor . . . But God has put the body together, giving greater honor to the parts that lacked it, so that there should be no division in the body" (1 Cor 12:23–25).

Paul's moral instructions to the Corinthian community are not rules defined by the Old Testament Torah, Roman law, or the upholding of universal moral justice. They are more akin to guardrails keeping Christians on the path toward relationships, community, and honor. "Whatever you do, do it all for the glory of God" (1 Cor 10:31). For Paul, glorifying God meant giving no offense to others and striving to please all (1 Cor 10:32). Shaming, demoting, or offending someone for whom Christ died nullifies God's work. Paul's teachings on head coverings in 1 Cor 11:2–16 offers another example of honor-centric ethics. Note the repeated honor-shame language. Every man who prays "with their head covered dishonors his head" (v. 4) "since he is the image and glory of God" (v. 7), and long hair "is a disgrace to him" (v. 14).

The women who prays "with her head uncovered dishonors her head" (v. 5), and since a woman's long hair "is her glory" (v. 15) "it is a disgrace for a woman to have her hair cut off or her head shaved" (v. 6). What is honorable is right; what is shameful is wrong. In this complicated passage, Paul appears to be denouncing the Greco-Roman liturgical practice of male head coverings because they reflected a cultic custom in the pagan temples and indicated hierarchical social prominence. But Paul mandates female head coverings as social symbols of distinct gender boundaries, moral propriety, and sexual modesty (Finney 2010). Paul does not discard honor and shame as moral rubrics, but reframes them for God's community in Corinth.

MINISTRY APPLICATIONS

The process of reforming honor codes begins at the earliest stages of interactions with people. Christians must consider how our professional activities, personal relationships, and even stories (Georges 2015) purposefully communicate true honor to people.

Your response to people during times of sin and conflict can also transform their honor code. Amidst these shame-inducing realities of life, embody God's gracious and welcoming honor. The western approach to conflict resolution is often shame-less. It prioritizes problems over people and confronts sin with little regard for face. Airing dirty laundry in the front yard is as wrong as sweeping the dirt under the carpet. Practicing restorative justice can help us mend broken relationships, form genuine community, and reintegrate the shamed (Gal 6:1–2). As we see in the life of Jesus, transforming honor codes is as simple, yet profound, as sharing a common table. Through these practices, we conduct ourselves in an honorable manner and rewrite destructive honor codes, dismantling the power and reality of illegitimate shame.

In evangelism, the proclamation of the gospel challenges traditional notions of honor and shame. The gospel declares the royal reign of God's resurrected messiah—the most shamed has become the most honored. The response required for participating in God's new honored community involves redirecting loyalty and honor toward God. Repentance is an "honor choice." A person with *pistos* grants exclusive allegiance to Jesus, not intellectual ascent to propositions. The New Testament term *pistos*—commonly (mis)translated as "faith"—involves loyalty and faithfulness, the obligations of a client to a generous patron (Crook 2004; deSilva 2000). Biblical conversion is transference of allegiance from one group to another, namely God and his community. A person changes their "court of reputation"—the group whose opinions and evaluations matter. Identity and status is not derived from socio-cultural systems of honor-accrual like kinship or ethnicity, but from participation in God's community and reception of God's honor.

This framework for salvation, characterized by honor-shame values, directly impacts a person's honor code. One cannot follow Jesus without reforming their honor code. In contrast, common evangelistic presentations emphasizing legal aspects of salvation are amoral. Simply "asking God for forgiveness" does not innately require new values, a new code of honor, a transfer of allegiance, nor a relational commitment. Western theology separates what God joined together—salvation and morality, evangelism and discipleship. Merely inserting the words "honor" and "shame" into evangelistic presentations does not challenge a person's honor code. Rather, evangelism should reconceive our problem as objective shame before God and reimage the nature of God's solution according to the moral values of honor-shame cultures (Georges and Baker 2016).

CONCLUSION

This essay pulled insights from multiple fields to explain the mechanics of ethics and moral change in honor-shame cultures.

But ultimately, the only sure way for ensuring moral change and ethical living is God's salvation.

Sin induces shame, and shame catalyzes more sin. The sinful heart plagued with shame (Gen 3) humiliates others (Gen 4) or exalts oneself (Gen 11). However, only God can save us from this tragic predicament (Gen 12).

God not only reveals a new honor code, he imputes a new honor (Ezek 16:14; John 17:22; 2 Thess 1:12). This divine honor frees us from cultural practices of status competition and face management. Having received God's honor, we extend it to others (Rom 15:7). God's honor enables us to resist false shame, honor others, and glorify him in all of life.[1]

References

Appiah, Anthony. 2010. *The honor code: How moral revolutions happen*. New York: W.W. Norton.

Augsburger, David. 1986. *Pastoral counseling across cultures*. Philadelphia, PA: The Westminster Press.

Bagby, Laurie M. Johnson. 2009. *Thomas Hobbes: Turning point for honor*. Lanham, MD: Lexington Books.

Barclay, John. 2014. "Grace and the countercultural reckoning of worth: Community construction of Galatians 5–6." In *Galatians and Christian theology: Justification, the gospel, and ethics in Paul's letter*, edited by N. T. Wright, Mark W. Elliott, Scott J. Hafemann, and John Frederick, 306–17. Grand Rapids, MI: Baker Academic.

Bediako, Kwame. 2004. *Jesus and the gospel in Africa: History and experience*. New York: Orbis Books.

---

1. A special thanks to Sandra Freeman, Werner Mischke, and Jackson Wu for their feedback on this article. Any shortcomings in this article remain entirely my own.

Benedict, Ruth. 1946. *The chrysanthemum and the sword: Patterns of Japanese culture*. Cambridge, MA: The Riverside Press.

Bonhoeffer, Dietrich. 1995. *Ethics*. New York: Touchstone.

Boutlier, Amanda. 2014. "Response to 'Healthy dose of shame' by Bootsy." Jan 10, 2014. http://breakingbootsy.blogspot.com/2014/01/do-fat-people-need-healthy-dose-of-shame.html.

Braithwaite, John. 1989. *Crime, shame and reintegration*. Cambridge and New York: Cambridge University Press.

Creighton, Millie R. 1990. "Revisiting shame and guilt cultures: A forty-year pilgrimage." *Ethos* 18 (3): 279–307.

Crook, Zeba A. 2004. *Reconceptualising conversion: Patronage, loyalty, and conversion in the religions of the ancient Mediterranean*. Berlin and New York: De Gruyter.

Cunningham, Anthony. 2013. *Modern honor: A philosophical defense*. New York: Routledge.

Demetriou, Dan. 2015a. "Honor ethics." *Honor ethics*. http://honorethics.org/.

———. 2015b. "Pinker on honor." *Honor ethics*. http://honorethics.org/2015/06/09/pinker-on-honor/.

Deonna, Julien A., Raffaele Rodogno, and Fabrice Teroni. 2011. *In defense of shame: The faces of an emotion*. Oxford and New York: Oxford University Press.

deSilva, David. 2000. *Honor, patronage, kinship & purity: Unlocking New Testament culture*. Downers Grove, IL: InterVarsity Press.

———. 1998. "Let the one who claims honor establish that claim in the Lord: Honor discourse in the Corinthian correspondence." *Biblical Theology Bulletin* 28 (2): 61–74.

Eisenberger, Naomi, and Matthew Lieberman. 2004. "Why it hurts to be left out: The neurocognitive overlap between physical pain and social pain." *Trends in cognitive sciences* 8 (7): 294–300.

Elliott, John H. 1995. "Disgraced yet graced: The Gospel according to 1 Peter in the key of honor and shame." *Biblical Theology Bulletin: A Journal of Bible and Theology* 25 (4): 166–78.

Fan, Ruiping. 2010. *Reconstructionist Confucianism: Rethinking morality after the west*. New York: Springer.

Finney, Mark. 2010. "Honour, head-coverings and headship: 1 Corinthians 11:2–16 in its social context." *Journal for the Study of the New Testament* 33 (1): 31–58.

Flanders, Christopher L. 2011. *About face: Rethinking face for 21st Century mission*. Eugene, OR: Wipf & Stock.

Freeman, Sandra. 2015. "At the edge of the Kalahari: Changing behaviour requires a change to the honour code." http://blog.zebrapost.net/2015/09/changing-behaviour-requires-change-to.html.

Furnish, Victor. 2009. *Theology and ethics in Paul*. Louisville, KY: Westminster John Knox Press.

Georges, Jayson. 2010. "From shame to honor: A theological reading of Romans for honor-shame contexts." *Missiology* 38 (3): 295–307.

———. 2015. "Reconstructing Central-Asian honor codes via orality." In *Beyond literate western contexts: Honor & shame and assessment of orality preference*, edited by Samuel E. Chiang and Grant Lovejoy. Hong Kong: International Orality Network.

Georges, Jayson, and Mark D. Baker. 2016. *Ministering in honor-shame cultures: Biblical foundations and practical essentials*. Downers Grove, IL: IVP Academic.

Goode, Erica. 2015. "Solitary confinement: Punished for life." *The New York Times*, August 3. http://www.nytimes.com/2015/08/04/health/solitary-confinement-mental-illness.html.

Gosnell, Peter W. 2006. "Honor and shame rhetoric as a unifying motif in Ephesians." *Bulletin for Biblical Research* 16 (1): 105–28.

Hari, Johann. 2015. *Chasing the scream: The first and last days of the War on Drugs*. New York: Bloomsbury USA.

Harper, Kyle. 2013. *From shame to sin: The Christian transformation of sexual morality in late Antiquity*. Cambridge, MA: Harvard University Press.

Hays, Richard. 1994. "Ecclesiology and ethics in 1 Corinthians." *Ex Auditu* 10: 31–43.

Hicks, Donna. 2011. *Dignity: The essential role it plays in resolving conflict*. New Haven: Yale University Press.

Jacquet, Jennifer. 2015. *Is shame necessary?: New uses for an old tool*. New York: Pantheon.

Jewett, Robert. 1997. "Honor and shame in the argument of Romans." In *Putting body & soul together: Essays in honor of Robin Scroggs*, edited by Virginia Wiles, Alexandra R. Brown, and Graydon F. Snyder. Valley Forge, PA: Trinity Press International.

Lewis, C. S. 2001. *The weight of glory*. San Francisco, CA: HarperOne.

Lichtenwalter, Larry L. 2014. "Toward the moral vision of honor and shame in biblical perspective: Worldview, identity, character." In *Shame & honor: Presenting biblical themes in shame & honor contexts*, edited by Bruce L. Bauer, 1–22. Berrien Springs, MI: Andrews University, Department of World Mission.

Marshall, Christopher D. 2001. *Beyond retribution: A New Testament vision for justice, crime, and punishment*. Grand Rapids, MI: Eerdmans.

Nordland, Rod. 2014. "In spite of the law, Afghan 'honor killings' of women continue." *The New York Times*, May 3. http://www.nytimes.com/2014/05/04/world/asia/in-spite-of-the-law-afghan-honor-killings-of-women-continue.html.

Olsthoorn, Peter. 2015. *Honor in political and moral philosophy*. Albany, NY: State University of New York Press.

Oppenheimer, Mark. 2015. "A Death Row inmate finds common ground with theologians." *The New York Times*, February 27. http://www.nytimes.com/2015/02/28/us/a-death-row-inmate-finds-common-ground-with-theologians.html.

Oprisko, Robert L. 2012. *Honor: A phenomenology*. New York: Routledge.

Ott, Craig. 2013. "The power of biblical metaphors for the contextualized communication of the gospel." *Missiology: An International Review* 42 (4): 357–74.

Piper, John. 2012. "Faith in future grace vs. misplaced shame." In *Future grace: The purifying power of the promises of God*. Colorado Springs, CO: Multnomah Books.

Richards, E. Randolph, and Brandon J. O'Brien. 2012. *Misreading scripture with western eyes: Removing cultural blinders to better understand the Bible*. Downer's Grove, IL: IVP Books.

Sessions, William Lad. 2010. *Honor for us: A philosophical analysis, interpretation and defense*. New York: Continuum.

Smedes, Lewis B. 1993. *Shame and grace: Healing the shame we don't deserve*. San Francisco: Harper.

Sun Wyler, Liana, and Kenneth Katzman. 2010. "Afghanistan: U.S. rule of law and justice sector assistance." *Washington D.C.: Congressional research service*. http://www.fas.org/sgp/crs/row/R41484.pdf.

Tangney, June Price, and Ronda L Dearing. 2002. *Shame and guilt*. New York: Guilford Press.

The ESV Study Bible. 2008. Wheaton, Ill: Crossway.

Thompson, Curt. 2015. *The soul of shame: Retelling the stories we believe about ourselves*. Downers Grove, IL: IVP Books.

Visser, Margaret. 2005. *Beyond fate*. Toronto: House of Anansi Press.

Whitsett, Gregory P. 2014. "Living in favor with God and man: Honorable Christian living in a Theravada Buddhist context." In *Shame & honor: Presenting biblical themes in shame & honor contexts*, edited by Bruce L. Bauer, 1–22. Andrews University, Berrien Springs, MI: Department of World Mission.

Williams, Kipling, Joseph Forgas, and William von Hippel, eds. 2005. *The social outcast: Ostracism, social exclusion, rejection, and bullying*. New York: Psychology Press.

Witherington, Ben. 1995. *Conflict and community in Corinth: Socio-rhetorical commentary on 1 and 2 Corinthians*. Grand Rapids, MI: Eerdmans.

Wu, Jackson. 2015. "Why the church lost 'face.'" *Mission Frontiers* 37:1.

Zehr, Howard. 2015. *The little book of restorative justice*. Intercourse, PA: Good Books.

PART TWO

COMMUNICATING IN FEAR, GUILT, AND SHAME CULTURES

*Let your face shine on your servant;
save me in your unfailing love.
Let me not be put to shame, Lord,
for I have cried out to you;
Psalm 31:16–17*

*I acknowledged my sin to you
and did not cover up my iniquity.
I said, 'I will confess
my transgressions to the Lord.'
And you forgave
the guilt of my sin.
Psalm 32:5*

*I sought the Lord, and he answered me;
he delivered me from all my fears.
Psalm 34:4*

4
Suitable Messages for Fear, Guilt, and Shame Buddhist Cultures

Alex G. Smith

Clash of cultures is normal and to be expected. For example, a western tourist is looking for the post office in Bangkok. He asks a Thai passer-by how to get there. The Thai politely gives him directions, but after meticulously following them, the foreigner does not reach the desired destination. He asks other Thai with similar results, until one knowledgeable Thai points him to the right direction. Not understanding Asian culture the westerner thinks "What liars these Thai are!" The Thai, however, tell him what they think he wants to hear, so that they don't lose face by revealing their ignorance. They feel potential shame if they do not know where their local post office is. The clash of the cultures of shame, fear, and guilt easily produces frustrations and misunderstandings, particularly between West and East. This results in cultural conflict as well as confusion in communication. Both are counterproductive to advancing acceptance of Christ's honored message among Buddhist peoples.

Serving in Thailand since the mid-1960s I was personally aware of Asian face-saving societies. But my first significant exposure to serious discussion on shame-orientation was in the mid-1970s through Lowell Noble's book *Naked and Not Ashamed* (1975). This was one of the earliest writings on shame. A second influence was Joseph Cooke's paper "The Gospel for Thai Ears." As a serious missionary I was seeking the most appropriate message to present to the Thai people in order to help them experience true enlightenment, liberty, and hope. Recognizing the intertwining of fear and shame among Thai Buddhists, I chose to emphasize a power-focused message, which is discussed later.

SEANET (a network for South, East, Southeast and North Asia) was launched in 1999. From its beginning, SEANET was concerned with effectively communicating the right Christian message in the right way, in order to produce people movements through church multiplication. At SEANET 2000 Steve Spaulding developed a helpful diagram of fear/guilt/shame cultures, proposing a useful summary of various comparative dynamics of the three cultures.

Since then, other contributors to SEANET have added insights for approaching folk Buddhists. Nantachai Mejudhon, a Thai pastor suggested "the way of meekness" as a witnessing approach in the friendly, gentle Thai culture. This method humbly presented the gospel in a non-aggressive and non-offensive form often lacking among western presentations (2005, 147–186). His model related more sensitively to shame cultures. Ubolwan Mejudhon, his wife, illustrated shame and conflict produced in Buddhist families when young individual converts decided to follow Jesus without discussing it with family. This showed a lack of respect and honor to parents. She recommended ways for reconciling these conflicts sensitively within Thai culture (2005, 217–251). Mark Dominey also contributed valuable cultural insights, expounding Japanese responses to the shame of abortion through *Mizuko* Rites in Japan (2005, 253–279).

My purpose here is to outline different dynamics of fear, guilt, and shame cultures, and to propose relevant messages for Buddhist peoples for each type. These will provide a basis for testing, experimentation, and evaluation. In the last decade much was written on these categories, therefore I will attempt to illustrate afresh some new insights on these issues. Let us review these three dominant culture types.

CULTURAL OBSERVATIONS

Fear, guilt, and shame are universals that may be found to some extent in any culture. Fear is a common emotion, though its intensity may differ from person to person, even culture to culture. Shame is common to all cultures, but in certain individuals it may be reduced or absent in those referred to as shameless (2 Sam 6:20; 2 Cor 12:21; Williams 1952, 381). Guilt can be a deeply significant feeling, though in some individuals it may be absent because of a "seared conscience" void of responsible remorse (2 Cor 5:11; 1 Tim 4:2). Relevant emotional responses to guilt may be shame (trying to hide the fact), sorrow, or remorse over committing moral or social infractions. Legally guilty persons may subsequently feel ashamed. Others may feel no emotive moral response. Some may suggest that guilt is not a feeling, but more like an intellectual reality governed largely by conscience. However, some westerners can be heard to say things like, "I feel guilty for over-indulging myself at dinner last night."

Responses of fear, guilt, and shame are universal to a certain degree. But all cultures are not affected equally by each. The preponderance of one of these modes of response varies from group to group. In some contexts fear, guilt, or shame may dominate and thereby characterize that people's culture. Western European cultures are generally identified as guilt-oriented. However, in the West's pluralistic societies where significant refugee and immigrant groups coexist, fear and shame may also be dominant among those minority groups. Eastern peoples, particularly of Asian cultures, seem in general to be more shame oriented, notably Buddhist and Hindu peoples. On the other hand, fear is prevalent and dominant among most tribal animistic groups. Buddhism frequently assimilates other belief systems. The resultant accommodation incorporates animism, fear of the spirit world and dread of ancestral ghosts in folk Buddhist contexts.

The challenge is to find suitable messages for proclaiming Christ's gospel effectively in this popular Buddhist amalgam.

Years ago in Thailand's Uthai Thani Province, a Thai Christian was wrongly imprisoned for many months, accused of murdering a man in his rural village. I visited him while he awaited trial. Joyfully he reported, "In this prison I feel like Paul, the apostle. Though I'm falsely accused, God has given me great opportunity to witness for him. Now we have a dozen Bible study cells in this jail. Some Buddhists have received new life and more are seeking." Nowadays, I wish I had asked this Thai believer what type of message he used to present Christ's gospel. Had he preached messages appropriate to shame, guilt, or fear? In jail all three might influence prisoners. Sadly I cannot determine which emphasis he used. After a couple of years, when his case came to court, scores of Thai Christians from the province crowded the court room. The judge was surprised at these believers amassed in his court. He listened carefully to the purported concocted testimonies of false witnesses from the village and speedily recognized the lack of concrete evidence. The Thai Buddhist judge summarily dismissed the case. The bold prisoner for God was freed.

BUDDHA ON GUILT, SHAME, AND FEAR

Buddha seldom refers to guilt in his teachings. However, in *Anguttara-Nikaya*, the Book of his Gradual Sayings, he discusses "two things that sear (the conscience)" (Hare 2006, 44–45 vol. I). This seems to relate to a sense of guilt from violation of conscience. By doing immoral acts of body, speech, and thoughts and /or omitting to do moral acts of body, speech, and thoughts, "he is seared (with remorse) at the thought: I have done wrong in body speech and thought. I have left undone the good deed in body, speech and thought. And he burns at the thought of it" (ibid.). Remorse and mental anguish are emotions of a guilty conscience. Guilt is also recognized as painful dejection felt through "the fivefold guilty dread" (Woodward 2005, 333 vol. V). These dreads are "the doom of Hell," rebirth in the animal world, rebirth in the realm of the ghosts, or experiencing "the Waste, the Woeful Way, the Downfall" (ibid.).

Buddha made reference to shame in *Samyutta-Nikaya*, another Buddhist scripture. At the "Bamboo Grove in Rajagaha" he told Maha-Kassapa to exhort the brethren. Kassapa responded that it was difficult to do so as they were intractable and indifferent to instruction. He spoke of inward shame, though a footnote suggested this may equate with conscientiousness (*hiri*). He then remarked,

> In whomsoever, lord, there is no faith in that which is good, in whomsoever there is neither inward shame nor outward discretion as to that which is good, in whom there is neither energy nor insight as to that which is good, of him, come day come night, decline in that which is good is to be looked for, not growth. (Rhys Davids 2005, 139 vol. II)

Buddha also talks of shame and shamelessness in *Anguttara-Nikaya*. He notes two states that are dark: "shamelessness and recklessness" and two states that are bright: "Sense of shame and fear of shame" (Hare 2006, 46 vol. I). He added that the latter two protect the world.

Buddha referred to fear frequently. I found at least fifty references to fear or its derivatives in the *Tripitaka*. In contexts of punishments and two consequent "faults" Buddha declared immediate retribution: "Thus scared at the thought of a fault (which has its result) in this very life, he goes not about plundering others' property." Retribution in the next life was anticipated as well. Buddha recognized hell as a deep fear of his followers. He continued his instruction about future retribution saying,

> Evil in the future life is the fruit of bodily offence.
> Evil is the fruit of offence by word, by thought,

in the future life. If I offend in deed, in word, in thought, should not I, when body breaks up, after death be reborn in the Waste, the Way of Woe, the Downfall, in Purgatory?

Thus scared at the thought of a fault to be atoned for in a future life, he abandons immorality in deeds of body and practices morality in deeds of body: abandons immorality in the practice of speech and thought, and cultivates morality therein and conducts himself with utter purity. (Hare 2006, 43–44 vol. I)

Buddha therefore saw fear of future hells as a motivation to do good, make merit, and live rightly. He himself was seen to be without fear of these things, through his enlightenment (Rhys Davids 2005, 1, 193–194).

Elsewhere Buddha talked of other fears: death, cemeteries, suffering, power, blame, self-reproach, and others' reproach. Further discussion is limited here. But note that the last three also cause shame. One surprising, unusual view of Buddha about fear was his startling comparison between a black snake and a woman. He described identical disadvantages for both of them: "unclean, evil-smelling, timid, fearful, betrays friends" (Hare 2006, 191 vol. III). Buddha explains the "deadly poison of a woman is this: she is almost always very passionate. The forked tongue is this: she is almost always slanderous in speech. And the betrayal of friends is this; she almost always commits adultery" (ibid., 192). Was he talking of women in general here or of prostitutes? Could he not have said similar things to fear about men?

Some fears arise out of Buddhism in conjunction with its various powers and influences. These powers are both mental and physical. Throughout the *Tripitaka*, Buddha's teachings are replete with scores of references to a variety of powers, including *bala*: the five powers, forces, or strengths (confidence, effort, mindfulness, concentration, wisdom) and *iddhi*: the four bases of power that are supranormal, psychic, or spiritual (intention, effort, consciousness, investigation). These *iddhi* manifest themselves in various forms of magic powers such as levitation, walking through doors or on water, body transformation, teleportation, kinds of astral projected travel, or recalling and remembering multiple former births (Woodward 2005, 236–237, 251 vol. V). Cultivating mindfulness, particularly through practicing breathing yoga (*hatha*), allows one to "enjoy in diverse ways manifold forms of magic power" (ibid., 269). These include reading minds of others, seeing via trance states, hearing sounds of gods and men, and gaining insight to special knowledge. Buddha warned that such practices could divert seekers, distracting them from fully attaining enlightenment. Overcoming such fears demand use of caution and discernment. Some spirits (genies) magically absorb cosmic energies before finally being born on earth. These spirits with other gods, devas, wrathful deities, fearful demons, hungry ghosts, and multiple *Naraka*-hells expand the scope of powers to be feared in Buddhism. The *Abhidharma-kosa* describes Theravada's sixteen hells, eight cold *Narakas*, and eight hot *Narakas*. Chinese Mahayana recognizes eighteen major hell chambers, nine east and nine west.

In the modern era, the majority of Buddhists face internal battles against fear, shame, and even guilt each day. Fear from many sources particularly controls folk Buddhists. Compounding these is a dread of consequences from irreversible karma, ardently pursuing them from past lives. Fear is a potent, devastating poison, paralyzing the whole person. Fear cripples emotions, defeats the mind, confuses the intellect, subjugates the soul, depresses the spirit, and immobilizes the body.

People in fear cultures tend to invent ways to deceive the spirits, pacify the demons, and manage the ancestral ghosts by placating them. They invent a multitude of various power devices. They solicit help from benevolent spirits to help avert attacks from evil spirits and to protect their families and themselves from marauding malevolent specters. By these means they manipulate adverse evil powers and spirit forces, often with the assistance of shaman, mediums, and spirit doctors. To propitiate the spirit world they offer animal sacrifices, make promises of devotion and offerings, appropriating gifts, food, flowers, incense, and other objects. Frequently the devotee dupes the deceiving spirits by offering token replicas of the gifts promised. They look and hope for a message that will free them from fear. Nevertheless, fear still dominates people, families, and societies across the Buddhist world.

When I visited Luang Phra Bang in Laos several years ago, the inhabitants told me about a very strong spirit they greatly feared in the area. On the opposite side of the river is high ground with a mountain (*Phu Sii*). A Buddhist monastery (*wat*) is located there. Each month the monks beat a gong on the fifteenth day of the lunar month, coinciding with the Buddhist holy day (*Wan Phra*) and a strong fearsome spirit reputedly comes out of the mountain. The local people are extremely afraid of this spirit and are careful how they conduct themselves. They teach their offspring to fear this mountain and its powerful angry spirit. This is only one of multitudinous illustrations of fear that frequently plagues folk Buddhists.

I have observed that Buddhists also rely upon concepts such as resident *mana* power (*phra*) and earned merit (*bun*) to counter unseen and sometimes visible dark forces. Multiple varieties of offerings to the spirit world complement these, in order to control or ameliorate sickness, disasters, and even delay death. Some of these power practices relate to individuals, families, the clan, tribe, or the whole village. These indigenous beliefs in power efficacy are deemed to be resident in guardian spirits, images, bushes, gods, deceased ancestors, Buddha, and spirit practitioners. Devotees resort to and call upon all of them for help. This animistic conglomerate predisposes folk Buddhists to a message of power over fear. Their hope for some power to conquer their fears becomes a launching pad for Christ's gospel. Scripture portrays absolute power in the all-powerful Creator, his miraculous operations as Lord over all, the resurrection power of Jesus, and so forth. Next, we observe the virile complexity of interpersonal ties that produce the dynamics undergirding fear, an ingredient in protecting community honor.

DYNAMICS OF EASTERN RELATIONSHIPS

Asian Buddhism is heavily laced with interwoven relationships. In China, Japan, Korea, Taiwan, and Vietnam, the influence of relational concepts from Confucianism, integrated into Mahayana Buddhist cultures, has a dominant sociological emphasis. Different levels of threats attempt to infiltrate these relationships and strongly disturb the interaction of members communicating in their tight social networks. These also carry over into avid filial piety, which is expressed in ancestral veneration and worship in Mahayana. In Southeast Asian Buddhist lands like Thailand, concepts of paired relationships pervade. Everyone has a set of respected people above them that are seen as superior. Everyone also is in a superior position to a set of relationships below them (Smith 2013, 155–60). This ripples throughout Buddhist societies in secular, business, religious, familial, and governmental realms. Through these complex networks of multiple paired superior-inferior roles, Asian societies function, producing levels of honor given to those above, and receiving respect from those below. Usually, Asian women in Buddhist contexts have an inferior place to men in public, in homes, and in the Buddhist sangha. For example, women are expected to walk a distance behind men when in public. On the other hand most Asian women control the family finances.

These honor relationships are particularly obvious in teacher-student relationships, where pupils kowtow to their teachers in formal annual rituals, like Teacher's Day (*Wan Wai Khru*) in Thailand. Similarly, students across the continent bow to teachers at beginning and end of the school day. The same pattern is also ingrained within families in many countries of South and East Asia, where children show deep respect to parental figures, bowing before them morning and evening.

A similar model of high respect persists in Tibetan Buddhism where devotees honor their lamas and master-mentors of meditation too. Officials and Buddhist monks of high position are shown honor with extended periods of respect during elongated periods of funeral or cremation rites at their death. Some are virtually "deified" in monumental images placed in temple grounds, where due honor and sometimes offerings are presented the deceased regularly.

The propensity of Hindu families toward honor killings still exists today, not only in India, but also in lands to which Hindus migrate, including the West. When a member goes against the relatives' values, familial wishes, or expectations, Hindu families feel dishonored and often take drastic retributive action through honor killings, which western societies deem to be murder.

In Eastern cultures the individual does not give meaning to the family, rather the family gives meaning to the individual. Consequently, individual actions may not only bring dishonor personally, but also to the family, clan, and even whole tribe. Primarily Buddhism is focused on the individual who must help him or herself individually since no one else can, not even Buddha! But the East's complex societal values are even stronger than the religion when it comes to losing honor or face in the community. Violation of accepted statuses and roles, particularly in hierarchical families or clans intensifies dishonor. Honor is normally of paramount value in highly relational social networks and communities. Fear of losing face is to be avoided rigorously. Being accused of dishonoring elders is a drastic judgment to be eschewed at all costs.

This contrasts with the West where independent individualism flourishes, often with domineering traits, where familial relationships have lower expectations than those in Asia. This is especially true with regards to extended families and also to deceased ancestors. Some level of honor may be given to significant familial members at Western funerals and subsequently through occasional visits to their graves. This, by no means, is comparable to Eastern ancestral rites of honor to the dead. These require elaborate rituals and ceremonies at certain regular periods as well as daily worship at family shrines or *butsudan* altars in Asian homes.

Another humiliating hurtful aspect of shame/honor cultures is losing face. Thai people fear this loss of face (*khaai naa*) above all injuries. It is a grave personal insult to lose face. To have your face scratched (*thuuk chiik naa*) is even more drastic. Grammatically, "scratch" (*chiik naa*) is active mood when done to others, but with *thuuk*, it becomes passive—a disturbing experience received. This feeling is deeply devastating, painfully personal, and grievously hurtful. One often-neglected observation in honor writings is the effect of shame on one's identity. Serious personal loss of face has significant consequences on identity, which affects self-image. It not only shames and dishonors the person, but also deeply violates and demeans their identity. Mischke agrees, "Simply stated, shame is about who I am; guilt is about what I've done" (2015, 63). Attacks on one's personal identity fuel a person's anger, unforgiveness, and vengefulness, usually unremittingly so. One Thai Christian felt she had been so dishonored that she refused to forgive the accused offender, even when counseling using scriptures about forgiveness brought her to tears!

Guilt is more dominant in western cultures. Their societies have meticulously coded legal systems, stringent moral standards, and often a dichotomy of societal and personal values. For example, an outsider can hardly comprehend American culture without realizing its penchant for categorical opposing twin values: right or wrong, guilty or innocent, black or white, Democrat or Republican, North or South (persisting since the Civil War), and so forth. This dichotomous view considers everything in dualistic values. Most Asian cultures tend to have a broader spectrum of choices to identify matters, with more shades of grey rather than only a narrow choice between two! A sensitive Christian in the West may feel personally guilty for even breaking small traffic infractions of the law, such as speeding above the limit or parking in non-parking zones. But an Easterner feels he/she has broader latitudes, especially when it comes to crossing over marked driving lanes in Bangkok or Manila, while waiting for a traffic light to change. This clash of cultures sometimes produces conflict of feelings that demand an adequate message of healing.

EMOTIONAL CONFLICT IN FEAR/ GUILT/SHAME CONTEXTS

Anthropological statuses and roles sometimes encounter "role conflict" when people who function together mutually have two or more sets of roles, such as the husband and wife who are also in business as boss and secretary. A conflict in values and emotions in guilt and shame cultures produces a similar effect. War always devastates emotions and increases tensions of fear, guilt, and shame, if not during, then certainly afterwards. The distorted events and abnormalities of these conflicts challenge values, leading to conflicting emotions.

For example, in April to May 1945 fear and shame gripped the hearts and minds of Germans as brutal Russian soldiers occupied East Berlin. Tensions between national honor through pride in Hitler's invincible army, and looming ignominious defeat under the Allies, especially by the cruel Red militia, caused deep emotional conflict in many Germans. Thousands committed suicide, including whole families, for fear of vengeful, Soviet savagery, coupled with the shame of being mass raped. In its History of World Wars episode on "The Battle for Berlin in World War Two," BBC televised the story of mass rapes and suicides: 100,000 women were raped, 10,000 of whom died, either as a result of mass rape or suicide. Many chose to die at their own hand rather than live afterwards with fearful shame. Historians claim the overall number of women raped on German soil under the Soviet Army was higher, possibly even as many as two million (Ash 2015).

Another classic example of emotional conflict was the Indian Emperor Asoka. Following his Buddhist conversion, this hardened warrior became a great patron and propagator of Buddhism. Through his efforts, Buddhism subsequently spread throughout the world. What contributed to the reformation of this great conqueror, who massacred hundreds of thousands of men, women, and children? Certainly, one cause was likely his fear and concern over his massive accumulated karma from slaughtering so many, particularly the merciless decimation of myriads during the Kalinga war. Combinations of fear, guilt, and shame possibly contributed to his change of heart. The fear of karmic retribution and being born in hell (*narakas*), a sense of guilt, seared with remorse from murdering multitudes, plus the consequent shame thereby attached to his warrior's conscience produced deep anguish. At his royal palace in Pataliputra (Patna today) Emperor Asoka, plagued by these intensified anxieties, invited the monk Nyagrodha to preach Buddha's dharma to him. Afterwards he took the three refuges from the monk in commitment to Buddhism (Piplayan 2005, 48–63).

More examples from World War II vividly come to mind. For example, Japanese soldiers commonly resorted to suicide rather than surrender. To give up, under any circumstance, was seen as dishonoring the emperor, the nation, the family, and even oneself. Shame was to be avoided at all costs. The consequence of national dishonor and personal shame was more feared than death itself. Suicide was preferred to capture or surrender. Even the general population of the Japanese mainland and its territories imbibed this attitude. Thus, when the American forces landed in Okinawa, many of the local inhabitants jumped off high cliffs to die on the rocks or sea below. Japanese tend to follow an amalgam of Buddhism (following moral codes), Confucianism (honoring ancestors) and Shinto (propitiating nature spirits). Although Buddhist tenets commanded the Japanese to avoid taking life, nevertheless the influence of state Shintoism mobilized the populace for decades of war legitimized the violent taking of life without compunction. During this period, established worship of Japan's emperor as the earthly descendent and representative of the sun goddess, Amaterasu Omikami, was instituted. Thus, hierarchical control of military generals imbibed a sense of Japanese invincible superiority in which aggression was propagated and brutal killing was accepted. Emotional conflict over Buddhist non-aggression was subdued as worship of the sun goddess and honoring the emperor superseded individual and family mores. The fear of shaming goddess, emperor, nation, and family saturated emotions and virtually dominated Japan's warriors. Suicide rather than surrender prevailed. The national shame of final defeat by the allies caused significant social changes that reversed and dismantled state Shintoism. Consequently, today's Japanese are a very different breed than that past era and generation. In conferences in Asia countries, I have heard many Japanese pastors and Christian leaders humbly ask forgiveness for their nation's cruel and aggressive acts in that World War. This catharsis has helped ameliorate conflicting emotions, and has brought about reconciliation and personal restoration for many Japanese.

The allied call to arms also produced emotional conflict. The biblical command against killing affected many Christian soldiers. Some opted to avoid killing even in what seemed a legitimate war, claiming conscientious objection. Others, while personally rejecting killing, served as stretcher-bearers, medical corpsmen, or chaplains on the front lines rather than as warriors. In this way, they avoided violating their moral conscience. After the war ended, many Christian soldiers were conflicted over the killing they had inflicted. Feelings of guilt continued to possess and plague them.

Some found relief through going back to their former enemies to ask forgiveness. Thus reconciliation was effected. As a kind of spiritual catharsis, some Christian GIs, driven by a sense of mixed guilt and compassion returned to Japan and elsewhere as missionaries. A good illustration of this conflict resolution is recorded in Laura Hillenbrand's *Unbroken*. It recounts the experiences of USA Olympic runner Louis Zamperini as a prisoner of the Japanese in World War II. The climax of the book occurs when Louis returns to Japan to face and be reconciled with his former tormentor. Hillenbrand concisely wrote, "At that moment, something shifted sweetly inside him. It was forgiveness, beautiful and effortless and complete. For Louie Zamperini, the war was over" (2010, 379). Forgiveness is a potent message, often resulting in reconciliation between conflicting parties, as occurred afterwards in this case.

SOME BIBLICAL PERSPECTIVES

Scholars have done much scriptural analysis pertaining to culture types, particularly with honor-shame cultures. I will not repeat their good research. Nevertheless, throughout this text I have sprinkled in some biblical insights. There are more than double the references to shame than guilt in the Bible. However, fear likely dominates the others in the Bible. More could be written on this. The epistles of Paul identify fear in those helpless, impotent, and powerless (Rom 5:6–7); guilt in sinners and lawbreakers (Rom 5:8–10); and shame in those dishonoring God and self (Rom 1:18–2:2). God's solution for all three is redemption through faith in Christ by means of God's grace, producing peace, hope, love, power, reconciliation, and salvation (Rom 5:1–5).

Fear in Scripture has both a positive and negative slant. To "fear God" is frequently encouraged. The Bible often commands us to be in awe of the Lord for he is awesome, holy, and perfect. He is omnipotent, omniscient, and omnipresent. His word is immutable. He is the sovereign Lord of all. Therefore, God alone is to be worshipped, honored, praised, and given glory. In the Apocalypse the angel flying in mid-heaven preaches to all on earth from every nation, tribe, tongue, and people. He loudly proclaims the eternal gospel: "Fear God, and give him glory [honor], because the hour of his judgment has come; and worship him who made the heaven and the earth and sea and springs of waters" (Rev 14:6–7). Another reason to fear God alone is that he "is able to destroy both soul and body in hell" (Matt 10:28). Thus, humans should have respectful, healthy fears of God as righteous judge, as well as the dire consequences of sin, failures before a holy God, and an eternal hell.

A clear biblical understanding of power underlies an apt message, particularly for fear, but also relevant to guilt and shame. Although some value is resident in the word "empower," I suggest, for reasons below, it should be utilized cautiously.

While power is a significant primary gospel message, missiologists and leaders should be careful about using some power terms. In church, mission practice, and leadership training, Christians sometimes too readily incorporate concepts such as visualization, empowerment, transmission, mindfulness, channeling, or similar power practices. These terms are integral to Buddhist worldviews, beliefs, and ritual practices. They focus on humanistic approaches to life, using human agents and human processes rather than dependence on Creator God. In mid-twentieth century British historian, Arnold Toynbee predicted the "interpenetration of Buddhism and Christianity" (Lai 2001, 128). This intermixing may be subtle, but it can undermine true spiritual dynamics essential to mission and church in Asia. Spiritual discernment is certainly needed.

For example, the term "empowerment" has become a common modern management goal, used popularly since the mid-1980s. Subtly, in the last half-century Buddhist influence has been seeping, like a leaking tap, into many business and church circles in the West through yoga, martial arts, and empowerment practice. Modern secular theorists on leadership and management particularly emphasize empowerment. Potterfield observes that many organizational leaders in society recognize employee empowerment as one of the most important and popular management concepts of our time (1999, 6). Webster defines to empower as to give power to (someone). Empowerment is "promoting the self-actualization or influence of someone" (SEUIR 2015, 1). This occurs by "encouraging and developing the skills for self-sufficiency, with a focus on eliminating the future need for charity or welfare in the individuals of the group" (Epps 2012, 60). Pragmatic forces behind such empowerment are clearly human in origin and effort. Present day Christians tend to import concepts from secular writers, adopting them into the church, mission, or seminary as part of spiritual practices and leadership training, without necessarily realizing their deep Buddhist connotations.

For hundreds of years Buddhism emphasized empowerment, a practice and technical term used in transmission during meditation and initiations (Tib. *wang*). In particular, the *Vajrayana* (Tibetan) vehicle utilizes rituals to empower various stages of meditation associated with particular deities (Tib. *yidam*). These are commonly guided by vajra masters. "All the rituals in an empowerment serve one function: to temporarily transform our normal way of perceiving reality" (House 2015, 2). This means transitioning from ordinary to sacred perception. Four main ceremonial purifications are performed to ripen the Buddha nature within the initiate. At the end of empowerment ceremonies, symbolic *mandala* offerings of "one's body, speech, mind, wealth, and existence to the vajra master" seal the commitment (House 2015, 2–3). Webster's Dictionary gives a more positive usage of the term: "to empower is to give power or authority to, authorize, to give ability to, enable or permit" (Guralnik 1984, 459). The vital discerning question is, "Who gives this power and ability?" Is its basic source human or divine? Practitioners or trainers must be careful how the term they use is defined and employed in training or discipling believers.

Sadly, modern leadership books or training programs frequently ignore or relegate to a lower priority the essential legitimate power of God's Spirit. Often little emphasis is placed on the indwelling power of the Holy Spirit required in the Bible—his operating that comes through the genuine empowerment and authority of God. In the frantic world of frivolous social media, today's church and society have little time or place for a sovereign, empowering God. Yet the one absolute essential qualification for biblically-oriented living is total reliance on the power of God and his Holy Spirit (Zech 4:6; Acts 1:4–5, 8; Eph 3:16; Col 1:11, 29; 1 Thess 1:5; Phil 4:13). As Oswald Sanders writes, "A touch of the supernatural was required" (1980, 30). This is indispensable.

In *Ephesians: Power and Magic*, Clinton Arnold points out that Ephesians 3:7 teaches us that "the divine enablement of the apostle" is through the gift of the grace of God "that is by the working of his power" (1992, 161). The Apostle Paul instructs the Ephesians to "be strong in the Lord, and in the strength of his might" (Eph 6:10) before he lists the believer's armor. He also recognizes the contrary spiritual bondage of "the elementary principles of the world" (Gal 4:3, 9; Col 2:8, 20). These are "spirits, angels, planets, the ABC of this world" (Williams 1952, 19). The folk Buddhist worldview comfortably aligns with them. But since Christians experience opposition from evil powers (Eph 6:10–20), Arnold declares that Paul calls for them "to acquire divine strengthening for the purpose of engaging the spirit-forces of evil" (1992, 103). He observes this "need for divine power in vv. 10, 11, 13, and 16. In no other single passage in the epistles attributed to Paul is there such a number and variety of terms for power: nine terms in all encompassing six different word groups" (1992, 103). Asian Christians, coming from a Buddhist background where one only depends on oneself, need adequate training on God's almighty power to counter deceptive evil spirits. Therefore, declare a message of the true source of power and empowerment in Christ. Jesus said, "the branch cannot bear fruit of itself, unless it abides in the vine" (John 15: 4).

Consequently, it is absolutely crucial to stress continuous, close relationship with Christ Jesus, along with full reliance on the Holy Spirit. Faithful believers live in the Spirit, rely on the Spirit, and walk with the Spirit. Therefore, teach with energy the spiritual disciplines, like meditating on God's word, praying constantly, depending on the Holy Spirit, and working under God's direction. These prerequisites are integral to the power message by which Buddhist peoples everywhere can be reached and blessed.

KEY RECONCILING MESSAGES FOR FEAR/ GUILT/ SHAME CONTEXTS

Some may advocate using one single biblical gospel message to bring about reconciliation for all. But like the variegated reflecting facets in a diamond, God's precious redemption is portrayed in different ways throughout the scriptures. Jesus dealt with people by varied means in each spiritual encounter. Therefore it is legitimate to apply various approaches and facets of the Bible to fear/guilt/shame contexts. Multiple cultural dynamics may likely require different approaches for each, but the heart message remains constant and focused on Jesus Christ.

Fear is overcome by finding faith, power, and hope in Christ's power. This can be accomplished through trusting his person, depending on his love (1 John 4:16–18; 5:4–5), and having confidence in his supreme power over all his creation. God is uniquely our all-powerful provider, protector, and preserver. By faith in Christ as our substitute, we exchange our fearful weakness for his mighty strength. Scripture is replete with references to God's power and its efficacy. The Amplified New Testament says "we hold fast *and firm to the end* our joyful *and* exultant confidence and sense of triumph in our hope [in Christ]" (Heb 3:6; emphasis added). The message people need to hear becomes a trusting response to be "mixed with faith [that is, with the leaning of the entire personality on God in absolute trust and confidence in His power, wisdom and goodness]" (Heb 4:2). Furthermore, "the word that God speaks is alive and full of power—making it active, operative, energizing and effective; it is sharper than any two-edged sword" (Heb 4:12). Meeting fear by trusting God's strength can increase faith, power, and hope. This in turn produces victory in and through the name of Jesus, who provides all essentials for body, soul, and spirit.

Dealing with guilt requires a strong message of forgiveness and restoration, both of which come through Christ's substitutionary sacrifice for our inadequacy and sins. That debt we are unable to repay. The innocent, holy "Lord of all" paid the full price for our guilty, unclean sinfulness. God is the loving redeemer. He forgives the repentant, guilty ones because he loves humans so much that he gave up his best and only Son to die, in order to provide salvation and restoration for all.

That message which combats shame and restores our honor is that Jesus, a holy and perfect sacrifice, is our substitute. Our new identity is "in Christ," making us part of his heavenly family. Being rejected, despised, and put to death, Christ bore our shame for us. His shame covers our shame. Through the sacrifice of himself for humanity, he restores relationships by saving our face before others and reconciling us to God. He sits in the highest heaven at God's throne as our advocate, in order to restore honor and intercede for us. He takes our lost honor on himself through his shame on the ignominious cross and exchanges it for our restored glory, honor, and face before our heavenly Father.

A POWER MESSAGE FOR FEAR

In 1970 I wrote a Thai manual for evangelization called *Multiplying Churches through Prayer Cell Evangelism*. It went through several editions and updates. An appendix added a suggested power model for witnessing entitled "The Power of Redemption for You." It affirmed the Bible was the revealed word of God, noting several simple affirmations of power: 1) The Lord Jesus Christ is the true, eternal God who created everything by his almighty power; 2) He created humanity in the image of God, giving humans the power to govern the world; 3) Mankind forfeited true power by rebelling against God and as a result came under Satan's power, enslaved to sin; 4) Christ came to earth to redeem humanity from the power of the devil and the curse of sin, by giving humans new power in the Holy Spirit (Smith 1970, 1971, 2003, 39–41). This power message suited Thai folk Buddhists. Day by day the spirit world influenced them more than Buddha's dharma, not unlike many other Buddhists across the globe.

In a later book on Buddhism, I refined and expanded this power encounter approach. Witnessing to folk Buddhists incorporated shame and fear in six simple axioms of a message on power:

First, God is the original source of all power and perfection. Jesus Christ is the all-powerful Lord, Creator, and Governor over all beings.

Second, God created humans in God's own image and gave them power to govern and care for the world. This first human couple was originally perfect, enjoying power and freedom in God's presence, without shame, sin or death.

Third, humans lost that power through willful disobedience and rebellion against God. As slaves of sin humans became slaves to karma. The human race came under the power of demonic evil spirits, resulting in suffering, shame, fear and death.

Fourth, Jesus saw humans had no way to free themselves from the power of Satan, shame, sin, or karma. Christ came from heaven to earth as man to break Satan's power over humans. Dying shamefully in place of humans, Christ bore the penalty of their sin and shame. He set them free from fear, restored their honor, reversed their karma, and redeemed their souls. The perfect sinless

Jesus reinstates God's power and honor in the lives of humans and their families, giving them new life connected directly to God.

Fifth, humans can regain this power through repentance and faith in Jesus as Lord. God's grace offers this power and honor freely, apart from human effort, one's own works, or earned merit. God grants this power through his Holy Spirit to all who obey him.

Sixth, God desires his children to share this good news of power, honor, and freedom from fear, karma, and shame with their families, friends, neighbors, and beyond to nations (2009, 92–93).

Asian folk Buddhists espouse fear of the spirit world, adopt a plethora of fearsome Buddhist hells, and accept irreversible generational karma. Socially, shame and saving face conditions them in daily living. Thus honor is of paramount importance to them and their families. Christ's gospel blends liberation, power, and honor in a message that suits folk Buddhists. The power of Jesus conquers all fear and overcomes influences of evil spirits. Jesus' voluntary sacrifice in shame restores face and honor to Asian Buddhist seekers.

MODEL MESSAGE FOR SHAME/ HONOR/FACE-SAVING CULTURES

Shame more than guilt is a paramount response among Asians. An excellent model of message for shame based cultures is a simple illustrated cartoon series entitled "Back to God's Village," which is produced by the Honor-Shame Network and is found at its website: www.honorshame.com/recommendations/. I recommend that workers in shame/honor Buddhist cultures experiment with this method and research effective applications of this message, particularly among Mahayana groups. This prime approach needs intense testing and evaluation. It might be greatly enhanced by applying it to whole families and clans, rather than only to individuals (a western orientation). God created families, which have been the building blocks of tribes and nations since the beginning of time. In his grand redemptive plan throughout Scripture God also revealed his concern for families. One Passover lamb for the household was sufficient for the protection and salvation of the whole family and their servants. The Lord spared Canaanite Rahab and her whole family at the fall of Jericho. Asian Buddhists are deeply family-oriented. For more on this family approach, see *Faith and Family in Asia* (de Neui 2010).

Early 2016, flying from Beijing, China to Thailand, I happened to be seated next to a college student from China. I politely began to chat with her. Noticing prayer beads on her wrist I asked how she used them. She replied she was a Buddhist! "Oh," I said, "That is interesting. I am a believer in Jesus." She promptly retorted, "Oh, Christians believe everyone is a bad sinner!" I wondered how best to gently answer this Chinese Buddhist scholar. Remembering my writing this chapter, I responded in a way befitting shame cultures: "Actually the Bible declares God created the first human beings perfect, without sin or shame, having great honor and unhindered access to creator God." Her attitude changed. She immediately began to listen intently. Then I explained that a problem arose when they chose to dishonor their Creator by rebelling, accepting the lies of Satan, God's enemy. The first humans disobeyed their Creator, thereby shaming themselves and God also. Then I explained that God lovingly provided a way to reverse their shame. He sent his only Son from heaven as a perfect honorable substitute to die in the place of all humans. Through the sacrifice of his Son, God reversed their shame and provided a way for humans to regain honor with God. God pleads with all humanity to call upon him. He can take away their shame and restore their honor with him. As soon as I finished explaining the gospel she quickly turned to her boyfriend, who also wore Buddhist *mala* prayer beads, and retold what I had just shared with her.

Reconciliation from shame before God and returning to honor and peace with God is identified clearly throughout Scripture. Notably the incarnate Christ, the Creator of all, wholly fulfills the intermediary role of high priest before Father God on behalf of shamed humanity. Jesus was perfected through suffering our shame so he could bring many humans to glory (Heb 2:10). The Amplified New Testament affirms,

> But we are able to see Jesus, who was ranked a little lower than the angels for a little while, crowned with glory and honor because his having suffered death, in order that by the grace (unmerited favor) of God [to us sinners] he might experience death for every individual person. (Heb 2:9)
>
> Therefore he is able also to save to the uttermost—completely, perfectly, finally and for all time and eternity—those who come to God through him, since he is always living to make petition to God *and* intercede with him *and* intervene for them. (Heb. 7:25)

CONCLUSION

Below is my contrasting summary of three different mega-categories. I included Christ's role from Spaulding. Apply these to develop appropriate messages for each culture type.

Model Type	Fear	Guilt	Shame
Dynamics	Spirit World – enslaved	Law – bound by legal rules	Relationships – affects identity
Characteristics	Powerless – helpless	Concealing – hiding	Vengeful pride, loss of face
Focus	Heart – why anxious	Conscience – what I did	Identity – who I am

Model Type	Fear	Guilt	Shame
Concern	Being slave to the spirits	Being found out	Being scorned, rejected
Need	Revolution – resistance	Reconciliation – forgiveness	Restoration – of lost honor
Message	Power – Victory over fear	Mercy – He died for me	Repair – replaces shame
Christ's Model	Slave bearer	Sin bearer	Shame bearer
Christ's Mode	Sovereign (controller)	Substitute (redeemer)	Sacrifice shamed for me
Christ's Role	Potentate, Master, King	Prophet, Messenger	Priest, Mediator, Peace Maker
Salvific Product	Faith, freedom, hope	Redeemed from curse	Restored face, honor, allegiance, relations

From the works of Noble to those of Mischke, much has been written on honor-shame approaches for mission. The dominance of shame in about three-quarters of the global population is inescapable, but often ignored. It is sadly significant that most preachers and theologians, even those from the East, still focus on messages to counter and heal guilt. The Christian mission's more challenging message should center around the paralyzing preponderance of fear affecting most peoples on all continents. This includes the West, where fear of one's guilt being found out is deeply ingrained. Like the biblical account of fear found in Achan and his family (Josh 7), Westerners and Easterners do everything they can to cover up their guilt and fear of exposure, a kind of face-saving.

Fear universally grips all three mega-culture types. Proclaiming a message of power over fear clearly identifies the strongest common gospel of general good news. The answer to fear of the spirits, fear of shame, and fear of guilt is power—

God's power and consequent victory over fear that results in freedom, confidence, and hope. Christ died "that through death he might render powerless him who had the power of death, that is the devil; and might deliver those who through fear of death were subject to slavery all their lives" (Heb 2:14–15).

Scriptures' prescription for overcoming fear, shame and guilt is an exchange model of "transference from . . . to." For example, to "turn from darkness to light and from the dominion of Satan to God" (Acts 26:18; I Pet 2:9; Eph 5:8); "He delivered us from the domain of darkness, and transferred us to the kingdom of his beloved Son" (Col 1:13); from being "not a people" to "now a people of God"; from "not received mercy" to now having received mercy" (1 Pet 2:10).

In 1934 Ethelwyn (Mrs. Walter G Taylor) of Pacific Garden Mission in Chicago aptly wrote:

> Far dearer than all that the world can impart
> Was the message that came to my heart.
> How that Jesus alone for my sin did atone,
> And Calvary covers it all.
>
> (Chorus)
> Calvary covers it all,
> My past with its sin and stain;
> My *guilt* and despair
> Jesus took on Him there,
> And Calvary covers it all.
>
> The stripes that He bore and the thorns that He wore
> Told His mercy and love evermore
> And my heart bowed in *shame* as I called on His name
> And Calvary covers it all.

Ethel wrote this hymn soon after the conversion of Walter "Happy Mac" MacDonald, who had been addicted to alcohol. He told God his fears, "You don't know how bad I am, Lord.

Really I'm the worst man in the world. You can't save me; I'm too bad" (Cottrill 2013, 1). Ethel assured Mac that Calvary covers it all. Mac believed and found peace from his fears, his guilt, and his shame by accepting restored honor and freedom. His humble acceptance and exchange of Christ as his vicarious substitute and his total dependence on the all-powerful name of Jesus gave him the victory. The essential gospel message is Jesus Christ. He has absolute power to restore, save, forgive, and transform fearful, guilty, shameful humanity. The supreme answer to human fear, guilt, and shame is found in messages of God's full provision of grace, honor, and finality in Jesus Christ.

References

Arnold, Clinton E. 1992. *Ephesians: Power and magic.* Grand Rapids, MI: Baker Book House.

Ash, Lucy. "The rape of Berlin." British Broadcasting Corporation. Posted May 1, 2015. http://www.bbc.com/news/magazine-32529679

Cottrill, Robert. 2013. "Worldwise hymns." Posted June 19, accessed November 24, 2015. http://wordwisehymns.com/2013/06/19/calvary-covers-it-all/

Cooke, Joseph. n.d. "The gospel for Thai ears." unpublished paper.

de Neui, Paul H. 2010. *Family and faith in Asia: The missional impact of social networks.* Pasadena, CA: William Carey Library.

Dominey, Mark. "Abortion and *Mizuko* rites in Japan." In *Sharing Jesus Holistically with the Buddhist World*, edited by David Lim and Steve Spaulding. Pasadena, CA: William Carey Library.

Editorial Committee. 1958. *The amplified New Testament.* La Habra, CA: The Lockman Foundation.

Epps, Henry. 2012. *Leadership: Lead, follow or get out of the way!* Publisher: Lulu.com.

Guralnik, David B., editor-in-chief. 1984. *Webster's new world dictionary of the American language.* New York: Simon and Schuster.

Hare, E. M. 2006. *The Book of Gradual Sayings (Anguttara-Nikaya).* Delhi: Motilal Banarsidass Publishers.

Hillenbrand, Laura. 2010. *Unbroken: A World War II story of survival, resilience, and redemption.* New York: Random House.

House, William, ed. n.d. "An Explanation of Buddhist Empowerments." *Reverse spins.* Accessed May 22, 2015. http://www.reversespins.com/empowerment.html

Lai, Whalen & Michael von Bruck. 2001. *Christianity and Buddhism.* Maryknoll, New York: Orbis Books.

MegaCARE Missions. 2015. Website, p. 1. http://megacaremissions.org/empowerment/

Mejudhon, Nantachai. 2005. "Meekness: A new approach to witness to the Thai people." In *Sharing Jesus effectively in the Buddhist world*, edited by David Lim, Steve Spaulding, and Paul de Neui. Pasadena, CA: William Carey Library.

Mejudhon, Ubolwan. 2005. "The ritual of reconciliation in Thai culture." In *Sharing Jesus holistically with the Buddhist world*, edited by David Lim and Steve Spaulding. Pasadena, CA: William Carey Library.

Mischke, Werner. 2015. *The global gospel: Achieving missional impact in our multicultural world.* Scottsdale, AZ: Mission ONE.

Noble, Lowell. 1975. *Naked and not ashamed: An anthropological, biblical, and psychological study of shame.* Jackson, MI: Jackson Printing.

Piplayan, Madhukar. 2005. *Asoka the great.* New Delhi: Samyak Prakashan.

Potterfield, Thomas. 1999. *The business of employee empowerment: Democracy and ideology in the workplace.* Westport, CT: Quorum Books.

Rhys Davids, Mrs. C.A.F. 2005.*The book of the kindred sayings (Samyutta-Nikaya) part* II. Delhi: Motilal Banarsidass Publishers.

SEUIR. 2015. E-Repository: Main Library, South Eastern University of Sri Lanka. Sep.1.

Sanders, J. Oswald. 1980. *Spiritual leadership.* Chicago: The Moody Bible Institute.

Smith, Alex G. 2003. *Multiplying churches through prayer cell evangelism.* Chiang Mai, Thailand: OMF.

———. 2009. *A Christian's pocket guide to Buddhism.* Ross-shire, Scotland: Christian Focus Publications/OMF.

———. 2013. "Training indigenous leaders in Thai Buddhist contexts." In *Developing indigenous leaders: Lessons in mission from Buddhist Asia*, edited by Paul H. De Neui. Pasadena CA: William Carey Library.

Spaulding, Steve. 2000. "Our cultures, diverse creations: Cultures & kingdom," a diagram of three culture types in Introduction to SEANET (Powerpoint). Manila Philippines: Dawn Ministries.

Williams, Charles Kingsley. 1952. *The New Testament: A new translation in plain English.* London: S.P.C.K. and Longmans, Green and Co.

Woodward, F. L. 2005. *The book of the kindred sayings (Samyutta-Nikaya)* part V. Delhi: Motilal Banarsidass Publishers.

5
Transformational Mission in Fear Cultures in the Buddhist World and Beyond

David S. Lim

There is apparently a global Christian consensus on the theology of mission, particularly in the missiology of transformational mission (TM) which consists of evangelism and social concern. Since the 1952 Willingen meeting of the International Mission Council, which merged with World Council of Churches in 1961, the formulation of *missio Dei* (mission of God) has become a helpful foundational concept that has unified various missiological formulations across denominational lines. Christian missions are now defined by the range of concerns that God has in and for the world, usually set in the language of realizing or extending "the kingdom of God" on earth.

This *missio Dei* has been conceived and formulated as transformational mission (TM) in the official documents of the various global church bodies. This was already a common understanding in the early 1980s, when the World Evangelical Alliance (WEA) joined the Roman Catholic Church (RCC, *Evangelii Nuntiandi*, 1982) and the Conciliar Protestant and Eastern Orthodox churches in the World Council of Churches (WCC, "Mission and Evangelism: An Ecumenical Affirmation," 1982) in articulating such in "Transformation—The Church in Response to Human Need" at Wheaton 1983 (Samuel 1999, 228–29). TM has been repeated in the *Capetown Commitment*: "God commands us to reflect his own character through compassionate care for the needy, and to demonstrate the values and the power of the kingdom of God in striving for justice and peace and in caring for God's creation" (2011, 29).

Yet there seems to be not much TM and transformational results in the Buddhist world, even in the fear cultures which have a supernaturalistic worldview that is quite similar to that in the Bible. Fear cultures are those which live in extreme anxiety toward the perceived beings and realities in their spirits-filled worldview, often labeled "animism" or "folk religions."

Christians in the past 115 years who have excelled in witnessing effectively among such fear cultures have mainly been the Pentecostal denominations ("First Wavers"), the Charismatics in major denominations ("Second Wavers"), and especially the Neo-Pentecostal/Full Gospel (also called "Third Wavers," hereafter just Neo-Pentecostal) churches. This has primarily been accomplished through power encounters in various healing and deliverance ministries. Indeed several if not most conversions to Christ and church membership have been through "signs and wonders"—miraculous experiences of supernatural power that have led a great number to faith in Christ.

Yet, though these highly visible and dramatic phenomena before crowds in public gatherings have led to personal and family transformation, they have not resulted in mass conversions, people movements, and societal transformation. This is particularly clear among folk Buddhist people groups in predominantly Buddhist countries.

How can we do effective TM in forming Christ-centered transformational communities (CTCs) as we share the gospel in fear cultures that believe in supernatural beings and forces? Though I approach this issue from my experiences in ministry among predominantly folk Buddhist Chinese in the Philippines, I believe that its relevance extends to ministries among other peoples whose cultures include supernatural beliefs and practices, including those in perhaps all other "folk Buddhists" in particular and "folk religionists" in general. Perhaps the suggestions here may also be applied among those who live in fears that are common to all humans, even those in secularized societies, such as fear of loneliness, misfortune, sickness, death, making major commitments, uncertain future, failure, and others. My suggestions are also based on literature about church planting movements (Garrison 2004; Schattner 2014) and my observations on the historical people movements or mass conversions of Han Chinese in John Sung's ministry, the post-Mao rural villages in Zhejiang and central China, as well as among other "folk religionists." These, and others, have become Christianized populations in South India, the Philippines, Northeast India, and Myanmar.

In spite of their apparent success, the main reason why the Neo-Pentecostals have generally not been able to maximize the impact of their power encounters in fear cultures is their failure to be fully indigenous. Each context is different, and the response to each should be different as the spirit leads. The Lausanne Covenant states:

> Missions have all too frequently exported with the gospel also alien culture, and churches have sometimes been in bondage to culture rather than to the scriptures. Christ's evangelists must humbly seek to empty themselves of all but their personal authenticity in order to become the servants to others, and churches must seek to transform and enrich their culture, all for the glory of God. (Paragraph 10)

This chapter shows that TM requires full indigenization in all of the four dimensions as propounded by missiologists of indigenous church planting and people movements: self-governing, self-propagating, self-supporting, and self-theologizing. The first three dimensions were developed in the 1860s by Henry Venn and Rufus Anderson, effectively implemented by John Nevius in Korea in the 1890s and reiterated by Roland Allen in the early 1900s. The fourth was added in the 1980s by Paul Hiebert.

For TM to be effective, not just fixing the message (self-theologizing), all four of these elements are required.

A recent successful instance of TM in a fear culture is that of Food for the Hungry-Cambodia. They received a gold medal in March 2016 from the King of Cambodia for effectively transforming the regions in two provinces where former Khmer Rouge soldiers who massacred their compatriots from 1975–79 were isolated and "exiled" for their protection from avengers. Their local staff were able to bring hope and empowerment to this unreached people group from their fears and despair. They were told upon entry in 2010 that "If you mention the name of Jesus only once, we will kill you all." Yet almost all of these ex-traitors have become Christ-followers because within a month one of their leaders saw Jesus tell him in a dream that he must ask this team to tell them about him. A Christ-centered transformational movement has been launched from among them! How will this TM be replicated across the Buddhist world and beyond?

SELF-GOVERNING

First of all, to do TM, we should first determine who will lead the CTC, which requires that the leaders be indigenous and chosen by the people themselves (cf. Deut 17:14–15; Acts 6:3–6). Neo-Pentecostals have realized this concept of planting indigenous churches, with each setting their own policies and owning their own properties—a new way of being church for many denominations. Though hardly grabbing headlines since they are done by the poor (Escobar 2000, 40–42), these Neo-Pentecostal churches have sprung a big surprise by doing some significant TMs through indigenous leadership and thus indigenous ownership.

Upon entry into the community, indigenous leaders can be developed by simply befriending, evangelizing and discipling a "person of peace" (someone who welcomes us as the local host, Luke 10:6) and his family, while also seeking their help to befriend their community leaders, perhaps including the religious leader(s). Then when an opportunity arises, especially after a power encounter (with the permission of the head of the family of the person healed or delivered), as the community's attention and curiosity have been aroused, the missionary could catalyze a community organizing process by which the community defines a felt need and then chooses a few among themselves to be the leaders to address that need, with the blessing of the community leader(s). The leaders of this new "peoples (or community) organization" and the "person of peace" will constitute the core group to be evangelized and discipled to lead the TM in their community and region.

Since our objective is to disciple entire peoples to Christlikeness in their community, our strategy must be to win and disciple adults, especially the community and religious leaders, so they can lead in the evangelization, theologizing and education (and worldview and religio-cultural change) of the populace. Usually missed by most missionaries are the local healers and shamans, as well as Buddhist and Taoist monks and nuns. We should participate in the activities of their communities, including their religious festivals. As we join in civic and socio-religious affairs, we show our willingness to cooperate with people of good will and thereby "earn the right" to form CTCs with them. Besides, most animist societies make decisions as a group, usually led by the chief and/or elders of the community or tribe (Tippett 1973, 123–24).

Perhaps the best example is that of Bruce Olson (1973), who successfully turned a power encounter into a people movement among the animistic head-hunting Motilione tribe in Colombia. He befriended not just the tribal chief and the elders, but also the shaman. When "pink eyes" became an epidemic in their community, he had penicillin to heal the disease. But instead of dispensing it himself, he had it done by the shaman! When the shaman hesitated at first to use it, he infected himself with the disease, and showed the shaman that his "power" could heal him! After healing the whole village, the shaman became the first convert to share Olson's gospel to the tribal leaders and people, who in turn spread it to the rest of their tribe. The Motiliones are now among the best medical professionals in Colombia!

In contrast with the prevalent "extraction evangelism" of Christian missions, people movements encourage converts to stay in their families and communities, so that they can share their faith with their compatriots (cf. Lim 2010; Talman and Travis 2015). The focus is on conversions of adults, preferably leaders of households, clans, and even whole people groups. Most mission efforts have focused on the youth, who have been put under severe stress and persecution, often unnecessarily just because of our rejectionist and separatist stance. Not being major decision-makers, these converts are considered rebels and traitors when they refuse to follow family traditions. There is much wisdom in the early church's practice of conversions of household heads, responsible adults who upon conversion (and immediate baptism) include their whole families, thereby ensuring a solid beachhead for evangelization, and also avoiding unnecessary trauma and persecution of young converts. Hence young converts must be discipled on how to remain in their family and trained to win their parents as soon as possible.

Moreover, because of the strong family ties and ethnic solidarity in fear cultures, changes cannot be introduced from the outside. The expatriate must therefore yield leadership to the new believers to decide which beliefs and practices to adopt or modify and which ones to discard. The "person of peace" must remain an insider, and local leaders should be appointed and developed as soon as possible. Since they are usually responsible adults, their plans and decisions will often be correct and appropriate, based on the wisdom of their culture. Hence people movements can happen only when it is truly self-governing, preferably from the beginning. This can be done only through insiders.

SELF-PROPAGATING

Secondly, people movements are initiated and propagated by insiders. And Neo-Pentecostals are self-propagating. As fresh converts they have the excitement and zeal to share their faith effectively with their relatives and friends, and even strangers. Such spontaneous and contagious witness is often combined with experiences of healings (physical, emotional, and social) and deliverance from demonic oppression. Since they remain lay-led (only a few can effectively aspire to become educated clergymen) in small groups that are extensions of their church, their witness extends to government, business, media, and all sectors of society.

Such spontaneous lay mobilization has resulted in effective penetration of Christian values in the social, political, and economic sectors. Through their Pentecostal theology and active laity, these churches have been able to break the sacred-secular dichotomy. *The Cape Town Commitment* highlights the "falsehood of a sacred-secular divide" which "has permeated the Church's thinking and action," by affirming that "God is Lord of all of life." It labels this dichotomy as

> a major obstacle to the mobilization of all God's people in the mission of God, and we call upon Christians worldwide to reject its unbiblical assumptions and resist its damaging effects. We challenge the tendency to see ministry and mission (local and cross-cultural) as being mainly the work of church-paid ministers and missionaries, who are a tiny percentage of the whole body of Christ. (TCTC 2011, 35–36)

The Neo-Pentecostal experience of "personal identity transformation" helps people to overcome their marred identity and passive fatalism due to their sense of powerlessness (Myers 2015, 117–118). Such empowerment redefines oneself as a victor and not a victim, and in God's eyes as a somebody and not a nobody (Freeman 2012, 24–25; cf. Jayakumar 2011). This results in new moral behavior which is pro-transformational and challenges cultural practices and traditional religion which some missions hesitate to address for fear of charges of cultural imperialism. This also effects reconciled relationships in families and communities, which in turn creates hospitable environments and helpful lifestyles for the common good. Hence, "Neo-Pentecostal churches are embedded institutions that change people and their narratives, alter social behavior and create new meaning, vision and hope for the future" (Freeman 2012, 24–25).

Yet their potential for maximum mobilization for effective TM has been diminished by their retention of clergy and clergy-led structures. They still ordain pastors (preferably full-time), and their mission practice still consists of sending church-planters (ideally ordained career missionaries) to plant churches (often to transplant the sending church's pattern) in other places. Unless combined with great cultural sensitivity and ecclesiastical flexibility, such strategy will have slow and less effective results.

It would be more effective if they would adopt a mission strategy called disciple multiplication movement (DMM) in house or simple church networks (HCN). This follows the spirituality of Jesus and the apostles who made disciples and modeled servant leadership by just equipping all believers to live according to God's will (Mark 10:42–45; 1 Pet 5:1–3; 2 Tim 2:1–2). Following the pattern of how Jesus discipled his first group of followers (Mark 3:13–15), each Christ-follower just needs to be equipped with three discipling skills: (a) hearing God through prayerful meditation (or "quiet time" = *lectio divina*) to turn his word (*logos*) into a word (*rhema*) to be obeyed, (b) making their own disciples and being discipled through participating in a "house church" with fellow believers in sharing life and Bible reflections together and, (c) doing friendship evangelism by sharing what they learn of God and God's will with their networks of non-believing relatives and friends.

A transformed socio-religious culture will reflect more and more the simple faith of the Torah (Deut 6:1–11), even made simpler without blood sacrifices since they have been fulfilled in Christ on the cross (cf. Atherburn & Felton 2000, Cavey 2007, and Lim 2008). Simple religiosity helps sustain self-propagation; it is easy to replicate across borders and cultures in our globalized pluralist world even by unsophisticated "laypeople." The secularization process that has come along with modernization, urbanization, and globalization may help hasten the formation of CTCs. The super-naturalist worldview consists of so many unknowns and conjectures, where each one's subjective experiences can elicit varied interpretations which usually end up as superstitions. On the other hand, we must be wary of secularism which denies the reality of the supernatural and miracles.

HCN leaders need to equip *all* believers (cf. Eph 4:11–16) in small groups, usually in their residences and workplaces for a season. The best DMM combines with community development and radical contextualization strategies in what is labeled "insider movements" nowadays. As Christ-centered individuals and families will be "incarnated" in the structures of their communities, they will naturally rise in leadership as they love and serve their neighbors in practical ways. As they facilitate the transformational development of their neighborhood they enhance their proximate communities "from the inside out" as they share their blessings as servant-partners with other communities in establishing CTCs. Such simple mission strategy will surely lead to more rapid and sustainable self-propagation.

SELF-SUPPORTING

Thirdly, the simple self-propagating structure of the church will also make it easier to be self-supporting for TM. The Neo-Pentecostals are already indigenous not just in leadership and programming, but also in finances, not dependent on outside resources (Freeman 2012, 24; Myers 2015, 119). Often, they hardly need any training in basic TM. (On the transformational holism in Pentecostal theology, see Myers 1999, 61–81 and Tizon 2008, 92–97,141–148). Though generally poor and living in poor communities, their spontaneous lay mobilization has made their expansion happen without any need for external funding and fund-raising.

Yet to form CTCs through people movements, they also need to transform their understanding of biblical spirituality and stewardship, which will make them more sustainably self-supporting. Biblical spirituality is to grow in faith and love for Jesus Christ. The Holy Spirit will guide people to become less concerned with religious practices since they are freed from the fear of spirits and demons which cause superstitious practices that require much expenditure. Instead, they are to grow "unto Christ," liberated from sin (especially greed, Col 3:5) to become more generous (more caring toward and sharing with their neighbors), which is the "agape" law of Christ (Gal 5:13–23, 6:1–2; cf. Isa 1:10–18, 58:1–12; Mic 6:6–8; Amos 5:21–24; Rom 13:8–10), that takes away all fears (1 John 4:18).

The best way to demonstrate God's power in fear cultures is to love our neighbors, through our "good works," not "signs and wonders," which their shamans and priests can also do. This is what biblical spirituality is all about: to glorify God as His light in the world through our good works (Matt 5:16), which is the summary of the Torah in the Great Commandment (Matt 22:37–39) and in the Golden Rule to do to others what we want to be done to us (7:12). This is the positive and higher version of Confucius' dictum, "Don't do to others what you don't want to be done to you." This is perfected in Jesus' New Commandment which raises the standard to the highest level: to love one another as he loved us (John 13:34–35), which is self-sacrificial (1 John 3:16–18).

We should disciple all Christ-believers to devote their time, energy, resources, and skills to do community services, from their homes, offices, and any community. If needed and capable, they can build community ministry centers, and also turn existing church buildings (as well as temples, mosques, and synagogues) into such. There is really no need to build more religious buildings for conducting religious services, for any meeting at any place turns into a "visible church" (= Christ-centered worship/liturgy) when it includes prayer and Bible reflection/sharing (cf. Matt 18:19–20; 1 Tim 4:4–5; John 4:21–24), as those gathered urge each other on to "love and good works" (Heb 10:24–25; cf. 2 Tim 3:16–17). If Christ-followers are known as people who love, care, and share, there will most likely be a people movement that will spread to form CTCs quite organically or naturally, just like what happened in the 1980–90s in China, and perhaps in all TMs that have occurred among the poor. There's really no need to be "high tech"; we only need to be "high touch."

Yet TM aims beyond self-support, but also release from poverty without becoming entrapped in the consumer society of today's global market system. The prosperity gospel shared among the poor lifts their spirits and empowers them. But when Neo-Pentecostals (and other churches) preach personal empowerment instead of the generosity gospel among the rich and middle class, it leads to greed and pride if not social injustice and misrepresentation of Christ (Yung 2005, 53–54). Instead Christ-followers simply need to promote social entrepreneurship that will extend their love for their neighbors materially and socially.

Most of the global South, especially Africa (Easterly 2006), has remained economically poor in spite of billions of dollars of foreign development aid and rich national resources (Corbett and Fikkert 2009). To alleviate poverty, the poor have to be empowered to join the supply chain of the local and even global market. With microenterprise development and micro-credit loans (Bussau and Mask 2003), the poor can start savings-for-investment groups which will grow into cooperatives and social enterprises (Rundle and Steffen 2003). They can then link to the business as mission movement which considers businesspeople as ministers in the marketplace, with four bottom lines: financial, social, spiritual, and ecological (cf. Yamamori et al. 2003). They then become part of the global movement for opposing the dominant capitalist market economy and advancing the social solidarity economy, which advocates for social entrepreneurship and fair trade.

SELF-THEOLOGIZING

Last but not least, unlike the usual practice of most Christians who transfer their theology and spirituality to new converts, indigenous leaders should be encouraged to do their own theologizing. This is necessary because people like to become Christ-followers without crossing ethnic, linguistic, or class barriers (McGavran 2005). This can be done as they appreciate their primal worldview by maximizing commonalities, focusing on Christ, and reflecting on the Bible.

Maximizing Commonalities

There is a wide variety of folk beliefs and practices even just among folk Buddhists and animists in general. The rule is to listen carefully, and to accept their views (including religious ones) non-judgmentally, with gentleness and respect (1 Pet 3:15), even if they may be dead wrong. Corrections may come later, as they prayerfully reflect individually and corporately on the scriptures through the guidance of the Holy Spirit (John 16:12–15).

Perhaps the main reason for the effective evangelism of Neo-Pentecostals among folk religionists is that they share the same supernatural worldview, and thus communicating the gospel clearly is quite natural and spontaneous, with hardly any need for specialized study at all. For instance, most folk Buddhists, like Chinese Filipinos, believe in only one universal spirit whose manifestations (*hua shen*) include all the religious figures on earth (Buddha, Jesus Christ, etc.). They believe this spirit is the source of existence and is benevolent and effective, performs miracles, and brings good fortune (Uayan 2005, 70). The Chinese lean toward monotheism, although for many the supreme spirit (*tien* or *tao* = heaven or way/word) may not be clearly personal as in Judeo-Christian and other theistic faiths. They also believe the universe is permeated with the cosmic breath or life force called *Qi*, usually described in a bipolar manner as *Yin* and *Yang*. All things that exist result from the interplay of these two forces. Humans are but a feeble part of this cosmos and as such must live in harmony with the cosmological process. Infinite numbers of gods, deities, spirits, and ancestors make up the vast pantheon of Chinese religion (Tan 1996, 65).

Paul Hiebert has helped us understand the primal worldview. It has three tiers of reality: the bottom level is the empirical world as experienced through human senses; the top level includes cosmic realms beyond human experience. In between, one finds the "middle level": the unseen or trans-empirical realities of this world. These three levels emerge out of the intersection of this world (earth, universe) and other worlds (heaven, hell), of the seen (empirical) and unseen (trans-empirical). He also points out that the "boundaries between the categories are often fuzzy" and the "organic and mechanical analogies form a horizontal continuum with many shades between the poles" (1999, 50).

Thus for Christian communicators, unlike the predominant Christian rejectionist outlook, it is important to have an appreciative approach which highlights commonalities for relevance and contextualized witness. We should emphasize what unites not what differentiates us. Folk Buddhists should be viewed as seekers of the truth. Christ-followers can embrace their values and beliefs that do not contradict scriptures. We can recognize in their worldviews the face of Christ, hidden yet truly present and revealing some aspects of the mystery of God (cf. Richardson 1981; Sanneh 2003; Singh 1926). In fact, there are many commonalities in the Christian and animist worldviews on the spirit world

(Yong 2005, 102–110; Kung 1986; and Pieris 1993). Both believe there is more to reality than the material world that engages the senses. In fact, the supernatural world is intrinsically interrelated with the material realm. Both also believe that the demonic is often, if not always, the source of the experience of evil and suffering; hence suffering (*dukkha*) can be used as a bridge to evangelizing Buddhists (Lim 2011, 77–88).

Though monistic, Buddhist cosmology distinguishes between good and evil as well as between the demonic and evil. The premier Buddhist symbol of the demonic (Mara) is that of the tempter who arouses desires which lead to death. The identity of Mara clearly overlaps with the Christian view of Satan (Boyd 1975). Both also agree in the cosmological conflict between good and evil in the universe—with eternal consequences! To show some commonalities with Christian demonology, this work depicts the cosmic struggle as particularized in two representative Buddhist traditions of exorcism: the Theravada in Sri Lanka, and the Mahayana in China, esp. Tibet.

Theravada Buddhism is itself a complex tradition with various faces spread out throughout South and Southeast Asia (cf. Swearer 1995). Any attempt to understand Theravadin notions of the demonic would necessarily have to take into account data stretching from Sri Lanka to Myanmar (Spiro 1978), Cambodia (Coggan 2015) and Thailand (Tambiah 1970; Davis 1993; Barlow 2012; Johnson 2012; Smith 2012). We focus here on exorcism in Sinhalese Buddhism, which is itself dynamic and complex (Winz 1954; Kapferer 1983). The centrality of the Pali scriptures to Sinhalese Buddhism accounts in part for the basic features of its demonology and its rites of exorcism. In a complex, multi-tiered cosmos, human health and prosperity is most immediately implicated by the activity of various deities, devas, and petas (*yakkas*). When afflicted, the Sinhalese seek out various healers including holy men, Buddhist monks, astrologers, oracles, priests, traditional medicine men, and exorcists (*edura*). If the problem is diagnosed as originating from demonic sources, rituals of exorcism are performed.

Similar doctrinal and ritual structures can be found in the complexities of Tibetan or Tantric Buddhism (De Nebesky-Wojkowitz 1956; Fisher 1978; Lopez 1997) as well as Chinese Mahayana religion (Ching 1993; Yip 1999), which have their equivalents in Korean and Japanese traditions (Kiyota 1987; Fukuda 2012). A ritualistic and magical tradition focused primarily on this-worldly benefits, such religion is the convergence of indigenous Tibetan elements and almost all of the Brahmanic and Hindu deities into the stream of Mahayana beliefs and practices as the latter spread eastward during the first few centuries. Demonic figures are especially wrathful and terrifying, including vampires, witches, zombies, goblins, and other malignant spiritual beings. Tibetans turn to lamas, Buddhist monks and priests, and other specialists for help with their afflictions, misfortunes, and other tragedies. Hence, generally both Buddhists and Christians believe similarly that the demonic world is real and the demons can be confronted, engaged, and vanquished through rituals of exorcism.

Christians and Buddhists also share similarities in exorcism rituals. In both traditions, a supreme power is recognized: that of Jesus by the Holy Spirit and that of Buddha through the dharma and the sangha; the invocation of their respective names are central; the identification of the offending spirits is done; mantra-like repetitions of various phrases of prayer and exorcism formulas are used; visualization is frequently exercised; and clapping and other physical gestures are employed. Christians emphasize baptism (in water for non-Pentecostals and in the Spirit for Pentecostals) and a moral life of discipleship in the way of Jesus as an ongoing antidote, while Buddhists also emphasize the importance of righteous living according to Buddha's precepts in walking the Eightfold Path. Perhaps Christians can affirm appreciatively that successful attempts at exorcism through Buddhist monks and rituals are also God's common grace at work among those who are oppressed by the demonic. All victories against any form of evil can ultimately come from God alone.

Focusing on Christ

Of course there are also differences, sometimes glaring ones. Yet raising unnecessary difficulties for evangelism should be minimized by avoiding any criticism of other cultures and religions, especially when rapport has not yet been built. If any conflictive differences that we consider erroneous or false in the folk Buddhist beliefs and practices do surface, we can just take note of them and let them pass. There is no use arguing, since they are still blinded by Satan anyway, and winning an argument usually means losing a friend. Our approach should be marked with gentleness and respect (1 Pet 3:15; cf. Col 4:5–6).

There should be only one criterion for an allegiance encounter in evangelism: "Christ and Him crucified" (cf. 1 Cor 1:18–2:5). He is the fulfillment of the best of all religious searching and consciousness. Much of what constitutes other religions is *praeparatio evangelica*, seeds of God's truth from which all other truths are derived and developed. As Paul told the Lystrans, "[God] has not left himself without testimony" among all nations and was the one who answered their prayers to the pantheon of gods in their Greek and Roman mythologies (Acts 14:17). He appreciated the Athenians' religiosity rather than rebuked their idolatry (17:22–23). In this dialogic and appreciative approach, we show that we are willing to learn from other traditions, while also inviting them to listen to ours.

For most converts of and witnesses to a power encounter, their first allegiance will naturally be to "*Christus victor*" (the victorious Christ), in whose name they experienced his all-powerful victory over deities and spirits in their worldview. Such faith in Jesus is enough for their salvation (and baptism). There is even no need to include the doctrine of "vicarious atonement" aspect of salvation immediately. Neither do they need to completely understand the uniqueness and exclusiveness of Jesus as Lord and Savior (intellectual assent). They will learn of such truths through their own reading and study of scriptures later by the guidance of the Holy Spirit. Saving faith is simply to turn one's allegiance from "other gods" to God and Jesus who they got to know in the power encounter (cf. 1 Thess 1:9). Saving faith is just to "repent and believe in Jesus." Those who are in a hurry can point the convert to reflect on John 1:1–18 and Colossians 1:15–23.

For Chinese, their allegiance may be to Christ as the *Dao* or *Shen*. For Japanese, Christ may be known as the "the Great *Kami*" who is "more powerful than other *kami*," the life force, the head of the cosmos, who rules over the various gods and blesses Japanese life with life-giving power (Fukuda 2012, 183–192). To Theravada Buddhists, Jesus may be introduced as the *Maitreya* who has already come (Thaiwathcharamas 1983). To Mahayana Buddhists, he may be presented as the *dharma* that leads to the true *nirvana*, breaking the stronghold of *samsara* ruled by the law of *karma* (Lim 1983, 187–193). To Tibetan Buddhists, he may be shown to be "the lama of lamas," of a superior lama-hood than the Dalai Lama's tradition. The adoption of Buddhist concepts fits the use of the common Greco-Roman philosophical *logos* (word) in John's gospel and *mysterion* (mystery) and *pleroma* (fullness) in the Pauline epistles. In some contexts, folk Buddhists may be shown Christ as the supreme God of their traditional animistic religion; for example in Sri Lanka, where they believe in *Sakra* who is the unique omniscient god, whose seat of stone warms up when a human is in trouble (cf. Mendis 1990, 25). In all these cases, traditional usages have been adopted, and then infused with Christ-centered meanings.

After they come to faith in Christ, the Holy Spirit will guide them to all truth (John 16:13–15), perhaps with our help as we point them to reflect on appropriate biblical texts (Acts 17:11). New believers can learn of Christ and his teachings and unlearn all that are unbiblical in their worldviews in the discipling process.

Salvation is through their simple faith to follow Jesus, so they can come to him "just as they are," in their socio-religious context, with no requirement for immediate worldview change. Otherwise, who of us can claim to be saved, since our worldviews are not completely biblical yet (cf. 1 Cor 13:8)? Most of us expect too much from new believers, usually that they not only believe in Jesus, but also follow all the right beliefs and practices (actually our religious/denominational traditions) as soon as possible. Our objective at the start should be to impress our new friends that we are not a threat or enemy who came to change them, but we are friends who have come to improve their lives.

New believers should retain their cultural and religious background (cf. 1 Cor 7:18–19). This empathetic approach is the best way to develop indigenous theologies and to catalyze more effective people movements to form CTCs with no more fear of the spirit world. In relation to spiritual realities, this positive stance toward accommodating as much of indigenous folk religious cultures as possible would enable a better understanding of the excluded middle in varied contextualized theologies. Their fear of fate, gods, spirits, and ghosts is best viewed as folk religion and not idolatry. There's no need to deny or reject the existence of such beings. The good news for them is that in Christ, there is freedom from fear of such beings, which is the source of so much superstition.

These CTCs will show that although they retain most of the primal worldview of their community, they now relate to them with confidence in the unique power of Christ and no longer in fear of the spirits (cf. 1 Cor 8, 10), starting with appreciating 1 Timothy 4:4–5. Along with believing in the One Creator God and thanking him for his wonderful creation, they can sanctify all things and overcome evil and the demonic with simply two things: the word of God and prayer in Jesus' name. Both are considered in 2 Corinthians 10:4–5 to be the weapons to demolish strongholds so that "we can take captive every thought to make it obedient to Christ" (cf. Eph 6:17–18).

The theological framework for such self-theologizing is best expressed by the Apostle Paul: for expatriates "to become all things to all people" (1 Cor 9:19–23) and for local converts to remain in their socio-religious identities (7:18–19), so that they may not only be able to win some (especially heads of households, clans, and communities) and thereby disciple them to win the rest, but also to be true to the essence of the biblical faith that is multicultural. To do otherwise is to repeat the "heresy" of the Judaizers who expected Gentile converts to adopt Jewish forms (Taylor 2015, 380–383). To develop dynamic and relevant Christianity, the alternative to contextualization has produced very poor results. Walls perceptively notes, "Christian faith must go on being translated, must continuously enter into vernacular culture and interact with it, or it withers and fades," (1997, 152).

Reflecting on the Bible

How then can we ensure that all these self-theologizing projects will not fall into false teaching (heresy) and wrong practices (syncretism)? As long as we focus on making disciples who take the Bible seriously, we should not be afraid of heresy where there is faith in the supremacy and uniqueness of Jesus Christ. Nor should we fear syncretism as long as objects made for idolatrous and occult practices are destroyed. All the rest of religio-cultural forms can be adopted and "redeemed" for Christ-centered ends to fulfill indigenous functions and convey Christ-oriented meanings, as it was done in the Bible: anointing oil (Jas 5:14), Paul's aprons and handkerchiefs (Acts 19:12), Peter's shadow (Acts 5:15), and Jesus' garment (Luke 8:44). Such critical appreciation of what is already there is not lowering down to the lowest denominator, but leveling up to the highest possible revelation!

Since almost all fear cultures are also oral cultures, they have another built-in advantage that can guard against heresy and syncretism. This is using biblical stories to transform their culture. N.T. Wright avers that stories constitute the core of every culture's worldview (1992, 38–40). A culture houses its central convictions in its fundamental narrative, whether its narrative is implicit or explicit. The mythologies in oral cultures around the world are examples of this. Those stories answer four fundamental worldview questions: Who am I? Where am I? What has gone wrong? and What can be done about it? Every culture uses stories to tell what it means to be human, what kind of world we live in, why there is suffering and evil, and what we can do to deal with them. Christianity has its own distinctive answers to these questions. So to transform people's worldviews, we need to tell biblical stories that offer alternative answers to their questions. The Bible answers these questions with special vividness and power in Genesis. Moreover, when we tell stories chronologically, we are giving a powerful alternative worldview from the very start in our evangelism. Biblical stories and the worldview embedded in them can replace or refine the cultural stories and the worldview embedded in them.

Wright argues that this is why Jesus told stories, particularly parables. Jesus intended them to challenge the existing Jewish worldview and to provide an alternative picture of reality that was called the kingdom of God.

> Stories are, actually, peculiarly good at modifying or subverting other stories and their worldviews. Where head-on attack would certainly fail, the parable hides the wisdom of the serpent behind the innocence of the dove, gaining entrance and favour which can then be used to change assumptions, which the hearer would otherwise keep hidden away for safety. (1992, 40)

Wright also shows that stories lie at the core of a worldview; formal belief statements, including propositional and theological statements, grow out of those stories. Thus discipleship that offers only propositional teaching cannot transform the worldview.

If we give only propositional teaching and do not present biblical stories to challenge existing worldview stories, we run the risk of syncretism. The cultural stories will continue to comprise the core of the worldview, and discipleship will deal only with the peripheral dimensions of the person's life. Because propositional beliefs are generated by and reflected in the stories, those cultural stories will continually be challenging the Christian propositional content. We end with the tragedy of professing Christians who assent to biblical propositions, but whose essential worldview and value system are deeply tied to worldview stories that have gone unchallenged. That mix of contradictory religious beliefs and practices is the essence of syncretism.

To avoid syncretism, therefore, it is most important to provide a recorded "oral Bible" for each people group in their language. This is a recorded set of stories, biblically accurate and told in their worldview context. At a later time when a written Bible translation is completed, then it could be recorded to provide a standard point of reference. With an "oral Bible," the stories are communicated in natural, live situations by mother tongue "storytellers" from the people group, using the mannerisms and storytelling techniques which are appropriate to that people group. (ION 2005, 32–39). Telling a biblical story in an interesting and accurate way is a single but powerful manner of freeing disciples to process Scripture. They can do it with a minimum of interpretive baggage coming from the outsider's culture and experience of Christianity.

It takes generations to develop systematic theologies directly from the word of God. Andrew Walls (1997) has shown how theological contextualization proceeded historically. He identifies three stages in the process of conversion of Hellenistic thought by the patristic fathers, which spanned more than three generations. During the first stage, the Hellenistic church experienced the missionary stage, typified and led by Paul as he began to adapt Jewish vocabulary and forms to Hellenistic categories and vocabulary. The second stage in the contextualization process is the convert stage. The main feature of this stage is that of identity, and Justin Martyr is its representative. He was convinced that Christ can inhabit that Hellenistic world and work to transform it. He notes,

> Conversion . . . means to *turn what is already there in a new direction*. It is not a matter of substituting something new for something old—that is proselytizing, a method that the early church could have adopted but deliberately chose to jettison. Nor is conversion a matter of adding something new to something old, as a supplement or in synthesis. Rather, Christian conversion involves redirecting what is already there, turning it in the direction of Christ. (Walls 1997, 150)

The third and final stage in this process is called the refiguration stage, typified by Origen. This stage can be achieved only by a later generation, following after the convert stage, which had grown up in the Christian faith and yet was reconciled to its pre-Christian inheritance and was not afraid of either. The burning question for many Christians in non-western cultures is whether the Jesus preached to them by western missionaries can ever be at home in their native culture. Will they have to surrender their identity and culture to follow a native Jesus? In other words, does the conversion demanded by the gospel include changing their socio-religious identity? Or will vernacular translations of Jesus and the scriptures open the door for Christ to enter into and abide in their cultures?

The incipient CTC should do the self-theologizing patiently. As they prayerfully reflect on Scripture individually and corporately, they will develop all kinds of theologies, like in the West. We need not waste time and energy in perfecting our (and correcting others') theologies, but trust the Holy Spirit to guide everyone into all truth (John 16:13–15) over time. God delights in creativity and diversity. We must allow freedom of conscience and allow each believer and each group/community to find the formulations of their faith in light of the scriptures, and to avoid being judgmental or legalistic (cf. 1 Cor 1–4; Rom 14:1–15:7). This inclusivist stance differs from the general exclusivistic denominationalism and separatist ethos of most missions today.

So far, Neo-Pentecostals have already shown evidence of how even those from secularized and non-religious cultures in the West can develop their own theologies biblically and creatively. Perhaps one of the most developed is that of Charles Kraft (2002, 188–194): in his cosmology and demonology, he has classified the types of spirits, and shown that in each category there are spirits assigned by Satan and competing spirits (angels) assigned by God. On God's side are angels and archangels (Dan 10:13, 21), and on Satan's side are "wicked spiritual forces in the heavenly world, like principalities, authorities, world rulers and spiritual forces of this dark age" (Eph 6:12). Who among Christians and CTCs will agree with his detailed depiction of the spirit world? Very few, if there is any. Each Christ-follower and CTC has their own unique life experiences, biblical hermeneutics, church tradition, as well as religio-cultural background. We should expect and welcome a multitude of contextual theologies emerging from all CTCs as they discover truths from the scriptures for themselves.

CTCs should also be fully authorized to develop not just their own theology but also their own spirituality—to express and live out their faith in light of their prayerful reflection of Scripture. As they become more transformational (other-centered and ministry-oriented) and missional (cross-cultural-oriented), they will be freed from the fear of the demonic and fear of syncretism. The main principle of contextualization is to retain the existent socio-religious culture as much as possible (1 Cor 7:18–19). It is to integrate Christian faith with the religio-cultural identity of the people. Failure to do so has resulted in the transplanting of foreign churches, and not the planting of indigenous churches.

Such cultural dislocations invite real syncretism, even Christo-paganism. Hollenweger (1999) and Van Rheenen (2006) have shown that Christendom has historically been syncretistic, adopting different philosophical and ideological frameworks in their theologies, like neo-Platonism, Aristotelianism, Rationalism, Capitalism, and more.

Contextualization of spirituality follows the logic of the divine incarnational method. Jesus (with ceremonial washing), John the Baptist (with baptism) and Paul (with the altar to the unknown god, Acts 17) risked being misunderstood. They met their people where they were at in their understanding, and then built bridges of communication, taking them from the known to the unknown. This is the principle of "becoming all things to all people" (1 Cor 9:19–23). The alternative is either importing new forms that would most likely be foreign (which will be easily rejected) or just leaving a vacuum (which will create an "empty house" that will invite seven demons worse than the first). Of course, the content and meaning of all religious forms, rituals, and festivities (and secular ones, too, like Independence Day, Memorial Day, etc.) have to be constantly explained and reinterpreted, lest they lose their meaning and relevance.

There is often no need to introduce new rites or practices in place of old ones. There are already rituals and festivals within cultures that are of themselves purely cultural and amoral (the Reformers' *adiaphora*). These should be welcomed and used by Christians, because they are familiar and give a sense of solidarity and security for the people. The goal is to develop local theologies and expressions of faith which are culturally appropriate and wholesome; any other way would mean a perpetuation of cultural and theological imperialism. We must seek to use the existing religio-cultural expressions except when they distinctly clash with the gospel (Schreiter 1985, 144–158).

We must allow young believers to follow their family traditions, including bowing down in worship (Gen 18:2, 27:29, 33:3;

Phil 2:10), offering incense (cf. Mal 1:11), eating food offered to idols (1 Cor 8, 10) and making tablets or scrolls, just like Paul did not object to the Corinthian practice of "baptizing the dead" (1 Cor 15:29). Out of love, they must never cause their families, clans, and communities to stumble over socio-religious practices (1 Cor 10:32–33, cf. 8:9–13). For Japanese, Fukuda (2012, 219–30) suggests bowing down (*hainei/ojigi*), hand-clapping in patterned rhythm (*teuchi/sanbon-jime*), water (*mizu*), and salt (*shio*) may all be adopted and used.

Many Christians have a rejectionist theology of culture, so they do not appreciate indigenous ways, not realizing that most of their own socio-religious expressions have been baptized into Christian usage by their previously pagan ancestors. They deny and reject for others what their faith-ancestors have done. Instead they should follow Bavinck's view of *possessio*, to take possession of heathen forms of life, and make them new; retaining and enlisting so-called pagan practices in the service of Jesus Christ is perfectly proper (1960, 178). Tippett observes,

> In the process of incorporating converts into their new fellowship group or congregation, indigenous forms, rites, festivals, and so forth, which can be given a new Christian value content, have greater likelihood of finding permanent acceptance than foreign forms and rituals," and "when good functional substitutes have been proposed and accepted at the time of the primary religious change (conversion) . . . these have stood the test of time and proved effective. (1985, 185)

It is not syncretism, because the content and meaning focus on Christ and his work on the cross, as it emphasizes that the forms must be culturally-sensitive. Those who oppose this approach can be counter-charged with syncretism, with imposing the secularized Enlightenment worldview of science and rationalism that deny the existence and powers of beings in Hiebert's "excluded middle," as well as their denominational version of Christendom.

The forms of the Christ-centered spirituality in the new CTCs will probably differ from mainstream westernized Christianities. Many Pentecostal theologians and missiologists recognize that their theologies are still very American or western (Ma 2005, 68–69; cf. Wostyn 2005, 372–375). Are we ready for Asian theologies to use Buddhist, Taoist, Confucian, or Islamic worldviews as their framework? There is no divine or universal form of Christianity which is suitable for all believers at all times. This is not a "to each his own" uncritical theologizing. Caught in the tension of Scripture, church tradition, and one's culture, each believer must choose their ways to follow Christ and obey God's word in their context. The Holy Spirit will use the word to illumine and direct all believers to be God's priests, prophets, and kings in Christ. It is the insider-believers themselves who will make the decisions. Some errors may arise, but the CTCs around them will keep them in check.

CONCLUSION

So, what should we do to form CTCs through TM in the Buddhist world and beyond? Christ-centeredness must be indigenized in fear cultures in order to transform Chinese, Buddhist, and similar folk religious communities from within through people movements and HCNs. In Asia, and perhaps in the world, most HCNs are Neo-Pentecostal in theology, so we may rightly consider them the "Fourth Wave" and perhaps the "Last Wave" of the Holy Spirit. And interestingly, if all the HCNs in Asia were one denomination, they would constitute the largest denomination in Asia today. With the rise of new religious movements, mostly with primal worldviews in our postmodern globalized world, this approach may be the most relevant and effective mission strategy globally in the twenty-first century, too.

Thousands of CTCs were formed through TMs in the rural villages of central and southeast China in the post-Mao era, as the HCNs learned to practice the priesthood of all believers without the structures of Christendom or denominations. Some of these people movements remain missional through the Back to Jerusalem movement, but most have lost their momentum as they became part of Christendom again, especially with the return of ordination (clergy-laity dichotomy), seminaries (formal leadership training), church buildings (sacred-secular dichotomy) and imported discipleship materials (back to dependency!). Perhaps there needs to be another strong religious repressive regime to help David relearn how to fight Goliath simply with a slingshot, rather than sophisticatedly in Saul's armor?

TM should be initiated in these fear cultures to break the traditional strongholds that have kept multitudes of folk Buddhists and folk religionists from indigenous faith in Christ. New brands of Christianity in folk religious contexts have begun, but we need to multiply CTCs through more people movements and HCNs. The integrity and credibility of Christ and his victory on the cross in the animistic pre-modern world is at stake. Without this shift, we condemn two billion folk Buddhists and folk religionists to reject Christ through a Christianity that is perceived to be foreign and irrelevant to their spirit world and devoid of power to transform their communities from the bottom up and from the inside out. May God find us faithful in doing and supporting TMs, which are forming indigenous CTCs in fear cultures in the Buddhist world and beyond.

References

Atherburn, Stephen, and Jack Felton. 2000. *More Jesus less religion*. Colorado Springs, CO: Waterbrook Press.

Barlow, Jane. 2011. "Suffering, death, and funerals in Thailand." In *Suffering: Christian reflections on Buddhist dukkha*, edited by Paul de Neui, 93–114. Pasadena, CA: William Carey Library.

Bavinck, J. H. 1960. *An introduction to the science of missions.* Philadelphia, PA: Presbyterian & Reformed Publishing Co.

Boyd, James. 1975. *Satan and Mara: Christian and Buddhist symbols of evil.* Leiden: Brill.

Bussau, David, and Russell Mask. 2003. *Christian microenterprise development: An introduction.* Oxford: Regnum.

Cavey, Bruxy. 2007. *The end of religion.* Colorado Springs, CO: NavPress.

Ching, Julia. 1993. *Chinese religions.* Maryknoll, NY: Orbis.

Coggan, Philip. 2015. *Spirit worlds: Cambodia, the Buddha and the naga.* Oxford: John Beaufoy Publishing.

Corbett, Steve and Brian Fikkert. 2009. *When helping hurts: How to alleviate poverty without hurting the poor and yourself.* Chicago, IL: Moody.

Davis, John R. 1993. *Poles apart: Contextualizing the gospel.* Bangkok: OMF Publications.

Easterly, William. 2006. *The white man's burden: Why the west's efforts to aid the rest have done so much ill and so little good.* New York: Penguin Press.

Escobar, Samuel. 2000. "The global scenario at the turn of the century." In *Global missiology for the 21st century: The Iguassu dialogue,* edited by William Taylor, 25–46. Grand Rapids, MI: Baker.

Fisher, James, ed. 1978. *Himalayan anthropology: The Indo-Tibetan interface.* The Hague: Mouton Publishers.

Freeman, Dena, ed. 2012. *Pentecostalism and development: Churches, NGOs and social change in Africa.* Basingstoke: Palgrave Macmillan.

Fukuda, Mitsuo. 2012. *Developing a contextualized church as a bridge to Christianity in Japan*. Gloucester, MA: Wide Margin.

Garrison, David. 2004. *Church planting movements*. Midlothian, VA: WIGTake Resources.

Hiebert, Paul, R. D. Shaw, and Tite Tienou. 1999. *Understanding folk religion*. Grand Rapids, MI: Baker.

Hollenweger, Walter. 1999. "Syncretism and capitalism." *Asian Journal of Pentecostal studies* 2, no. 1: 47–61.

International Orality Network & Lausanne Committee for World Evangelization. 2005. *Making disciples of oral learners*. Lausanne Occasional Papers No. 54. Bangalore: Sudhindra.

Jayakumar, Christian. 2011. *God of the empty-handed: Poverty, power and the kingdom of God*, 2nd ed. Victoria, Aust.: Acorn Press.

Johnson, Alan. 2011. "Investigating Laypeople's Conception of *Dukkha*." In *Suffering: Christian reflections on Buddhist dukkha*, edited by Paul de Neui, 147–62. Pasadena, CA: William Carey Library.

Kapferer, Bruce. 1983. *A celebration of demons: Exorcism and the aesthetics of healing in Sri Lanka*. Bloomington, IN: Indiana University Press.

Kiyota, Minoru, ed. 1987. *Japanese Buddhism*. Tokyo: Buddhist Books International.

Kraft, Charles. 2002. "Contemporary trends in the treatment of spiritual conflicts." In *Deliver us from evil*, edited by Scott Moreau, et al., 177–202. Monrovia, CA: MARC.

Kung, Hans, et al. 1986. *Christianity and the world religions: Paths of dialogue with Islam, Hinduism and Buddhism*. New York: Doubleday & Co.

Lim, David. 1983. "Biblical Christianity in the context of Buddhism." In *Sharing Jesus in the two-thirds world*, edited by V. Samuel and C. Sugden, 175–203. Grand Rapids, MI: Eerdmans.

———. 2008. "Biblical worship rediscovered: A theology for communicating basic Christianity." In *Communicating Christ through story and song: Orality in Buddhist contexts*, edited by Paul de Neui, 27–59. Pasadena, CA: William Carey Library.

———. 2010. "Catalyzing 'insider movements' in Buddhist contexts." In *Family and faith in Asia: The missional impact of extended networks*, edited by Paul de Neui, 31–46. Pasadena, CA: William Carey Library.

———. 2011. "Continuities with suffering as a bridge to evangelizing Buddhists." In *Suffering: Christian reflections on Buddhist dukkha*, edited by Paul de Neui, 77–90. Pasadena, CA: William Carey Library.

Lopez, Donald, Jr., ed. 1997. *Religions of Tibet in practice*. Princeton: Princeton Univ. Press.

Ma, Wonsuk. 2005. "Asian (classical) Pentecostal theology in context." In *Asian and Pentecostal: The charismatic face of Christianity in Asia*, edited by A. Anderson and E. Tang, 59–91. Oxford: Regnum.

McGavran, Donald. 2005. "A people reborn: Foundational insights on people movements." *Mission Frontiers* 27, no. 5 (September–October): 16–17.

Maggay, Melba. 2005. "Toward contextualization from within." In *Doing theology in the Philippines*, edited by E. Acoba et al., 37–50. Mandaluyong City: OMF Literature.

Mendis, Lalith. 1990. *Unashamed*. Colombo: Christian Professionals Forum.

Miller, Donald, and T. Yamamori. 2007. *Global Pentecostalism: The new face of Christian social engagement*. Berkeley, CA: University of California Press.

Myers, Bryant. 1999. *Walking with the poor: Principles and practices of transformational development.* Maryknoll, NY: Orbis.
———. 2015. "Progressive Pentecostalism, development and Christian development NGOs: A challenge and an opportunity." *International Bulletin of Missionary Research* 39, no. 3 (July): 115–20.
Olson, Bruce. 1973. *Bruchko.* Chicester: New Wine Press.
Pieris, Alysius. 1993. "Does Christ have a place in Asia? A panoramic view." In *Any room for Christ in Asia?*, edited by L. Boff and V. Elizondo, 33–47. Maryknoll, NY: Orbis.
Richardson, Don. 1981. *Eternity in their hearts.* Ventura, CA: Regal.
Rundle, Steve, and Tom Steffen. 2003. *Great commission companies.* Downers Grove, IL: InterVarsity.
Samuel, Vinay. 1999. "Mission as transformation." In *Mission as transformation*, edited by V. Samuel and C. Sugden, 227–35. Oxford: Regnum.
Sanneh, Lamin. 2003. *Whose religion is Christianity?* Grand Rapids, MI: Eerdmans.
Schattner, Frank. 2014. *The wheel model: Catalyzing sustainable church planting movements.* William Jessup University.
Schreiter, Robert. 1985. *Constructing local theologies.* Maryknoll, NY: Orbis.
Singh, Sadhu Sundar. 1926. *The spirit world.* Madras: Christian Literature Society.
Smith, Alex. 2011. "Suffering and compassion in Buddhism and Christianity." In *Suffering: Christian reflections on Buddhist dukkha*, edited by Paul de Neui, 57–76. Pasadena, CA: William Carey Library.
Spiro, Mulford. 1978. *Burmese supernaturalism,* expanded edition. Philadelphia, PA: Institute of the Study of Human Issues.
Swearer, Donald. 1995. *The Buddhist world of southeast Asia.* Albany, NY: SUNY Press.

Tambiah, Stanley Jeyaraja. 1970. *Buddhism and the spirit cults in north-east Thailand*. Cambridge: Cambridge University Press.

Talman, Harley, and John Jay Travis, eds. 2015. *Understanding insider movements: Disciples of Jesus within diverse religious communities*. Pasadena, CA: William Carey Library.

Tan, Chiu Eng. 1996. "The cosmos, humans and gods: A comparison of non-Christians and Christians on Chinese beliefs in MetroManila." PhD thesis: Trinity International University.

Taylor, David. 2015. "Contextualization, syncretism, and the demonic in indigenous movements." In *Understanding insider movements*, edited by H. Talman, and J. J. Travis, 375–383. Pasadena, CA: William Carey Library.

The Cape Town Commitment. 2011. Peabody, MA: Hendrickson.

Tippett, Alan. 1973. *Verdict theology in missionary theology*. Pasadena, CA: William Carey Library.

———. 1987. *Introduction to missiology*. Pasadena, CA: William Carey Library.

Tizon, Al. 2008. *Transformation after Lausanne: Radical evangelical mission in global-local perspective*. Eugene, OR: Wipf & Stock.

Uayan, Jean. 2005. "Chap chay lo mi: Disentangling the Chinese-Filipino worldview." In *Naming the unknown God*, edited by E. Acoba, 65–77. Mandaluyong: OMF Literature.

Van Rheenen, Gailyn, ed. 2006. *Contextualization and syncretism: Navigating cultural currents*. Pasadena, CA: William Carey Library.

Walls, Andrew. 1997. "Old Athens and New Jerusalem: Some signposts for Christian scholarship in the early history of mission studies." *International Bulletin of Mission Research* 21, no. 4 (October): 146–53.

Winz, Paul. 1954. *Exorcism and the art of healing in Ceylon*. Leiden: Brill.

Wostyn, Lode. 2005. "Catholic charismatics in the Philippines." In *Asian and Pentecostal: The charismatic face of Christianity in Asia*, edited by A. Anderson and E. Tang, 363–83. Oxford: Regnum.

Wright, N. T. 1992. *The New Testament and the people of God*. Minneapolis, MN: Fortress.

Yamamori, T., B. Myers, and Kenneth Eldred, eds. 2003. *On kingdom business: Transforming missions through entrepreneurial strategies*. Wheaton, IL: Crossway.

Yong, Amos. 2005. "The demonic in Pentecostal/Charismatic Christianity and in the religious consciousness of Asia." In *Asian and Pentecostal: The charismatic face of Christianity in Asia*, edited by A. Anderson and E. Tang, 93–128. Oxford: Regnum.

Yung, Hwa. 2005. "Indigenous Chinese Pentecostal denominations." In *Asian and Pentecostal: The charismatic face of Christianity in Asia*, edited by A. Anderson and E. Tang, 37–57. Oxford: Regnum.

6

How to Communicate the Gospel in a Shame Culture

SOME THOUGHTS ON THE SKILL OF JAPANESE "NOH"

Timothy Hwang Taeyun

Western universalism dawned in the age of Enlightenment, reached its peak in the nineteenth century and was the ideological basis of colonization of the non-western world (Maffesoli 2008, 151). Needless to say, missions during that era was operated within the same framework, characterized in the pursuit of quantitative expansion using the tools of rationalism (Dyrness 1983, 25), systematization of missions, and efficiency with massive productions of the gospel message.

By the twentieth century, however, the two world wars destroyed all confidence in human rationality and western universalism. The disappointed world turned its eyes to the East for alternatives where former colonies were leaping forward as independent countries, yet remained seemingly healthy in traditional values and customs. The recognition of the failure of human reason and the collapse of the existing system led the trend of thought to relativism and uncertainty (Maffesoli 2008, 149–156), and was scientifically supported by the quantum mechanics of Einstein's Relativity Theory and Heisenberg's Uncertainty Theory. A unilateral declaration or a dialectic approach of mission (often done in a condescending manner) proving the superiority of a western Christianity was no longer acceptable. Yet the message of God's loving nature and promise must still be shared. How this is done must be relative to the culturally available means of building a bond of sympathy and interest between the messenger and the listener.

The conventional way (or the era of universalism) focused on the content, the essence of being rather than the means of expression. The form of expression was neglected as it was considered merely superficial and phenomenal, and could be changed at any time. In a missionary-sending country, the passion for spreading the word of God was identified with the brave hearts of missionaries, justifying mistakes in the area of cross-cultural communication. However, in the postmodern society, this system of cultural idealism is regarded as extremely limited and paternalistic. Instead, there is now a focus upon the aesthetic point of view that must consider all areas of life, including ethics (Maffesoli 2008, 149–156). There are no longer clear lines between right and wrong. It seems that everyone of this era does her or his best to be content with an individual sets of rules expressing him/herself. Now, the task given to the messenger is how to get the seemingly old and fossilized message of the gospel to reach into the hearts of recipients of this new era without compromise or distortion. It is clear that the unilateral declaration or dialectic approach does not work anymore. We need to be able to communicate with all people. It is essential that we recognize, in the same way of sending a radio signal, what are our receptors' frequencies and then tune into the right ones.

This paper is written to suggest one humble example of a way of tuning into another culture's frequency as a learner. For that purpose, I will use the Japanese traditional musical drama "Noh" as a tool of study. First, I will look briefly into the development of Noh, then the value of expression in Noh more deeply, concluding with some thoughts to consider for application in mission to a shame-oriented culture.

JAPANESE CULTURE REVEALED IN NOH

Keeping in mind the fact that no culture can be completely categorized by only one concept, we can generalize Japanese society primarily as a shame-oriented culture. This was first claimed by Ruth Benedict in her book, *Chrysanthemum and the Sword*, although her study was limited historically and geographically. In a shame culture, where people give the priority to the fulfilling of group expectations over individual conviction, personal opinion appears to be buried under the thick crust of the group. Japanese scholar, Hamakura answered this assumption, "It is not true that the Japanese (as an individual person) has neither self-opinion nor self-identity. We do not raise our voice like the westerners do. We only use highly refined manners in the way of expressing ourselves in public" (Aoki 2003, 129). Actually, the "self-expression in highly refined manners" as Hamakura emphasized can be found in various aspects in Japanese culture; for instance, the garden as spatial structure, the floor mat, the traditional form of poetry "Haiku," the traditional dress "Kimono," the traditional musical drama "Kabuki" and "Noh."

The essence of the expression in Noh should be understood in relation to the time-space concept which draws from this three-dimensional approach, including its Buddhist ideals. However, since the purpose of this paper is to suggest an example of how to communicate with another culture, I will focus only on the skills of expression.

Noh was listed as an Intangible Cultural Heritage by UNESCO in 2001. The storyline of a Noh play is nothing special; it is generally about the vanity of human ambition and the passionate struggle to get there. The highest value of Noh, however, is in its emotional expression. A Noh actor must not express his emotion in a descriptive way, but in a symbolic and metaphorical way. The goal of Noh acting is to attain the perfect form of expression beyond individual details, which is classical rather than popular in methodology. Noh has been performed continuously for over six hundred years and still continues to satisfy something within the Japanese nature today (Lee 2004, 22–23).

THE DEVELOPMENT OF NOH

The prototypes of Noh were much more raucous than its present form, and were closely related to popular entertainment. It was formed from three different types of entertainment: *sarugaku* (a shrine pantomime ritual play), *sangaku* (altered *sarugaku* with Chinese origin), and *dengaku* (field music about rice planting dances performed by peasants). Later, in the Kamakura period, Noh actors came to seek peace from war and moved into Buddhist monasteries where Noh was polished with Buddhist ideas (Lee 2004, 101).

Kan'ami Kiyotsugu, one of the most famous men of Noh history, adapted a form of storytelling dance into Noh which drew great patronage from the aristocratic circle of the time including Hojo Takatoki, the last shogun of the Kamakura period. Patronage of Noh by the noble class continued through the next period of Muromachi, and under their favor and protection Zeami Motokiyo, Kan'ami's son, established Noh in the standard form that remains today.

THE VALUE OF EXPRESSION IN NOH

The word "noh" derives from the word meaning "skill" or "talent," that is the ability of the performer. This "ability" is not only the skill of dancing and singing, but more importantly, the ability of empathizing with the audience. Noh is not incremental with a particular level that must be reached, nor is it a certain technique that is to be mastered. It is more like capturing energy or a spirit that stays in tune with the audience. The performer must devote his whole life to it in order to achieve this. The highest goal for a Noh player is to draw the audience to the mysterious world beyond the real.

Stylization

Every element of Noh is patterned extremely carefully. You can cut it into the small pieces of a puzzle if you choose to try.

The stage is standardized and each role has its own position. The basic posture of the actor has a standard form called *kamae*, which has him ready for any move. He uses a particular style of walking when he moves. Noh is well known by its art of walking, and any movement cannot be made without this particular style of walking, called *suri ashi*. That is why the Noh play looks so slow. Actually, it takes quite a long time for the performer to come out on the main stage through the corridor using this *suri ashi*. Moreover, every movement of the dance has a particular form in accordance with the intended meaning, which is called *kata*. All those patterned pieces find their own places coming together in a beautiful masterpiece, and yet one that is dynamic, full of energy, and unique every time.

Minimization

There are almost no props in a Noh play other than a fan, which may represent various objects in the same play. When any props are used they will be extremely simplified. A Noh play clearly aims for the simple minimalism of Zen Buddhism. The same goes with the way of expression of the actors as well. It is a humiliation for a Noh actor to leak any unnecessary residue of emotional expression onstage. The number of people appearing on the stage together can be counted on the fingers of your hands, sometimes only one hand.

Collaboration

There are four primary character roles in a Noh play: the *shite* (protagonist), the *waki* (supporting actor), the *hayashi* (chorus and music), and the *kyogen* (comical interlude). At first glance, Noh appears to be a monologue led by the beautifully clothed protagonist in an elaborate embroidered garment and wearing a grotesque mask. But as the play proceeds it becomes clear that all the parts are subtly woven together to synthesize an exquisite piece of visual, musical, poetic, and dramatic art. Every role must pursue its own beauty, yet should not stand out. Take the *waki* for example, who is called the "silent light, left hand, unmoved focus" by Noh experts (Lee 2004, 15). His role is to draw the audience into the space-time of the play pulling up the drawbridge. However, he cannot draw the audience's attention to himself. He is only the medium between the audience and the play.

Symbolization

A Noh play is full of symbolism. For the most part, there is no elaborate scenery on the Noh stage except for an old pine tree as a metaphor representing eternal life. If any props are needed they are present only in outline form suggesting the real objects. The physical size of the stage is very small and confined. In that way, the audience can jump straight into the heart of the play without distraction. Anything that gets in the way of concentration must be eliminated. Even the emotion of the actors cannot be exceptional. The use of masks maximizes this effect. The eyeholes of the masks are too small for the actors to get full sight which promotes the actors' concentration. A slight tilt in dim light can dramatically change the originally neutral expression of the mask. A Noh mask alone is a beautiful piece of art which is handed down over many generations and some of them are national treasures of Japan. There is no specific classification for masks for each play. The actor chooses a mask according to his own assessment. After choosing it, he sits down in front of a mirror in the *kagami no ma* (mirror room) reflecting himself into the mask until he becomes the mask itself. The whole process needs great concentration and self-control. Noh dance does not mime actions, but evokes the emotion of the action's ultimate meaning with various sequences of limited patterned forms. The repetitive solemn chant is also intentionally abstract.

Emptiness

There are moments of emptiness in a Noh play when an action begins or comes to an end, or in the interval when there is no action and no sound at all. This is called *ma* (negative space). One of the founders of Noh, Zeami himself, confessed that the moment of no-action is the most enjoyable because of the underlying spiritual strength of the actor which unremittingly holds the audience's attention. If the strength is so obvious that the audience can see it, it would not be a successful *ma*. *Ma* should make a linkage between the actions entering the state of mindlessness and also between the play and the audience. It is complete stillness and emptiness, but yet it is full of energy to move the audience beyond imagination. This is often referred to as the core of the expression in a Noh play. Such emptiness of feeling may also be experienced in the hearing of the sound of *utai* (song, chorus) pronounced not by the throat, but from the bottom of the belly of the singer, the sound of restricted emotion.

Yugen

This whole concept of *ma*, or simply Noh, is pursuing one of the highest points of the Japanese esthetic view, *yugen*. The original concept of *yugen* was derived from Buddhism, meaning the profound and mysterious truth of the universe. *Yugen* is the taste that lingers even after the end of the taste of something, such as that found in poetry or the tea ceremony. *Yugen* in Noh is the beauty of the innermost nature of things, the beauty of hidden truth. And its metaphor is the Hidden Flower. In one of a series of Noh teachings, Zeami wrote the following called "Fushikaden": "If it is hidden, it is the Flower, if it is not hidden, it is not the Flower. The knowledge of this distinction is an essence of the Flower" (Zeami, 156). And he explained it like this: if the Flower was exposed as "something unique," the audience would expect it and seek the "something unique" through the whole play and they would find it. Then it—the something unique—cannot be the true Flower. An actor's Flower will appear because the audience is not expecting it. On the other hand, the audience may see something extraordinarily skillful and interesting, but will not know that it is the Flower, then this is precisely the actor's true Flower. According to Zeami, the true Flower can draw out a feeling that people had not expected to have, and it is meant to be appreciated by any audience regardless of their sense of art.

REFLECTIONS ON NOH AS A MODEL FOR CHRISTIAN COMMUNICATION

It is apparent that not all of the Bible is written in an apologetic or dialectic style. The silent and visual communication of Queen Esther, the poetic metaphors used throughout the Book of Psalms, personal letter writing, historical documentation, storytelling, and parables are examples of non-apologetic styles. Each style is important in that it complements the weak points of other styles. The Song of Songs written in the style of romantic drama is no less powerful than the Greek style of rhetoric used in the book of Romans. The stories of Ruth, Joseph, and so many others in the Bible are drama plays explaining God's message in a variety of styles. We, in our daily lives, also communicate in the same ways that drama does. We, here on earth, are in God's Play. We need to learn from this.

In the history of Christian expansion by modern missions, various kinds of methods of Christian evangelism have been developed, such as: "The Four Spiritual Laws" of Campus Crusade for Christ, Evangelism Explosion, Discipleship Manuals, Mass Evangelism, Total Invitation, and apologetics. All were created to provide good reasons for believing in Christ. However, they are all, at least to people from shame-oriented cultures, one-way directed, persuasive, and theologically oriented. These methods show sharp division between the subject and the object. Thus, the whole process of evangelism ends up with a teaching and learning session. It is noticeable that the style of evangelistic and discipleship materials tends to be a replica of that of the missionary's home culture rather than drawing from the subtle hearts and means of communication found among those in our mission fields.

To return to the context of Japan, in the mid-1970s Japanese socio-economists declared that progress was over. Throughout the younger generation of Japanese society there grew a movement of "3 Lows" (Seeking life of low risk, low price, and low dependency). They were looking for self-help in life, not depending upon any theoretical basis or socially approved lifestyle (Kuma and Niura 2012, 16–18). It seems that the highest value of their life was not to be found not in public reason, but in self-existence, while at the same time not wanting to be any hindrance or burden upon others, still upholding the shame-orientation of the society. This seems to be a unique mixture of Zen-oriented individualism and Samurai shame-based culture. To communicate the gospel effectively with this younger Japanese generation, the search for more subtle ways of its communication is mandatory.

CONCLUSION

My emphasis in studying Noh is to put more weight upon the skills of indirect expression. I understand that it is not easy for some Christian groups to make use of these Noh skills for Christian evangelism due to their own theological reflection or cultural limitations. In fact, total acceptance of these skills is beyond my expectation. At least here, the intention of my paper can be extended to the point that we may learn how to appreciate the beauty of communication skills found in a rich foreign culture regardless of its religious background or what the culture is based upon. As outsiders, we tend to quickly refuse any cultural value without any appreciation, especially when we feel we know its native religious background. The problem is that such presumptions poison us with prejudice and make us into self-righteous, grumpy people who are always trying to rectify others. We are called to build God's kingdom. Kingdom life is not made of conceptual messages only. We cannot afford to mess up God's business by confusing God's ends with our means.

As I mentioned earlier, one unilateral declaration is an anachronistic method. We have to communicate through building mutual understanding. In a society where the most significant things are hidden under a mundane agenda, we must lessen the weight of articulated adjectives in words. Instead, we must find ways to reveal the invisible reality that is concealed under the mundane agenda. In this way, Japanese society may consider the message we hope to communicate as truly a significant matter.

In discussing all kinds of Noh skills, Professor Lee Sang Yong stresses the need for the actor to be able to be completely open to any emerging feelings of the audience. A player cannot attain the Noh skill if his thoughts are imprisoned by stereotyped expression. The mind of a player should be ready to flow like water, as being filled with appreciation of the audience. The spirit is no longer spirit if it is stereotyped. The same spirit might enlighten us as to attitudes intercultural Christian communicator should be adopting.

References

Asoki, Tamotsu. 2003. *Nihon Bunkaron no henyo* (Change of Japanese culture). Seoul: Sohwa Publisher.

Berkouwer, G.C. 1977. *A half-century of theology*. Grand Rapids, MI: Eerdmans.

Dyrness, William. 1983. *Christian apologetics in a world community*. Grove, IL: InterVarsity Press.

Hume, Nancy G., ed. 1995. *Japanese aesthetics and culture*. New York: SUNY Press.

Jerome, Binde, ed. 2008. *Ou vont les valeurs?* (Where values go? Gachineun Eadiroganyunga?). Seoul: Munhak kwa Jesungsa.

Kim, Chungyoun. 1997. *Literature of Japanese traditional romanticism.* Seoul: Uni. Press.
Kuma, Kengo and Miura Atsushi. 2012. *Three low-ism.* Seoul: Aan-graphic.
Lee, Eunhee. 2010. "A comparative study on mask plays of Japan and Korea," *MunmyungYeonjee.* Vol. 25.
Lee, Sangkyung. 2004. *Esthetics of Noh-Kabuki.* Seoul: Taehak Pub.
Lee, Sangmoon. 2010. *Merleau-Ponty: Being and expression.* Seoul: Sangkakeunau Press.
Maffesoli, Michel. 2008. "Toward post-modern ethics of esthetics of inner person." In *Qu'est-ce que la culture?* Seoul: Sikongsa.
Michaud, Yves et al., eds. 2003. *Que'st-ce que la culture?* (What is Culture?). Seoul: Sikongsa.
Viladesau Richard. 2001. *Theological aesthetics: God in imagination, beauty and art.* Seoul: Hankuk sinkak yoonkuso.
Yoon, Boeun. n.d. *A Study on the traditional aesthetic consciousness reflected on the contemporary fashion.* Daechon, Korea: A thesis of Chunnam University.

7
Christian Observation of Buddhist Fear Expressed in a Devil Dancing Ceremony

G. P. V. Somaratna

Demons and spirits are an important part of Buddhist worldview. They are primarily powerful and malicious spirits of nature, who require recognition and appeasement. They cause fear and sickness. Fear of demon attacks is an ever-present factor in the day-to-day lives of Sinhalese Buddhists. As a means of alleviating this fear, there are several demon ceremonies practiced by the Buddhists in Sri Lanka for healing purposes. Buddhists choose demonic festivals in times of sickness that is suspected to come from evil spirits whether they live in cities or villages. One such event is a Tovil dancing ceremony. Tovil is considered an event where demons appear in greatest force. This ritualistic dance is an important aspect of folk religion that has been adopted by the Sinhala Buddhists.

Anthropologists have regarded it as folk superstation (Gombrich and Obeyesekere 1988, 221). However, the practices are widespread and exist amicably with canonical Buddhism. The Tovil ceremony, which receives attention in this paper, is one of the major healing rites. It is conventionally used in the field of medical anthropology. Many anthropologists have published excellent books and articles on this subject. Among them is the anthropological research by Seligman (1911), Perthold (1930), Paul Wirz (1954), De Silva (1980), Obeyesekere (1969, 1984), Kapferer (1983, 1997), and Larson (2008).

Spirit possession is a term for the belief that demons, extraterrestrials, gods, and spirits can take control of a human mind and body. The concept of spirit possession however, is not confined to popular Buddhism in Sri Lanka as it is found in other folk religions in the world (Lewis 2003, 28). The purpose of this paper is to observe some aspects of this ritual from a Christian point of view, which may help evangelists deal with these encounters in their ministry in Buddhist Sri Lanka.

INTRODUCTION

The intrusion of demons and spirits upon personal and social life of the Sinhalese is a widespread belief. The disruptive and malicious activities of these supernatural forces often manifest their presence by causing illness in individuals. Demons are regarded as evil, therefore they bring disorder, disaster, and harm. They use devious means to achieve their own evil purposes. The Sinhalese believe that misery, hardship, illness, disease, and plague can come from the malevolent demonic powers. They are harbingers of death.

It may come as a disclosure to those who equate Buddhism solely with its intellectual and mystical teaching to learn that demons are a central feature of its history. Buddhism was more successful than any of the other missionary religions to coexist with the demonology that it confronted in its introduction to Sri Lanka. The sangha either turned a blind eye to existent demon-deity cults or accommodated the practice. Animist aspects flourished concurrently with canonical Buddhism.

It may come as a surprise to those who equate Buddhism solely with its intellectual traditions to learn that demons are a central aspect of its belief. Observers have found that the "demons" of Asia are primarily powerful, ancient spirits of nature, who require recognition and appeasement. Fears of demonic attacks remain an ever-present reality in the Buddhist's life. All supernatural forces, gods, planetary deities, demons, and spirits are feared because they are believed to harm people.

The devil dancing ritual known as Tovil is a healing ceremony to counter the ill effect of demon possession (*avesa*) and their gaze (*disti*) on individuals. It is a demonic ritual primarily exorcist in character. In its exorcist form it is meant to control and drive away countless hosts of wicked spirits. The evil forces are believed to be capable of bringing about harmful pathological conditions of body and mind. In addition to the demons of the folk Buddhist pantheon departed spirits of the malevolent type also can bring disaster therefore they are also brought under the exorcist power of Tovil.

The rituals relating to Tovil are an important aspect of folk religion of the Sinhala Buddhists. Religious approval is given to this folk religious element, and it has become a part of Buddhism. Sri Lankan Buddhist ritual practice aims at two goals. The canonical Buddhism of the Temple is to lead one to transcendence from this world (*nirvana*), and the lesser tradition leads to success in activities in this life. The latter satisfies the religious needs of the masses, which canonical Buddhism lacks.

Demons are usually malevolent beings prevalent in Buddhist teaching as well as folk religious tradition (Kapferer 1979, 147). These evil and harmful supernatural beings are usually associated with darkness, danger, violence, and death (Kapferer 1979, 147). They are considered as unclean spirits of known and unknown types.

CANONICAL BUDDHISM

Canonical Buddhism has many references to fear caused by malevolent spirits and the ways to eradicate them. The Buddha accepted that the *yakkhas* (demons) and other related non-human beings have the power to make their victims ill in various ways. Buddhist texts also mention that they can disturb human life by possession leading to illness. In this connection Buddha is referred to as the dispeller of the dread (*ubbega*), panic (*uttasa*), and fear (*bhaya*) emanating from these spiritual powers (Rhys Davids 1890–96, 148).

The *Dussila Sutta* also records many specific fears discussed by the Buddha on several occasions. Fear is caused by a string of desires like *piya* (desire), *pema* (affection), and *tanha* (craving). In the discourse on fear and dread (*Bhayabherava Sutta*) craving for power, lust, jealousy, and pride are also given as causes of fear (*Samyukta Nikaya*, V, 386). Another ancient tradition says even gods suffered from fear. It is stated that Dadimunda was the only deity who did not run away in fear at the time of Siddhattha's struggle with Mara, the demon of death, just before the enlightenment, while the other gods escaped in fright (Kariyawasam 1996, 67).

The Buddha cautioned his followers regarding the methods and resources used to combat fear of demons and other fears. In the Dhajagga Sutta Buddha is said to have admonished his followers, stating that when fear arises in the mind they should recall the *tisarana* (triple gem), which is Buddha, Dhamma, and Sangha. On another occasion Buddha stated that by cultivating faith in the tisarana, meditating, and following the eightfold noble path bhikku can attain arahatship, where fear would be eliminated (Rhys Davids 1890–96, 192). The absence of fear is the characteristic of a fully spiritually developed personality. According to the teaching of Buddha, recollecting dhamma enables people to be freed from sufferings, such as fear of demons and of robbers, fear of disease, and the fear of samsaric sufferings. A person who is free of lust, not affected by hatred, and who has overcome evil would have no fear. *Dhammapada* v. 39 states that "If a man's thoughts are not dissipated, if his mind is not perplexed, if he has ceased to think of good or evil, then there is no fear for him while he is watchful." Buddhist spirituality in the Theravada tradition recommends *samatha-bhāvanā* (Cultivation of Tranquility), which is considered to lead to the development of mental tranquility to overcome fear (Malalasekera 1990, 223).

Dhammapada further states, "Men, driven by fear, go to many a refuge, to mountains and forests, to groves and sacred trees for help" (Narada 2010, 188). *Atanatiya Sutta* of the *Digha Nikaya* Buddha gives a poem to his followers to recite for protection from evil spirits. This verse is used by many Buddhists for preventing sickness or danger from non-human beings, such as demons (Rhys Davids, 1890–96, 189, 195).

Although the canon is very clear on the ill-effects of fear, the means proposed for eradicating it is beyond the ability of the common man. The remedies of the Buddha call for a highly disciplined mind. These solutions are applicable mostly to the sangha. In the case of modern man, practice of *bhavana* (meditation) is for the educated Buddhist who is capable of disciplining his mind.

DEMONS

Buddhism looks at demons in the samsaric context. The demons in the Buddhist scriptures are sub-human with anthropomorphic nature. They are believed to have monstrous features. They may have a head, claws, and tails of ferocious animals. In the Jataka stories demons have hairy bodies, disheveled hair, red eyes, fat bellies, large mouths, and jutting out long sharp teeth (EB IV, 371; Sutherland 1991, 116). The Jataka stories further state that demonic power is manifested in humans through fear and ignorance.

In other Buddhist texts demons are depicted as very tall and their complexion is dark. They are presented as man eaters. They have supernatural powers. They can change their appearance. They sometimes appear in human form or animal form. They are ferocious and use their powers for evil purposes. Demons are generally described as filthy, contemptible, and despicable and possess various types of abnormalities. Their motives are malevolent (Sutherland 1991, 124). Yakkhas are mysterious and have a quality of strangeness that generates a sense of fear among the humans.

Buddhist canonical literature also refers to various categories of sub-human beings. The ghost world (*pittivi saya*) is one of them. *Digha Nikaya* uses the word *yakkha* in the sense of demons (D II, 346). They are filthy and dreadful diabolical creatures. They are skinny, deformed, and perpetually hungry. The narratives found in the sutras and the Jatakas show that they are in that state because of their bad karma in their lives as human beings. Demons, like other beings, are subject to rebirth. In *Mahasamaya Suttanta* the leader of demons is the demon of death, Mara, who is the most feared demon (EB IV, 371). Therefore one can see that the canonical Buddhism as well as local animist views heavily influences the demonology in Sri Lanka.

Buddhism teaches the reincarnation and transmigration of souls according to one's karma. The dead suffer punishments before being reborn. Humans after death roam as lonely, often evil, spirits for a length of time before being reborn. At this stage they are especially harmful to their relatives or other associates as they can possess them. They are as awful as disrupting demons and other evil spirits.

LAITY

The average Buddhist laity is immersed in worldly life. Therefore in times of difficulty they seek refuge in popular forms of religious activities. The rituals of folk religion are within their capabilities. They cannot practice meditation amidst their daily struggle for existence. There are centers for practice of meditation in Sri Lanka. They are costly. Long periods of stay are required in these centers to learn meditative practice under a master. The person affected by fear is in no way ready to learn Buddhist texts to expel fear. The society persuades them to consult demon priests for healing rituals. These animistic practices have Buddhist religious sanction. Folk religious elements have crept into normative Buddhism to supplement whatever is lacking in the canonical

Buddhism to satisfy the religious needs of the masses. As seen earlier, canonical Buddhism is otherworldly and has no teachings to help people in their daily struggles (Gombrich and Obeyesekere 1988, 265).

FEAR

Fear is the most common emotional state which is associated with demonic illness. Mental attitude is weakened by this unbalanced emotional state. Fear makes the person vulnerable to malevolent spirits. It is observed that there is a propensity for women to be more vulnerable than men to demonic illness (Kapferer 1991, 147; Salgado 1997, 213; Nabokon 2000, 298). If these symptoms remain unchecked the fear connected with malign spirits would increase to cause personal and mental distress to the individual as well as the family. The behavior of the demon-possessed person with fear can hinder the peace and harmony in the household (Obeyesekere 1990, 11; Kapferer 1991, 71; Caplan 1989, 55).

Social scientists have noted that a demonic attack causes emotional, mental, behavioral, and even hormonal imbalance (Bilu 1979, 364). Fear of a demon may cause panic attacks, because of the helplessness of the patient to cope with the situation. The possession of a deceased relative or friend, acute sexual desires, envy, jealousy, hatred, and unforgiving nature are also considered to be symptoms of fear and eventual demon attack (Nabokov 2000, 307).

FEAR-CAUSING DEMONS

In Sinhalese folklore, Mahasona is a well-known demon that haunts the spirit world. The name Mahasona means "great demon of the cemetery" (Liyanaratne 1987, 188; Smith 1976, 92). It is the most feared and most dangerous demon in Sri Lanka (Gombrich and Obeyesekere 1990, 117). Mahasona is believed to haunt graveyards and lonely places, looking for human prey.

This demon is believed to be surrounded by human corpses. As demons are foul spirits, their favorite food is human entrails, dead carcasses, etc. Junctions where three roads meet are hunting grounds of this demon. He is able to spread infectious illnesses like cholera and dysentery. The other demon feared is Ririyaka. It is a blood-thirsty, vindictive demon. Kalu-Kumara (black prince) is the demon of lust. Huniyam is the demon of sorcery. They are black in color. Their bodies are covered with coarse fur.

POSSESSION

Demon possession depends on certain assumptions about the internal states of mind of people who become possessed. "All the really interesting and significant processes are taking place in the mind of the possessed" (Stirrat 1977, 133). This is where anthropologists cannot venture. The sick person may get into a state of ecstasy due to a demon's control of the personality, which involves an apparent loss of physical and mental control (Salgado 1997, 213). Some shamanic practices here are clearly against Buddhist teaching. One of the main activities of the Tovil ceremony is to kill a cock to appease the blood-thirsty demons. This violates one of the five main precepts of Buddhism (Gombrich and Obeyesekere 1988, 142). There are reports of local gods, who are territorial spirits; taking possession of individuals. Normally possession is caused by malevolent spirits rather than by gods (Gombrich and Obeyesekere 1988, 333). However, it is to be noted that word god is used interchangeably with gods and demons by Sinhalese Buddhists.

Reasons

Demon possession, which is an outcome of fear and terror, is caused by feeling of loneliness and helplessness brought about by the absence of a personal relationship with a dependable divine being in the Buddhist religion. It is noted that demon attack of fear comes when individuals are alone. When a person is physically or emotionally removed from the company of others they can become vulnerable to demonic fear. This is known in Sinhala as *tanikama* (loneliness) (Obeyesekere 1969, 176; Kapferer 1991, 70). Isolation from others is one of the preconditions for demonic attacks of fear. Encounters with demons are reported at night, in dark places, lonely places, cemeteries, lonely times in public bathing wells, and even lonely places in hospitals. People have reported that they were away from human habitation when the demon attacked the individual with fear and terror. The person may feel that powerful demons and spirits are dominating them with supernatural powers. The otherwise healthy person senses the power of a control from outside which they feel is demonic (Kapferer 1991, 70).

It is important to restate the fact that Sinhalese Buddhism lacks a personal relationship to a deity. Buddha is dead and cannot help anyone living. Their gods and demons are not considered beings with whom human can maintain a relationship. In fact, there is no difference between some of their gods and demons with regard to their evil nature. They cannot be contacted for help at a time of distress. As a result, the Buddhists resort to the use of foul language when they feel that they are in the presence of a demon. In this manner, both holy as well as profane means may be used at the same time.

People have reported seeing mysterious figures appearing in black or white colors. Some people have reported that they saw demons as a pregnant woman or a mother with a baby in dark lonely places. Foul, disgusting stench, rocks and stones falling, sand thrown into their meals, snakes crossing their path, and dark ferocious dogs trying to attack them are also some indications of demon presence. It is interpreted that some force from the demon world outside the human perception is attacking them. This is considered to be a demonic gaze (*disti*) and demon possession (*avesha*).

Physical Symptoms

Biochemical activity, which is thought to determine a person's physical and mental qualities, becomes imbalanced when demon possession is present. Symptoms like rapid pulse, palpitation, high fever, bloodshot eyes, blood in feces and urine, vomiting, and headache would become visible. Dysentery, stomach aches, and pain in limbs also have been reported. There are different symptoms attributed to different demons. As seen earlier, most commonly known demons who bring mortal fear to people are Mahasona, Ririyaka, Sanniyaka. There are eighteen manifestations of Sanniyaka associated with eighteen kinds of illnesses. Many other lesser known demons and spirits attack people with terror and fear (Gombrich and Obeyesekere 1988, 115).

Fear-causing demon attacks may also cause sudden depression. This is sometimes severe or very subtle. The individual may feel that life is not worthwhile; therefore suicidal thoughts might haunt them. Having severe arguments with one's spouse or friends without any perceivable reason also may occur. Feelings of hopelessness also are reported. Feeling like some external power is controlling, someone or something is pressuring to do certain acts, and the feeling of someone touching, scratching, or attacking can also be experienced. Hearing one or multiple negative, persuasive, or commanding voices in the head to do something may also occur.

The possessed individual may experience personality changes. Frightening feelings are common. One's own house or the neighborhood may elicit negative and oppressive feelings. Scratching sounds, things falling off walls or shelves, religious or spiritual items being moved about, and feeling physically attacked have been reported. This feeling of being attacked may come with physical pain that is medically inexplicable. Therefore one can notice that possessed people communicate with other beings that are unseen by normal people.

DEMON PRIEST (*yakadura*)

A Tovil ritual traditionally requires a retinue of at least seven. This retinue would include at least three performers, *yakadura* (demon priest), several assistant priests, a dancer, and a drummer. The number of the retinue may vary according to the demand of the situation. The demon priest is a specialist exorcist who leads the ceremony, while the dancers impersonate the demonic force. The demon priest, being a sorcerer, advices the team. He is thought to have abilities to summon and control demons through magical ritual practices. They are members of a drummer caste specialized in this art. They usually organize the troupe to perform in the ritual drama. They have a long tradition of involvement in exorcism. These individuals learn the essential skills of exorcism from the older generation of exorcists. The responsibility of the *yakadura* is to dance, chant, and act the ritual. He and other dancers personify the demons wearing masks and other clothes and ornaments. The impersonation of demons indicates the actual presence of the demon.

DEVIL DANCE

Tovil is a healing and purification ceremony, which emerges from the belief of Buddhists of Sri Lanka in the power of supernatural beings and the healing power of magical rites. This ritualistic healing ceremony primarily belongs to folk religion. It is a demonic ritual mainly exorcist in character. It is a public healing ceremony conducted at night, as demons are believed to be active in the dark (Ambos 2011, 249). It is intended to drive away fear-causing evil powers as the malevolent demons who are capable of bringing about physical and mental illness. The departed spirits of the malevolent type, may also be brought under the exorcist power of Tovil. Possession by a departed spirit is one of the prominent fears in the Sinhala Buddhist society, especially in the aftermath of a funeral.

The Tovil rite can be categorized as a rite of affliction. Major parts of the Tovil ceremony comprise a dance. It is also known as devil dance (*yak natuma*). The dance is accompanied by chanting mantra spells, music, texts, mime in performance and comic drama (Kariyawasam 1996, 31). The Tovil dance is performed for the benefit of the patient. Since it is a public performance an audience is present while the demons and spirits are invited.

Exorcists, who would have observed the behavior and appearance of the sick individual, would trace the onset of demonic attack. Then he would advise the family to obtain items according to a list, which are needed for the exorcist ceremony. The demon priests have to prepare the ground for the presence of demons that they would invite in the course of Tovil performance. Anyone who visits would feel an aura of demon presence while the Tovil dance is in progress. This is the time that the demon priests detect the presence of believing Christians in the audience. There have been occasions when the demon priest has stopped the dance and ordered the Christians to leave the precincts of the Tovil ceremony. On one occasion at Kurunegala the demon priest detected the arrival of the pastor at the entrance of the compound and informed the people in the house that an enemy has come. The family members who came to see who that person was, found the pastor. When there were prayerful Christians within the compound where the devil dancing was going on, the devil priests have complained of their inability to perform their rituals.

REASONS FOR THE EVENT

The Tovil ceremony is conducted for two reasons. One is for the healing of a person affected by fear, anxiety, and terror. The other is the event performed as a purely cultural event. The latter event is conducted by cultural societies as well as for the entertainment of tourists. They do not have the healing elements attached to them. Our attention in this paper is on the former, where households make arrangements to conduct elaborate devil dancing ceremonies mainly for the purpose of getting relief from the fear of demons.

The full-scale Tovil ceremony usually begins at dusk and ends at dawn. The event commences with offerings made to different spirits and demons in the presence of the patient. The first ritual activity of exorcism procedure is solely on the patient together with the members of the patient's family. On this occasion the main offerings are given to ghosts and demons. This is accompanied by the chanting of protective and curative mantras. It is believed that through this ritual the relationships between the patient and harmful spirits and demons are magically cut off. The exorcist performs a central role as a mediator between the patient and the spirits, which are causing the illness. This is before the public performance of rituals. However, the audience eventually assumes a greater importance in the ritual.

They in fact become highly involved in the performance. This is followed by a succession of elaborate dances. The Tovil performance consists of a series of comic dramatic acts. Each deals with a particular demon causing the illness. Other demons are also propitiated in the ritualistic acts. As a result the whole arena is used at that stage. Exorcists bring the patient into a direct confrontation with the supernatural forces causing the illness. It is believed that the person for whom the ritual is arranged goes into a trance (Brow 1996, 146).

The dances and dramatic scenes presented in the performance are an integral part of the ritual. There are times in the night allocated to a particular demon. Such times are taken to placate the demon with dramatic performance. The exorcisms contain sequences of dances with dramatic masks. The dancers who represent demon characters in some stages of Tovil ceremony are masked in this manner. In the case of one Tovil ceremony, known as *daha-ata sanniya*, eighteen disease-spreading demons are portrayed. In this ritual each demon has a specific mask associated with the exorcist performance.

The comic drama is the most popular part of the devil dancing ceremony. It occurs toward the middle of the night. By this time about six hours of ritual activities and chanting have taken place. Following which is the comic drama period, lasting about three hours, when the audience is brought into an active involvement in the ritual proceedings. This is an entertaining interlude where the whole audience laughs with the demon. The exorcists extensively use humor. The improvised lines often used to address the demon include wit and even vulgar humor. This is a description of an act performed by the demon causing diarrhea witnessed by an observer (Pieris 2001, 26–27). "He danced his way into the arena in a frightening manner and suddenly became the laughing stock of the crowd as he feigned to be suffering from that disease. The disgusting effects of diarrhea were acted out with such vivid crudeness that no room was left for the imagination. The scene was so hilarious that it triggered convulsions of hysterical laughter" (Pieris 2001, 26).

Two important facts that emerge from this brief description of Tovil are the theatrical value present in these rituals and the way in which religious sanction has been obtained for their adoption by the Buddhists. The dance is performed in order to appease the particular demon. Food and other offering are also made for that purpose. Throughout the ritual the demon priests invite the demons causing the patient's suffering to come out into the open (*vidiya*). They plead with them with food and treats, and they command them to give up the patient before moving away at the end. It is believed that the patient who is possessed of the devil is set free by the Tovil performance in the end.

DEMON CHASING DEMON

Tovil ceremonies are events where more powerful demons are used to oust the demon or demons harassing the patient. For example, if Ririyaka possesses the patient, another powerful demon named Maha Sona would be brought in by the devil priest to chase Ririyaka. Basically it is one demon used for chasing another demon. This process could be trickery or facade to appease the demon causing the illness. The demon priests say that they use trickery, cheating, and persuasion to get demons out. It may bring about an immediate, temporary relief. Having tricked the demon, which brought immediate relief to the family, demon priests leave soon after the event is over. It is a known fact that rituals on a lesser scale would be needed to be continued for complete healing. This usually brings the family to an economic poverty. It is only at this stage that Christians could intervene.

SOCIAL

Ceremony usually has a climate of joy in the home of the patient, temporarily dispelling the fear of demons. Men and women of all ages enjoy a freedom normally absent in villages. The atmosphere is socially friendly and one would be able to see groups gathered under trees. Even though it is dark, the meetings take place within socially accepted norms (Pieris 200, 26).

THE PATIENT

The patient (*aturaya*) is given an important place in the ceremony. He or she is given recognition they've never had before. The entire village would visit the sick person and wish them well. This would give the person some psychological comfort and help him in inner healing in some way. The festive mood is found everywhere. The patient sees and meets many who wish him well. This is one occasion when even the neighbors who are in enmity with the patient's family would come and even offer help. Usually on occasions like this, neighbors help the house where the ceremony is held by loaning chairs, tables, cutlery, etc. They would come to assist the family in the preparations.

INVOLVEMENT OF CHRISTIANS

Sri Lanka has a considerable presence of ecumenical, liberal, and liberation theologians. They have written a substantial amount of research publications on peaceful coexistence with other religions. Ecumenical Center for Religion and Dialogue in Colombo, the Tulana Research Center at Kelaniya, and several university researchers keep a close relationship with Buddhist scholars. What is noticeable in these relations is that their dialogue is confined to the philosophical aspect of Buddhism. None of the ecumenical Christians have dared to keep in contact with the practitioners of folk Buddhism. Their relationships are with the Buddhist elite. The popular level Buddhism is not within their ecumenical relationships.

From the missionary times, Christians have avoided Tovil ceremonies and other activities where a demon presence is intended. The same idea is present today. Many pastors advise their flock to avoid such events. As we mentioned earlier, the presence of Christians has interrupted the Tovil ceremonies. Many pastors have reported that the demon priest has conveyed his inability to perform rituals because of the Christian presence. Two pastors at Hambantota in the south of Sri Lanka were requested recently by the chief householder to leave the premises because of the request of the demon priest. The demons that are consulted to reveal secrets in a necromancy situation have refused to talk to Christians.

Pastors also inform that the demonic forces are present in Tovil situations in full force. It is harmful for the Christians to be present unless they are equipped and willing to combat the demons spiritually. Taking all these factors into consideration, there is still room for Christians to intervene to bring relief to these families who are haunted by fear and exhausted financially and spiritually. Although the devil dancing ceremony is a time that the demons are present is full force the opportunity comes immediately after the end of the ceremony.

LAST RESORT

People embark on a Tovil ceremony usually as a last resort when every medical avenue has failed. They do not have other forms of help to turn to. Therefore they consult astrologers and search for a demon priest who could perform the rituals to heal the sick person. From that time onwards the family has to incur expenses. The preliminary work before the performance of the ceremony entails a significant outlay. The visits of demon priests to the house, which would take place several times, need to be paid for.

COST

A Tovil ceremony requires a considerable sum of money. The demon priest requests the head of the house to purchase numerous items needed in the ceremony. The chief demon priest and his helpers and drummers have to be paid. Since the demon priests do not get a regular income they charge a large sum when they get work. The ceremony is an occasion for the visit of friends and family members. Relatives may come from distant places and stay with the household for some days. The visitors have to be provided with food and drinks. There has to be people to serve them. Thus a Tovil ceremony is a costly affair. At the end of the ceremony the family may be in debt. The expenses for the provision of food and drinks during the period of the ceremony are a heavy burden to the family.

EXORCISM

Exorcism is considered to be dangerous even to the demon priests who act as mediums. In spite of its dangerous nature it is regarded as necessary, for demons must be brought under human control by attracting them to a ritual place. In a Tovil ceremony the demons are chased out by the power of a stronger demon. Buddhists believe that it is in the name of the leader of demons that all rituals are performed. The other demons are commanded to obey their leader who is brought under the orders of the exorcist (Karayawasam 1996, 53). Therefore, the ailments caused by demon possession will disappear as the demons leave. The devil priest can magically sever the demons' connection to a patient by banishing them from the scene. They are only banished. They can reappear in the same patient or in any other person in the family (Kapferer 1979, 147).

It has been observed that the symptoms of demon possession have a tendency to reappear in about three months time because another demon, that is not bound by the demon priest, will appear in the patient. Then the cycle may repeat. The family will face a helpless situation. Another Tovil would cost a similar amount or more. The explanation of this predicament given by Jesus is found in Matthew 12:45 (RSV) stating "Then he goes and brings with him seven other spirits more evil than himself, and they enter and dwell there; and the last state of that man becomes worse than the first." The real solution is to chase away the demons completely. The folk Buddhist rituals are unable to bring about a lasting relief. This is where the Christian minister can come to rescue the family.

Buddhists will not willingly come to accept Christian help because of their prejudices regarding Christianity. They may be under the impression that Christian exorcism also may need money. Pastors do not get directly involved in the initial stages. They usually use a believer of the church to communicate with the family to convince them of the true situation of Christianity. One has to be gentle in dealing with the patient's family as they are already tired of numerous kinds of healing procedures.

It is at this stage that the families may communicate with the pastor in the village. The pastors may be requested to visit the house and exorcise the demons. On such occasions the pastors should give clear guidelines to the family with regard to the Christian attitude to demons. The pastor has to lay down his conditions. The patient needs to be brought to the church as the church is beyond the reach of the fear-causing demons. It is only later when the patient is moderately relieved of demonic fear that the pastor goes to the house to pray.

Once they decide to come to church and receive healing, they may try to offer money and other gifts. Busloads of people will come to church merely for the sake of getting healed. Such people treat Christ like their own gods who have to be paid for their work. Thereafter no relationship is maintained. Casting out demons is inadequate for healing. It is after the healing begins that a clear relationship with Christ has to be introduced, where fear-causing *tanikama* (loneliness) would no longer bother them.

Pastors have to be vigilant in such circumstances. The patient and the family should be informed that this is not a business deal but a relationship with the living God. There are many places in Sri Lanka where such Christian healing work is undertaken. However, those exorcisms, which have not been followed up with Christian instruction, have not brought about any positive results to the Christian church. Building a relationship with Buddhists who are engaged in Tovil ceremonies may be a difficult task. Yet they also need to know the gospel. Connections with them have to be undertaken cautiously.

There are many people who have sought the help of Tovil ceremonies to get rid of the fear-attacks caused by demons but who have not received any healing. Some have solicited the help of Christians and received deliverance from demonic fear and been given physical healing. This is a phenomenon present mostly in the evangelical churches. There are even full-time pastors who have come through this avenue, now serving many churches. This shows that Christians should not ostracize those who have formally sought the help of Tovil ceremonies to receive relief from fear.

In this connection one has to remember that the Christian pastor will now move on to the subject of power encounter. It has its own rules and practice clearly spelled out in the Christian Scripture. It is a large subject in its own right. It is not covered in this paper, as its content is limited to the Tovil ceremony as it deals with the fear factor caused by demons.

CONCLUSION

Devil dancing, known as Tovil, is performed by Buddhists to free individuals from the psycho-physical symptoms of fear caused by attacks of demons and evil spirits in Sri Lanka. It is a widespread practice, which has a long historical background. Christian missionaries from the early sixteenth century have had a role in dealing with people professing to be possessed by demons. Traditional Christian denominations have ceased to take part in exorcism of demons. The new evangelical churches, however, have had to face the repercussions of incidences of Tovil ceremonies and their aftermath. Their success in making use of the incidences of Tovil ceremonies have been remarkable although the numbers may not be very large. Those who have been delivered in their ministries have been able to live a normal life. Some even have taken an active role in the Christian church for its growth. This will be an ongoing struggle that the church will face in the context of Buddhist beliefs in Sri Lanka.

References

Ambos, A. 2001. "The changing image of Sinhalese healing rituals: Performing identity in the context of transculturality." In *Transcultural research: Heidelberg studies on Asia and Europe in a global context*, 249–69. Springer.

Ames, M. 1964. "Magical-animism and Buddhism: A structural analysis of the Sinhalese religious system." *Journal of Asian Studies* 23 (3): 21–52.
Bartholomeusz, T. 1994. *Women under the Bo Tree*. Cambridge: Cambridge University Press.
Bell, R. 1987. *Holy anorexia*. Chicago: University of Chicago Press.
Betty, S. 2005. "The growing evidence for demonic possession: What should psychiatry's response be?" *Journal of Religion and Health* 44, issue 1 (April): 3–30.
Bilu, Yoram. 1979. "Demonic explanations of disease among Moroccan Jews in Israel." *Culture, Medicine and Psychiatry* 3, issue 4 (December): 363–80.
Bloss, L. 1987. "The female renunciants of Sri Lanka: The Dasasilmattawa." *Journal of the International Association of Buddhist Studies* 10 (1): 7–31.
Boddy, J. 1989. *Wombs and alien spirits*. Madison: University of Wisconsin Press.
Bond, G. 1988. *The Buddhist revival in Sri Lanka*. Columbia: South Carolina Press.
Brow, James. 1996. *Demons and development: The struggle for community in a Sri Lankan village*. Tucson: University of Arizona Press.
Caplan, L. 1989. *Religion and power*. Madras: CLS.
Carrithers, M. 1979. *The forest monks of Sri Lanka: An anthropological and historical study*. Delhi: Oxford University Press.
Carter, J. R. and Mahinda Palihavadana, eds. and trans. 1998. *The Dhammapada*. New York: Oxford University Press.
De Silva, Lynn. 1980. *Buddhism: Beliefs and practices in Sri Lanka*. Colombo: Ecumenical Centre for Study and Dialogue.
De Silva, Padmasiri. 1976. *The psychology of emotions in Buddhist perspective*. Kandy: Buddhist Publication Society.

Devendra, K. 1988. "Establishment of the Order of Buddhist Nuns and its development in Sri Lanka." In *Sakyadhita: Daughters of the Buddha*, edited by K. L. Tsomo, 258–66. New Delhi: Sri Satguru.

Eliade, M. 1969. *Yoga: Immortality and freedom*. New York: Princeton University Press/Bollingen Foundation.

Feer, L. and Mrs. C.A.F. Rhys Davids, eds. 1884–1904. *Samyutta Nikaya*, six volumes. London: PTS.

Gombrich, R. and G. Obeyesekere. 1988. *Buddhism transformed*. Delhi: Motilal Banarsidass.

Kakar, S. 1982. *Shamans, mystics and doctors*. Boston: Knopf Doubleday Publishing Group.

Kapferer, B. 1979. "Entertaining demons: Comedy, interaction and meaning in a Sinhalese healing ritual social analysis." *Social Analysis: The International Journal of Social and Cultural Practice*, 108–52.

Kapferer, Bruce. 1991. *A celebration of demons: Exorcism and aesthetics, a healing in Sri Lanka*. Berg: Smithsonian Institution Press.

Kyokai, B.D. 1986. *The teachings of Buddha*. Tokyo: Bukkyo Dendo Kyokai.

Larsen, Hege Myrlund. 2009. "Buddhism in popular culture: The case of Sri Lankan 'Tovil dance.'" PhD dissertation, University of Bergen, Norway.

Lewis, I. 2003. *Ecstatic religion: A study of shamanism and spirit possession*. London: Routledge.

Liyanaratne, Jinadasa. 1987. "Sinhalese medical manuscripts in Paris." *Bulletin de l'Ecole française d'Extrême-Orient* 76 (1): 185–199

Malalasekera, G.P., ed. 1990. *Encyclopedia of Buddhism*. Colombo: Government of Sri Lanka.

Nabokov, Isabelle. 2000. *Religion against the self: An ethnography of Tamil rituals*. New York: Oxford University Press.

Obeyesekere, G. 1969. "The ritual drama of the Sanni demons: Collective representations of disease in Ceylon." *Comparative studies in society and history* 11 (2): 174–216.

———. 1970. "The idiom of demon possession: A case study," *Social Science and Medicine* 4 (1): 97–111

———. 1977. "Psychocultural exegesis of a case of spirit possession in Sri Lanka." In *Case Studies in Spirit Possession,* edited by V. Crapanzano and V. Garrison, 235–94. New York: John Wiley.

———. 1990. *The work of culture: Symbolic transformation in psychoanalysis and anthropology.* Chicago: University of Chicago Press.

Pieris, Aloysius. 2001. *Prophetic humour in Buddhism and Christianity.* Colombo: Ecumenical Centre for Study and Dialogue.

Rahula, W. 1978. *What the Buddha taught.* London: Gordon Fraser.

Rhys Davids, T.W., trans. 1890–1896. *Dialogues of the Buddha: Dighanikaya*, Vol. II. London: PTS.

Salgado, Nirmala S. 1997. "Sickness, healing, and religious vocation: Alternative choices at a Theravada Buddhist nunnery." *Eathnology* 36, no. 3 (Summer): 213–26.

Seneviratne, H. L., and S. Wickremeratne. 1980. "Bodhi-puja: Collective representations of Sri Lanka youth." *American Ethnologist* 7 (4): 734–43.

Shirkey, J. C. 2008. "The moral economy of the 'Petavatthu': Hungry ghosts and Theravada Buddhist cosmology." PhD thesis, volume one. Chicago: University of Illinois.

Southwold, M. 1983. *Buddhism in life: Anthropological study of religion and the Sinhalese practice of Buddhism.* Manchester: Manchester University Press.

Spiro, M. E. 1967. *Burmese supernaturalism.* New Jersey: Transaction Publishers.

Stirrat, R. L. 1977. "Demonic possession in Roman Catholic Sri Lanka." *Journal of Anthropological Research* 33, no. 2 (Summer): 133–57.

Sutherland, G. H. 1991. *The disguises of the demon: The development of the Yaksa in Hinduism and Buddhism.* Albany, NY: SUNY.

Tambiah, S. J. 1970. *Buddhism and the spirit cults in north-east Thailand.* Cambridge: Cambridge University Press.

Thera, Narada and C. A. Pereira, eds. 2010. *Dhammapada.* New York: Kessinger Publishing.

Wirz, P. 1954. *Exorcism and the art of healing in Ceylon.* Leiden: E.J. Brill

PART THREE

RESTORING TO FREEDOM FROM FEAR, GUILT, AND SHAME

If anyone is in Christ, the new creation has come:
The old has gone, the new is here!
All this is from God, who reconciled us
to himself through Christ
and gave us the ministry of reconciliation:
that God was reconciling the world to himself in Christ,
not counting people's sins against them.
And he has committed to us the message of reconciliation.
We are therefore Christ's ambassadors,
as though God were making his appeal through us.
We implore you on Christ's behalf:
Be reconciled to God.
2 Corinthians 5:17–20

8

Reconciliation Through Purification Rituals in Communal Cultures

Cristian Dumitrescu

Any visit to an Asian country will impress you with its rituals. In fact, rituals are what trigger the realization that you are in the midst of people with different worldviews and values. From Turkey to Japan and from Mongolia to Papua, Asians act and react based on worldviews that emphasize values of purity and honor. In cultures where Buddhism is the majority religion, peace and harmony are added as fundamental values. Conflict and alienation are to be avoided as much as possible, and rituals are provided in order to restore purity, peace, and harmony. Christians find it challenging to communicate the gospel to Buddhists, not only because their worldviews are different, but because the meanings and expressions of values are also unalike. This chapter will look at ways in which values are expressed in different religious worldview rituals, particularly in Christianity and Buddhism in order to find bridges to communicate the gospel.

RELIGION AND PURITY

Purity is a basic value for most religions and is the opposite of defilement. David A. deSilva defines purity as:

> Fundamentally concerned with ordering the world
> and making sense of one's everyday experiences in
> light of that order, which is usually conceived as

being a divine ordering of the cosmos (and thus "the way things are and have to be"). It tells us "what and who belong when and where," and thus enables us to know when order is being maintained and when something is out of place. (2000, 246)

When a defiling agent penetrates a community, thus breaking a rule or a prohibition, the expected reaction is either rejection or purification. As defined by Merriam-Webster's *Encyclopedia of World Religions*, purification entails the "use of ritual techniques to protect against what are held to be unclean, sinful, or otherwise undesirable situations." The whole community feels affected. All societies have rituals of purification. In the religious realm, "rituals of purification may entail the use of water (as in baptism), mutilation (as in circumcision), fasting, prayer, and confession" (891).

Over time, religious communities often go through a process of accommodation to the demands of the surrounding society, thereby losing the "purity" of their message or ritual. As a reaction, sects and offshoots claim to restore the purity of the original design, protesting the compromise of the mother church. They usually mark the separation from the original group by a defined ritual, either by public announcement or a dramatic departure from the original site. Offshoots of offshoots, or sects of sects, continue the same process in the name of preserving purity of doctrine or practice (orthodoxy and orthopraxy).

In Hinduism, it is impossible to become pure or impure by moving up or down within the caste structure. The lower the caste one is born in, the more impure one is. Money cannot help someone change status in society. A Brahmin will remain Brahmin, regardless of the wealth or poverty an individual may experience. Martin A. Mills notes that "Indian society is fundamentally hierarchical, organized according to an understanding of social life that seeks always to distinguish between the pure and the impure" (2003, 237). If you are impure, you are considered untouchable, shameful, and this shame can never be completely washed away. One can improve the purity status for the next life by ethical intentions, by good deeds, and by ritualistic behavior.

In contrast, in Mahayana Buddhism the human mind is considered pure, because it has all the capacities and objects of knowledge in itself and therefore has no need for change. In his article "Platform Sutra of the Sixth Zen Patriarch" H. Dumoulin uses the metaphor of the sun and clouds to describe the Buddhist perception of purity:

> The sun and moon are always bright, but if they are covered by clouds, although above they are bright, below they are darkened, and the sun, moon, stars and planets cannot be seen properly. But if suddenly the wind of wisdom should blow and roll away the clouds and mists, all forms of the universe appear at once. The purity of the nature of the mind in this world is like the blue sky; wisdom is like the sun, knowledge like the moon. Although knowledge and wisdom are always clear, if you cling to external environments, the floating clouds of false thoughts will create a cover, and your own nature cannot become clear. (quoted in Mills 2003, 255)

The body may become impure and cloud the beautiful and pure mind. Rituals are intended to cleanse the person and help maintain purity. Ritual actions include washings, meals, or sacrifices. In Buddhist practice, the mind needs to be able to focus on the goal of knowledge and purity, so all senses are used in the rituals: sounds, sights, smells, motions, and tastes. Felicitas D. Goodman believes that "the religious ritual . . . is the most exalted form of human communication, and recognizing this kind of deep structure restores to it that dignity that is lost in the desiccated categorizations of earlier years" (1988, 33).

For Southeast Asian cultures, visual language is always more powerful than audible language. Goodman notes that "in ritual of any kind, gesture always takes precedence over the spoken word" (1988, 16). For example, the mantras or the incantations of a shaman are of less importance than the gestures or dances performed. This is why a Christian prayer does not have the same attraction and credibility for a Buddhist as a shamanistic ritual. Even within Christianity, liturgical or Pentecostal rituals involve more than words, and engage the participants more than those of other Christian denominations.

Biblical writers often refer to holy people or to the chosen nation or remnant in terms of purity (Deut 23:9; Isa 65:1–5; Jer 23:3–8; 31:7, 17–19; 42:15, 18; Mic 4:6,7; Zeph 1:4–6; Acts 10:14, 15, 28; Eph 5:3–5; 1 Thess 4:1–7; Rev 21:26–27). Ethical norms are described as purity standards. In a culture of honor and shame, purity is regulated and defended at any cost. As deSilva explains,

> Pollution is a label attached to whatever is out of place with regard to the society's view of an orderly and safe world. Purity has to do with drawing the lines that give definition to the world around us, distinguishing, for example, what belongs to an individual from what belongs to others, and then defending these lines from being crossed by unwelcome forces. (2000, 243)

The problematic aspect comes from our ignorance regarding our own moral norms and values, which are based on the same purity dynamics, although in different forms. The western obsession with cleanliness is based on the same root of purity. However, as deSilva points out, "defilement for us has become largely microbial" (2000, 244).

Unfortunately, humans tend to associate only with people who share the same understanding of purity, so social barriers are created. We divide time and space according to the activities performed, and feel someone pollutes these domains if the rules are broken. Class and race are another illustration of purity dynamics in society. Most people consider homeless persons as dirty or unclean, and associating with them is seen as polluting, requiring basic purification rituals such as washing and sanitizing hands or taking a shower.

WORLDVIEW AND RITUAL

Rituals have a social origin, being agreed upon by a group of people and also becoming prescriptive in time. Rituals embody relationships and lead to social solidarity. For example, participants in initiation rites:

> Experience a common bond or feeling of *communitas* that they do not encounter outside the ritual experience. As a result, there is a sense of community and social solidarity that takes place among the initiates that enables them to become aware of the interconnectedness and equality among them. (Ring et al. 2012, 158)

As a social dimension, ritual takes the form of communication that may be dramatic and performative. "Religious ritual, properly viewed, has a special task, namely, expressing all or part of the complete drama of human life" (Goodman 1988, 6). In Gerald Klingbeil's words, "rituals are the 'Sistine Chapels' of communication" (2007, 241).

Religious rituals provide rhythm and order to a group's life in accordance to the accepted values of the group and their understanding of the sacred in the universe. Erik Cohen notes that "Pervasive changes can take place only collectively, not individually, as long as social controls, effective through the mechanism of shame, are intact" (1991, 124). Stephen K. Bailey advises that in Buddhist societies, "social allegiance to the group and the rules of social engagement within the group are issues that must be accounted for if the gospel is going to be communicated with impact in this context" (2006, 106).

In many non-western cultures, community is the natural domain where religion is lived. In fact, this is one of the major social barriers Christian missionaries face when they work in such cultures. Allegiance to family and larger community is stronger than any intellectual assent. Family and closest friends offer "the closest possible relationships that offer the greatest possible security to any individual" (Wagner 2006, 215). Buddhist men may not want to become Christians because of their duty to become temporary monks and make merit for their parents. In many cultures, religion, ethnicity, and nationalism blend into the identity of a person. To be Thai is to be Buddhist, to be Indian is to be Hindu, and to be Hebrew is to be Jewish.

Each ritual has meaning in a context marked by time, geography, action, and audience. Nancy C. Ring, Kathleen S. Nash, Mary N. MacDonald, and Fred Glennon believe that, "Like all symbolic action, our rituals can have different meanings depending upon the context or our experiences" (2012, 96–97). A purification ritual may have less impact when a person thinks there is no need for one, compared with the moment when the same person commits a wrong and the shame or lost face presses upon his or her honor.

Rituals embody values and worldviews. When worldviews or values change, the rituals performed by communities also change, either in the form or the meaning. However, ritual is conservative and tradition-building, and, in time, communities transform ritual into law and custom. Although ritual may change, such change is painful and disturbs life's order if not guided carefully. Rituals are grouped in three categories: rituals of separation, transition, and incorporation. Purity rituals are considered rituals of separation because they require shame or shame factors to be excised so that order may be restored.

SHAME, RITUAL, AND RESTORATION OF PURITY

In East Asian societies there is an intricate relationship between ritual and ethics that goes beyond the guilt felt by conscience. Any action that is contrary to the moral order asserted by a group or a religious tradition triggers a strong sense of shame. Douglas J. Davis points out that:

> In some indigenous religious traditions, when the harmony in the universe is out of balance there is an assumption that someone or some group has acted contrary to the moral order of the universe. The only way to set things right, to restore the balance, is by means of ritual action, which may include some divination process as to the cause of malaise. (2011, 159)

Such restoration rituals are not restricted to East Asians and their worldviews. For example, Yom Kippur, the Day of Atonement, was the yearly ritual in Judaism when the problem of individual or corporate sin and the shame it accompanied was addressed. The desire of both God and the community was to restore purity. Blood was required in order to wash away shame, and ritual sacrifices took place for the purification of the community. Isaac Kalimi calls Yom Kippur "the hope for freshness and a new beginning for individuals and for the collective" (2011, 71–72). It was a time of reconciliation between Israel and God, as well as reconciliation between individuals. The ritual was community building, uniting Jews and increasing their spiritual unity.

The whole ceremonial temple system at Israel's sanctuary was built to teach onlookers and participants about the solution to impurity and defilement and restore their lost honor (Ex 29:36–37, 30:10; Rom 3:22–26; Heb 2:17, 8:1–6, 9:11–12). "Its ritual and festivals also illustrated the larger issues of the cosmic conflict between God and his opponent, involving issues of divine justice (or theodicy), a public investigation and judgment, and, ultimately, the elimination of sin" (Klingbeil 2015, 113).

Christianity requires private and public confession in which a person or group takes ownership of and responsibility for wrongdoings or mistakes. Such confession is done in the name of Jesus and through his blood, which removes shame (1 John 1:9). But Christians perform other purification rituals such as baptism by water. The meaning of baptism is expressed as "forgetting the past" and beginning a pure new life (Rom 6:4). "Many religious traditions associate the act of bathing with purification and cleansing before coming into the presence of the sacred" (Ring et al. 2012, 100).

As deSilva noticed, "some of the least popular portions of [Christian] Scripture include the lengthy discussions of how purity is lost and how it is to be regained" (2000, 241). He draws attention to the fact that contemporary Christians consider the Old Testament as passé because it is referring to rituals and ritual laws. He is also concerned that Protestant Christianity no longer pays attention to rituals due to the strong Enlightenment influence of reason and, as a result, discards purification rites. Since God can be approached directly, without an intermediary, people lose sight of God's holiness and human sinfulness that is expressed through purity/impurity terminology. The problem is not only losing perspective of God's purity and holiness, but "we frankly regard any culture that still has such regulations as primitive" (242).

Buddhism also requires purity of mind for the self to be able to join nirvana. However, Buddha's sitting position, purifying his own mind through meditation, contrasts with Jesus on the cross in excruciating pain cleansing humanity's sin with his blood through atonement. Although the two purification processes may seem radically different, they are symbolic of the desire for purity. Both processes try to solve the problem of attachment: Buddha from the desires, Jesus Christ from the power of sin. In both religions there is an external force or identity that opposes the desire for purity. For Christians, Satan or the devil is the leader of evil and disobedient spirits; his name's meaning being the adversary. Its counterpart in Buddhism is *Mara* who "typifies one such evil antagonist of humans, and especially of Buddha in his progress toward enlightenment" (Davies 2011, 78).

Buddhist monks (sangha) are considered a pure community compared with the rest of the population. In the Zen tradition, sangha ritual is exacting and demanding. Dale S. Wright observes that, "Virtually, all life in a Zen monastery is predetermined, scripted, and taken out of the domain of human choice. . . All the routines of the Zen setting appear to be treated as essential to the life of Zen, and all life appears to be ritualized in some sense" (Wright 2008, 3).

When a person becomes a Buddhist monk, the ordination ritual benefits both the individual and the community. The ordained candidate "receives a sense of mission, vocation, and purpose; he becomes a member of the sangha, the community of monks who live together and participate in the practices and rituals that line the path that leads to enlightenment" (Ring et al. 2012, 103). But the results of ordination are expected to reflect at the community level, "especially for his relatives and those ancestors who may be suffering in hell. By renouncing all worldly pleasures, he becomes a storehouse of spiritual power that others can draw upon" (104). Even a monk's sexual purity and restraint is considered to improve the fertility of the lay community and the purity of offspring.

The desire for purity is also related to death in Japanese Buddhism. Before death and going to the Pure Land, Japanese devotees take a purifying ritual bath and chant the name of Buddha Amitabha. If the face of the dying person indicates happiness, it is considered a sign that the person was pure and entered the Pure Land. Purity and water are also connected in the Vesak celebration when participants bathe the Buddha. In the act of pouring scented water on an image of Buddha, the celebrant vows to attain purity of body, speech, and mind for the past, present, and future.

FUSATSU–A PURIFICATION RITUAL IN BUDDHISM

The Buddhist discipline of self-control and insight, of self-renouncing and spiritual growth resembles the purity sought in biblical atonement. The Buddha described his own experience in terms of purity, as it is recorded in *Anguttara-Nikaya II* (38–39), "As a lotus flower is born in water, grows in water, and rises out of water to stand above it unsoiled, so I, born in the world, raised in the world, having overcome the world, lived unsoiled by the world" (Burnett 2003, 25).

Unlike Christianity, which identifies sin as the cause for defilement, Buddhism indicates a twelve-source causality (*nidanas*) for impurity: spiritual ignorance, constructing activities, discriminative consciousness, mind-body, six base senses, sensory stimulation, feeling, craving, grasping, existence, birth, and ageing/death/sorrow. The difference between the two religious worldviews resides in the source of the solution: in Buddhism within the inner being of a person, while in Christianity through an external source. For Buddhists the human mind is pure and able to receive illumination, which can be obtained through the ritual of meditation.

As the final goal for Buddhists, nirvana is the pure state where change and impermanence (*anicca*) no longer exist. Impermanence is equivalent to insecurity and shame. The goal of Buddhism is to attain nirvana, a state of inexistence, which is the ultimate honor for Buddhists. They accept that human nature is imperfect and have no problems recognizing wrongs, acknowledging mistakes, or taking responsibility for harmful actions. This attitude reconciles the individual with his past and with the life of all beings. However, for a Buddhist, admitting a wrong does not require forgiveness.

In Zen Buddhism the *fusatsu* (observance) ritual is practiced for atonement and purification. When breaking a precept, one does harm to himself/herself and purification is attained by removing the causes that produced harm. One cannot apologize to themselves, but should meditate and vow not to repeat the wrong deed. Even when someone else is affected by the wrong and suffering, recognition of the wrong action is enough.

The *fusatsu* ritual involves burning incense, singing the liturgy, and confessing responsibility for the suffering produced to others. The purification ceremony creates resolution by renewing the vows: the Three Refuges, the Three Pure Precepts, the Ten Major Precepts, and the Bodhisattva vows. It is expected that the person undergoing the ritual becomes compassionate, manifesting wisdom at the intellectual level. There are no feelings involved, no guilt, and no shame implied. If Christian atonement ritual deals with wrong actions of the past, Buddhist atonement is intended to prevent such wrongs happening in the future.

THE CHALLENGE OF RECONCILIATION

Reconciliation involves both personal and community levels. First, an individual must address the reconciliation of the self. As imperfect beings, we break rules, transgress boundaries and laws, and act against our own standards of purity. As sinners, Christians find themselves alienated from God and in need of reconciliation. Confession is the first step in the process, followed by turning from the wrong and by reparation or repayment. But Buddhists may find themselves in a state of impurity as well. Reconciling rituals, such as *fusatsu*, open the way to restoration to a pure state even though Buddhists may not use the term "reconciliation" when talking about realigning their lives to the Eightfold Path.

For shame and honor cultures, restoration of self has to be marked by a public ritual. Reconciliation with oneself needs to be acknowledged by community witnessing either a public confession or a sacrifice or offering. Indeed, individual failures often affect community: relationships become tense, problematic, and even broken. Public confession is expected when the process of reconciliation takes place. Even when private confession takes place in the seclusion of a Roman Catholic confessional, the priest forgives and welcomes back the penitent in the name of the community. A ritual marks the closing of the reconciliation process. For example, in Judaism, Yom Kippur is the day when:

> Jews align themselves anew with the community and with the community's worldview. . . . If they admit to themselves that they have held a grudge against someone or have acted unjustly, they make amends to those involved. On Yom Kippur itself observant Jews fast from sunset to sunset. They gather in their synagogues or temples and spend the day in prayer. This attitude towards reconciliation is a development of the prophetic insight that the quality of people's relationships with others mirrors the quality of their relationship to God. At the conclusion of Yom Kippur, they participate in a celebratory meal. Reconciliation engenders joy and good comradeship, which demands social expression. The sharing of food is among the most deeply symbolic and reconciling rituals known to humankind. We don't eat with our enemies, and if we do, they usually do not remain enemies. (Ring 2012, 354–355)

Reconciliation often needs to go beyond the visible aspects of life. Most people recognize their need for reconciliation at personal and societal level. But purity is at the deeper levels of values and worldviews. The proposed new values challenge our allegiances. Purity is a domain where our presuppositions are tested. From considering Buddhism a pagan religion to accepting or even embracing Buddhism there is a huge leap. Some people stop somewhere in the middle of the process, where they feel they cannot go further. Sometimes we are faced with ideologies that are unacceptable when looked at from a biblical informed worldview.

As missionaries, we live in cultures that share a different worldview than the one we grew up with. We experience the constant challenge to adapt to the new values, traditions, and rituals. But we also find ourselves at odds with our initial worldview any time we step back into our native culture. We notice that old values diminish in importance as well as new ones coming to the fore. We may feel the urge to react in order to preserve our standard of purity or try to correct the trend in society when changes are sweeping. We then realize the only chance to live a normal life is to reconcile ourselves with the community and the new acceptable values. We need to embrace or adapt rituals that will mark our new identity.

Writing about an attempt of dialogue and reconciliation between Buddhists and Roman Catholics, Erik Cohen describes the challenges and limitations of the process:

> Members of the Catholic clergy in Thailand, particularly foreign priests of long standing in the country, consequently made a serious effort to reconcile the two religions to the greatest possible degree. Participation of Catholics and Buddhists in each others' rituals was encouraged. When interviewed, one Jesuit priest went so far as to agree that one can be concomitantly a Christian and a Buddhist; a Catholic nun argued in favour of Christians participating in Buddhist meditational exercises—without, however, reaching the highest stages, in which one has "to deny everything." But even those Catholics who keenly sought a *rapprochement* with Buddhism remained aware of the impossibility of a complete

reconciliation, owing to the unbridgeable gulf that exists between the basic presuppositions of the two religions. (1991, 128)

In a wider application of reconciliation, religious bodies can also initiate reconciliation processes. Christian-Buddhist relationships are not healthy in South Asian countries. Conflicts mark their history, especially when political or armed intervention was involved in addition to religious differences and has created deep wounds and scars.

CONCLUSION

The value of purity in the context of East Asian cultures offers a broad platform for dialogue, and reveals a potential bridge of communication between Christians and Buddhists. Purification rituals allow missionaries to address issues at both personal and societal levels. The Bible speaks of purity and contains indications for removing defilement. At the same time, Buddhism is concerned with purity and provides purification rituals. Missionaries should consider all these factors that support reconciliation efforts.

Several steps need to be considered in the process of using purification rituals in the reconciliation process:

- Similar purification rituals have to be identified in the practice of different religious groups.
- The meaning of the rituals and the significance of the symbols used (water, oil, smoke, etc.) needs to be clarified within each religious context.
- Reconciliation rituals should be agreed upon, after dialogue and according to the geographical and temporal context.
- In each instance, the standards of purity need to be clearly spelled out.

- Christians should make sure that the symbols and rituals agreed upon do not contradict the biblical worldview.

Dr. Jon Dybdahl, a veteran missionary who worked in Thailand, relates his story being invited to help a Buddhist monk create a plaster mural depicting the essence of Christianity. After considering several options, Dr. Dybdahl decided to introduce the artist monk to a ritual he may understand in the story of Jesus washing his disciples' feet in John 13. "Do you mean to say that the Founder of your religion washed His students' feet?" asked the monk looking with incredulity.

> The usually placid moon face with shaved eyebrows and head wrinkled up in shock and amazement. He was speechless, and so was I. I swallowed very hard several times, and we were both caught up in the drama of the scene. As I gazed at him, the look of incredulity on his face changed to a reverent awe. Jesus, the Founder of Christianity, had touched and washed dirty fishermen's feet! . . . There are, however, two present day living memorials. The first is in the heart of a Thai Buddhist monk who for the first time discovered God's condescension and the cross through feet. The second is engraved in the heart of an American missionary who rediscovered the dynamic power of the cross through feet and Thai culture. It began in Thailand with feet. It ended with an understanding of the cross (Dybdahl 1986, 28).

References

Bailey, Stephen K. 2006. "World Christianity in Buddhist societies." In *Communicating Christ in the Buddhist world*, edited by Paul de Neui and David Lim, 106–131. Pasadena, CA: William Carey Library.

Burnett, David. 2003. *The spirit of Buddhism*. London: Monarch Books.

Cohen, Erik. 1991. "Christianity and Buddhism in Thailand: The 'battle of the axes' and the 'contest of power.'" *Social Compass* 38 (2): 115–40.

Davies, Douglas J. 2011. *Emotion, identity, and religion: Hope, reciprocity, and otherness*. New York: Oxford University Press.

deSilva, David A. 2000. *Honor, patronage, kinship, and purity: Unlocking New Testament culture*. Downers Grove, IL: IVP.

Dybdahl, Jon. 1986. *Missions: A two-way street*. Boise, ID: Pacific Press.

Goodman, Felicitas D. 1988. *Ecstasy, ritual, and alternate reality: Religion in a pluralistic world*. Bloomington, IN: Indiana University Press.

Kalimi, Isaac. 2011. "The Day of Atonement in the Late Second Temple Period: Saducees' high priests, Pharisees' norms, and Qumranites' calendar(s)." *The Review of Rabbinic Judaism* 14 (1): 71–91.

Klingbeil, Gerald A. 2007. *Bridging the gap: Ritual and ritual texts in the Bible*. Bulletin for biblical research supplements 1. Winona Lake, IN: Eisenbrauns.

———. 2015. "God's 'show-and-tell': The didactic power of ritual in Scripture and missions." In *Ministering to mourners: Funeral rituals and Christian witness in East Asian contexts*, edited by Gregory and Amy Whitsett, 103–121. Silver Springs, MD: CEAR.

Mills, Martin A. 2003. "Hinduism and Buddhism." *A companion to religious studies and theology*, edited by Helen K. Bond, Seth D. Kunin, and Francesca Aran Murphy. Edinburgh, UK: Edinburgh University Press.

"Purification." 1999. *Merriam-Webster's encyclopedia of world religions*, edited by Wendy Doniger. Springfield, MA: Merriam-Webster.

Ring, Nancy C., Kathleen S. Nash, Mary N. MacDonald, and Fred Glennon. 2012. *Introduction to the study of religion*. Maryknoll, NY: Orbis.

Wagner, Paul. 2006. "Beyond Karma: A model for presenting freedom in Christ in the Buddhist context." In *Communicating Christ in the Buddhist world*, edited by Paul de Neui and David Lim, 210–32. Pasadena, CA: William Carey Library.

Wright, Dale S. 2008. "Rethinking ritual practice in Zen Buddhism." In *Zen ritual: Studies of Zen Buddhist theory in practice*, edited by Steven Heine and Dale S. Wright, 3–19. New York: Oxford University Press.

9
A Church Restored from Sin, Shame, and Fear in a Tibetan Context

Christian Gabre

In a world broken by sin, the three aspects, guilt, shame, and fear, can be traced to the very beginning in Genesis 3. All three taint the relationships, worldviews, and values of every culture. Adam and Eve left the Garden of Eden in shame, carrying the guilt of broken rules and fragmented trust, and filled with the fear of pain, the lack of provisions, and future hardships. The action by Adam and Eve was the original sin, and what they did was more than just breaking a commandment; it was also a wish to receive knowledge and to be more like God. We are still colored by this, and as long as we are in the world we will continue to face all of this. Scripture states we should not be of the world but we still get our hands and feet dirty by the broken world pushing itself upon us.

When we look at different cultures, one aspect of the three orientations of guilt, shame, and fear always seems to be more dominant. It is a popular opinion that most cultures in Asia are prevalent by the honor-shame aspect. We could expect shame-orientation to be dominant among Tibetan Buddhists too, but with the shamanistic side of Tibetan Buddhism the orientation is more toward fear among the common people. Through my ten years of working with Tibetans, in interviews and reflections, I have seen that a fear culture is predominant among many Tibetan Buddhists. This has also been expressed in testimonies and activities in fellowships. The reconciliation brought by God is a full restoration of the creation in all aspects and as such we cannot limit it to only one cultural orientation. The question is how can we embrace a holistic reconciliation in these three aspects in a culture dominated by one, as Tibetan Buddhism is dominated by fear? Can we allow one orientation to be the primary focus even when it is not the orientation toward forgiveness of sin and righteousness?

In Christ, sin's power was and is broken. Sin previously kept us away from God through our guilt, shame, and fear. Christ took all these upon himself and became one with sinners and the guilty. Crucified on the cross in shame, he descended into hell breaking the power of humanity's ultimate fear: death itself. It is not enough that death's power was broken and with that also sickness, but in the process the restoration of all humanity to righteousness was made possible. Through his victory we were brought to justification and sanctification. Christ's reconciliation broke guilt, shame, and fear and restored us to their opposites: righteousness, honor, security, and power. In my opinion the opposite of fear is not power, but security and wholeness, but more about this further down. In sanctification we were raised up with honor to be able to approach God's throne and rule with Him. Through sanctification we are also freed from any fear of bondage, death, or sickness and claim the power of being his children. This results in safety and security, opposites of the fear under which we previously lived.

What does the restoration of righteousness, honor, and power mean to God's church; our community and our family? It is easy to put this off to the sphere of the heavenly kingdom, and conclude that it is only for the future resurrected fellowship. But we can't ignore the fact that the church is Christ's body on earth here and now and therefore living in the paradigm of "the already and the not yet." In the same manner we are justified and free of sin already, but still not in full as it will be in heaven. As a church we have ignored all but the justification, and maybe sometimes get a taste of the others but it is not usually incorporated as part of the teaching and activities. In a culture of shame and fear, the restoration of honor, security, and power have to become more obvious or the church as a community will be weak and remain broken. God's desire is for complete reconciliation. In what aspects of the church life can we see the reality of the victory we claim and where do we need to put our efforts?

BROKEN CREATION

"The big white stupa broke at the foot, and yellowish pus poured out from the base of the stupa." It was clear for this woman that her dream was true and help was to be found with the Tibetan Pastor visiting the village. She had heard the gospel the day before, and the morning after the dream she went to the pastor who prayed and her useless swollen foot was healed. She also received Christ.

Sin is what separates us from God. I clearly remember how this was a challenge for me to understand in my early days. It was my Sunday school understanding that sin was breaking the law not breaking relationships. The dictionary still defines sin as, "an immoral act considered to be a transgression against divine law" (Merriam-Webster 2015, Sin). More commonly sin is described as rebellion against God. John Stott follows this line of thinking; "The essence of sin is man substituting himself for God, while the essence of salvation is God substituting himself for man. Man asserts himself against God and puts himself where only God deserves to be" (1984, 160).

Allister McGrath expresses sin in its relationship to God as, "something that separates humankind from God" (2007, 96). Consequently salvation restores the possibility of relationship with God in the same way the temple curtain was rent asunder to open up the way to the altar. "Salvation is the breaking down of the barrier of separation between humans and God on account of Christ" (96).

We can see how these descriptions of sin include more than the dictionary's definition of transgression of a divine law. The original sin led to expulsion from God's garden where Adam and Eve walked in God's presence. Apart from not being in God's immediate fellowship, sin also led to death, birthing pains, hard labor for food production, and sickness. In short the first couple was now forced to live in and with a broken nature. Many Tibetan brothers express that freedom from their fears of death, spirits, sickness, and suffering was the biggest impact of their salvation. "The biggest change for me was that I was free from my fears in the daily life" (Tibetan brother and believer for seven years in a private conversation).

It is necessary for churches everywhere to understand that sin is more than broken laws, and to see the different aspects involved in sin and the consequences of it. *"We all, like sheep, have gone astray, each of us has turned to our own way"* (Isa 53:6). This describes much more than the act of transgression, it expresses the rebellion against God. In trying to take the place of God, human beings try to claim the honor and glory that only God deserves.

In shame cultures relationships are the basis for the concept of shame and honor. It is not possible to have shame or honor individually but only "in the face" of others. Shame in itself creates distance in relationships, while honor strengthens ties and reinforces relationships with more honor as well. It is for this reason that people like to take photos with an honored person or desire to shake the hands of the famous. Association with a person of honor brings honor in the relationship and to self as well. Most Buddhist cultures understand this accordingly.

The flip side is also true. Public shaming is not reserved for individuals alone. China has expressed this very clearly in modern times in regards to any person not aligned with the government. Not only is the individual punished but anyone else related by blood, relationship, or association with the accused will also be punished through social isolation, public shaming, or even more severe measures.

This has of course affected Tibetans. It is part of their culture, even if not as public as in China. In literature about Tibet we find different reasons for public punishments for crimes ranging from stealing to failing to appear at a dance performance for the Dalai Lama (Norbu 2015, blog). Tibetans in Lhasa shamed criminal offenders during the early twentieth century by practicing *cangue,* placing the accused on public display with a door around the neck (Bell 1946, 62–63). Other shaming practices included physical mutilation such as cutting off ears, gouging out eyes, cutting off noses and hands, and public administration of additional pain and shaming. Using intoxicants while mutilating the offender demonstrates that the purpose was not necessarily to abate the pain felt, but rather to increase the shame that would follow. A criminal who had served imprisonment, would be put in shackles to publicly beg and be continually shamed (Norbu 2015, blog).

Similarly it is understood that forgiveness is very difficult to understand and to exercise. Revenge is a common concept and accepted as a way to remove shame. One mother of a *Rinpoche* (one declared to be a "Living Buddha" having reached enlightenment in a previous life and returning to guide people to reach the same) expressed that her son was now dead to her when he confessed faith in Christ (anonymous conversation). The shame she felt in the eyes of the society was unbearable, she would lose face not only for herself but she would lose all respect in society. Turned from being a mother of a Living Buddha to a mother of a Christian, she was now seen as a traitor of the religion and society. To her the only solution to facing dishonor was to have her son wished and declared dead.

One of the unique aspects of Tibetan Buddhism is the Bön religion. It has merged with and influenced Tibetan Buddhism thoroughly. It is simply explained as a form of shamanism from pre-Buddhist times. It takes an animistic approach to appeasing spirits by worshipping the rivers, mountains, and places in nature where powerful spirits are located. It is especially dominant among the common non-religious population outside Tibetan Buddhist monasteries. We need to see Tibetan culture as including a range between more shame-orientation in the areas of higher religion and more fear-orientation among the common strata of society, both the nomadic and the settled populations. Examples of this are the fear of darkness and respect for sacred trees described by Amy McIntosh (2015, 11).

For many Tibetans the first person they turn to for treatment and remedies when sick is the witch doctor or the shaman (Watters 2011, loc 1830–37). We have observed that the primary way Tibetans encounter Christ is through prayer and miracles. This type of power encounter holds strong attraction, and ministry in these areas is very much appreciated. Tibetan brothers and sisters have expressed to me their new reality of living in freedom from fear as a result. To see Christ's power at work personally in their lives is a strong pull toward salvation. It is worth noting that this experience is described as freedom from fear, and not as having power against fear, which expresses my understanding that it is an escape from fearful things to an area of safety and security.

In the opening story we can see the power of Jesus demonstrated to an older lady when the stupa in her dream broke and the pus revealed the rotten insides of the entire system. She needed to be released from fear and from sickness by a power stronger than the dedicated stupa which is the very essence and symbol of the Buddhist worldview containing what are considered to be powerful sacred relics. I love the way my Tibetan brother expressed the life prior to salvation as "a daily life in fear." With these words he captured the essence of Tibetan life, even for him as a monk of many years.

We can conclude that a personal awareness of sin and a resulting cultural orientation of guilt are very weak in Tibetan societies. The stronger cultural feature is fear-orientation, with a strong overtone of shame. Even as Buddhists are taught that they should be free from desire, we still see that there is high social honor (and therefore a desire) to becoming enlightened and having good karma. Let us now turn to what it means for a Tibetan Buddhist to be restored and reconciled to God when the culture is dominated by fear.

RECONCILED AND RESTORED THROUGH SALVATION

As explained above, the world and human beings are broken and fallen by original sin. Humanity in its rebellion against God needs holistic and full restoration. That is not to say that a holistic view of restoration has been neglected before, but the focus has been primarily on righteousness and justification. Jayson Georges summarizes that different concepts of reconciliation in historic systematic theology have brought a wider understanding of reconciliation than just the forgiveness of transgression (2014, loc 597–736).

In recent times there has been more of a focus on atonement and forgiveness of sin, but earlier in church history these concepts carried a wider meaning including healing and the reconciliation of relationships. When we only focus on one aspect of reconciliation it is like focusing on only one small part of the complex image in a *thangka* (a Buddhist painting composed of a main focus with many small figures) and forgetting that it belongs in a bigger picture. It is easy to get fixated by the idea that the forgiveness of transgression (the guilt/security dimension) has to be explained first as it is the core of Christian teaching of the cross and blood sacrifice. For a limited time or situation we may focus on one aspect of reconciliation (forgiveness, honor, and security-power) but for wholeness in reconciliation all three aspects of restoration have to be pursued.

To many this lack of understanding of the breadth of God's forgiveness becomes the first obstacle to cross before anything else can be shared. In this way cross-cultural communicators of the gospel (in Tibetan contexts and others) may be stuck trying to find different ways to explain one small area of focus and to make this aspect of God's truth understood when actually conveying a bigger picture is needed. A more biblical perspective would be to actually zoom out wider and see the other details of the picture first. By allowing a broader culturally appropriate understanding of reconciliation to be the focus first, the wider truth will grow from there.

The first step in contextualization is to identify our audience and to find common denominators for communication. One of these is the common ground we share in the path of the Via Dolorosa. We know Christ walked the earthly path of suffering before us and took upon himself the curse of our fallen nature in order to restore us to himself. He identified himself completely with the fallen nature of humanity, and not just from the perspective of punishment of sin and guilt, but also in shame and fear. When we look at Christ's way to the cross from the perspective of shame we can understand the Fall.

Start with the Palm Sunday expectation of a coming king. The multitudes cheered him, "Hosanna!" But only a few days later he was brought to Pontius Pilate, mockingly robed, crowned with thorns and sarcastically titled, "Jesus the Nazarene King of the Jews." The fall from honor was even deeper when Jesus was nailed naked to the cross, the ultimate punishment of shame. His shame was made complete as he was betrayed, denied, and abandoned, utterly alone on the cross, separated even from the Father. The defining point of shame is the loss of relationship with others, humans and God, and Jesus felt this ultimately just before death when he cried out to his Father, "Why have you forsaken me?" (Mark 15:34). This was expressed in Isaiah's words "He had no beauty or majesty to attract us to him, nothing in his appearance that we should desire him. He was despised and rejected by mankind" (Isa 53:2–3). The connecting point with the fall of mankind is naturally the shame Adam and Eve felt when they hid in their nakedness, but also the broken relationship with God. They had to leave paradise in shame unable to have fellowship with God as they previously had when they walked in the garden together.

To have fellowship with the Father in his glory and honor, is also giving honor to everyone in his presence, as expressed in Psalm 23:5 where a table of honor and oil of anointment is prepared for God's people. Restoration from shame is more than a restoration of honor, it is also the restoration of a glorious and honorable relationship with God our Father. This is expressed in Revelation as our eternal relationship with our God. "Those who are victorious will inherit all this, and I will be their God and they will be my children" (Rev 21:7). The same Tibetan brother who expressed the daily fear as part of living before he experienced salvation, added this second part, recognizing the honor of having a personal relationship with the Father in heaven. This full restoration of honor and relationship is waiting for him when he is brought to his heavenly home.

Restoration from shame to honor is also tangibly realized in the present through the honor of fellowship and community. Fellowship with the Lord is experienced through his gift of fellowship with brothers and sisters in Christ. Restored community is an important external part of the healing process of broken relationships.

As Jesus took the path of shame, he also took the path of fear. I took the opportunity to ask some Tibetan brothers and sisters directly what they were afraid of and what fears they were freed from at the time of salvation. They responded by sharing very practical fears, not limiting themselves only to metaphysical fears (which they included as well) normally associated with an animistic worldview such as in Tibetan Buddhism. The fears they expressed included the daily fears of darkness, sickness, hunger, lack of resources, loneliness, and death. These fears all stem from the Fall when nature and creation were cursed with death, suffering, pain, and lack of resources.

When Adam and Eve were expelled from paradise they began to suffer pain: the pain of childbirth (Gen 3:16), the pain of hard labor (Gen 3:18–19), and the pain of death (later expressed clearly by Cain in Gen 4:13–14). These were identical to words spoken to me by my Tibetan brothers and sisters which I rephrase as "lack of shalom" in its full meaning of health, peace, and fullness. The lack of shalom is the root of fear. It is the lack of safety and security in a world that is broken and full of pain and death. In this I deviate from Jayson Georges to suggest that restoration from fear is shalom, together with safety and security. I draw this from my experience with fear cultures in Asia, where most treat that which they fear with avoidance or attempts to appease spiritual powers.

Spiritual powers can be useful, but they can also be fickle and undependable. Most people in fear-oriented cultures will make a concerted effort to stay in a safe zone and avoid anything that could cause fear or disturb the cosmic harmony. Jesus in the garden of Gethsemane, sweating to the point of blood, expressed his fear by asking the Father to spare him, but he went to the cross, entered the kingdom of hell and broke the power of death. The ultimate power of fear was finally broken.

Salvation means full restoration to God's intended humanity and being in reconciled relationships. Again, this includes the forgiveness of the transgression of divine law. It is through the sacrifice of Christ we are made whole and holy. But forgiveness of transgression is only one part, albeit a very important part, of God's holistic reconciliation process.

Currently there is a growing emphasis in sharing the gospel through prayer and power encounter. This speaks directly to the Tibetans' heart of fear. Many welcome the prayer as they often recognize care and healing through spiritual encounter. Some Tibetans have experienced this from westerners who have learned certain methods through charismatic training. But other

Tibetans also minister frequently through prayer and healing, caring for people in a natural Spirit-led way not dependent on specific training. This is definitely touching the hearts of many Tibetans. A concern, however, is that without proper guidance into fellowship with God and other believers such experiences may remain as only one-time emotional encounters. Fear may have been dismissed temporarily, but growing into honor and understanding of righteousness and holiness may fall short, and may not ultimately result in a lasting relationship with the God Most High.

Another weakness I have seen in several Tibetan fellowships is a low level of scriptural knowledge. In preaching and teaching I try to be interactive and ask easy questions from the Bible but even these are not able to be answered at times. Tibetan fellowships have an active prayer life and strong community which addresses the areas of counteracting shame and fear-orientation. But an understanding that God's holistic reconciliation also includes justification and forgiveness of guilt caused by the transgression of God's law may be weaker.

Humanity is broken by sin and lacks the holiness required to enter into God's presence. The result of this broken nature is not only shame, dishonor, and loss of relationships but also fear resulting in burdens, pain, and death. Salvation breaks humanity's bondage to sin and restores humanity into the fullness of righteousness, holiness, honor, safety, and shalom. All this happens at the moment of salvation but is not always fully understood or experienced initially. Misunderstood salvation is weak in more than one or two of these aspects. Not until heaven will we understand the full breadth of God's reconciliation, but it is possible, even now, to understand and experience it more deeply than a mere fraction.

A major problem among Tibetan believers is backsliding and this is most often indicated by either leaving the faith or leaving the fellowship. It is a problem across the wide range of Tibetan peoples, and although much research has been done on this topic, results have been inconclusive. An obvious problem is the corporate identity and the pressure from society to belong and fit in. When you are a Christian you are normally isolated and you no longer belong in the society. The fellowship of Christians should be the new community, but over time it is often not enough for the wider corporate identity. The pressure from family, society, and structure wears down the believers to a point of giving up. Therefore I call for a refocus to work more deliberately on community and building the fellowship of believers. It is not necessary to focus on the negatives; instead let us give attention to the positive aspects of restoration as a community.

Below is a simplified table to express a schematic picture in the process described in this chapter. It is meant to be more of an inspiration and a starting point. It has been helpful to think about perception and feelings and letting theology be more clearly expressed in other places. As many have accurately pointed out to me, the terminology should be "guilt-innocence," "shame-honor," and "fear-security" to follow the pattern of brokenness and restoration, and holistically all three should come under the heading of "sin-shalom." But for the sake of simplicity I will stay with the traditional dichotomy concepts and explain shalom later.

Schematic of Restoration Process

Aspect of Culture	Sin-Guilt	Shame	Fear
Brokenness	Broken Rules	Broken Relationships	Broken world
Restoration into	Righteousness, justification (Rom 3:23–26)	Honor, glorification (Rom 8:16–17)	Shalom, wholeness (Col 1:20)
Human attempts at restitution	Regulations, justice, karma	Status, contracts, isolated communities, monkhood	Power, empowered items, shaman

Aspect of Culture	Sin-Guilt	Shame	Fear
Christ's restorative work on the cross	Fulfilling the law, forgiveness	New covenant, agape love	New creation, new home, all power given
Our tools	Forgiveness, truth, Scripture knowledge (Luke 7:36–50)	Love, honor, fellowship (Rom 12:10)	Faith, Holy Spirit, prayer (Matt 8:23–27)
Key for Tibetans	Need of Scripture and forgiveness	New fellowship and community	Prayer and miracles

RESTORED FELLOWSHIP

It is easy to express focus on that which is negative and broken, and to make this the major point of analysis. But through the work of Christ we have moved on from the negative aspects to focus more on the positive, the restoration and reconciliation of the human being. Reconciliation is all about the cross, particularly the wider and deeper understanding of the work of the cross. In the past I approached this topic in the style of western theology, although the cultural context of Tibetan Buddhists is not a sin or guilt-oriented culture. The traditional approach has been very systematic with a focus on the personal condition of the individual. Tibetan culture, however, deeply values a corporate identity and places great importance on the role of the community in everything. This is where shame-orientation plays a prominent role. Fear-orientation in this setting has also more of a corporate expression in the ways that common fears are shared, but individual fears are also strong in regards to fear of personal expression and fear of loneliness.

Therefore we need to move from individual concepts into corporate values, and for Tibetan Christians this comes through church fellowship. The fellowship of Christians is the new community. We see the importance of the new community, and how it is filling the role of a true family in the words of Jesus when he asked, "Who is my mother, and who are my brothers?" (Matt 12:48). The context following this verse is concluding that anyone doing the will of the Father is a brother to Christ. Obeying and following the Father's will is the basis of the new community, establishing God as our Father and seeking unity as we follow God's will together. This also establishes the close link, or inseparable understanding of obedience as part of guilt-oriented cultures as well as shame-oriented cultures. To disobey would not only be to break a regulation but also to shame the person giving the order, while to obey reconfirms the bond keeping us together with the Father.

For Tibetan churches who are wrestling with backsliding, fellowship needs to work on a holistic view of salvation, and what it means for the church. The natural way is to teach more, but to really make it meaningful for Tibetans (and any highly relational and fear-oriented cultures), teaching must be readily applicable to the work of daily living.

Most Tibetan churches and fellowships are very small and very young. They are usually caring communities that form strong ties to each other. But since they are small, the need for a larger supportive community, in sense of a corporate identity, is stronger. The society around becomes more of a threat than if the church was larger or if the whole village and surrounding area was also Christian. These fellowships have a deep sense of commitment to each other, and the care they exhibit toward each other is very strong. They are coming closer to creating a genuine feeling of family. One pastor told me,

> To be a pastor is to be more of a family father. You have to care about everyone and you look out for the children, giving advice to the parents in raising the children or school education but it is also to make sure the elderly are taken care of as well.

The pastor is not so much a teacher, as a real shepherd for church people. It is, of course, very challenging. Pastors get no time off when their role is like that of a father of a big family.

We all have different experiences of salvation. Just as God works in many ways, we all will experience and receive salvation differently. The lady mentioned at the beginning of this chapter was convicted by her dream and needed healing for her foot. This led to her first steps with Christ. But it was really just a first encounter. If dreams and healings were the foundation of salvation then many more would be saved, but they are merely first encounters with Christ and his love and power. Some people have found faith out of the pursuit of freedom from fear in their life. In Christ they find a place of safety where they can be free from fear. Real salvation brings them out of fear, but spiritual maturity and growth do not occur through a one-time encounter. The believer must live in the light of Christ away from darkness and areas of fear.

An important second step is to move into a fellowship where members help support each other stay out of areas of fear, and to fight against fear with faith and the Holy Spirit. Without going into a full discussion of spiritual battle, it is safe to summarize that fears have to be countered and conquered with Christ. The new Tibetan believer has turned away from a daily life of fear. Instead of going to the shaman to drive away evil spirits and sicknesses, she has now turned to Christ. Instead of fearing the darkness and death and the uncertainty of what will come, she has turned to the light and found safety. She has left the place where she felt unsafe and powerless, to the place of security in Christ with His power. Simply put "if God is for us, who can be against us?" (Rom 8:31).

Jerry Bridges says "Each of us must respond individually in repentance and faith to the gospel invitation. But although God saves us as individuals, He immediately incorporates us into the body of Christ" (2012, loc 628). The body of Christ is not a geographical location, but is a relational fellowship. A Christian fellowship is a place where we care for one another, honor one another, teach and pray for one another. At the moment of salvation we have left the state of fear, but we are still living in the world. But we are no longer of the world. Fear may still threaten us just as sin may continue to occur in the life of any Christian. Any Christian knows that even though he is forgiven he may still sin again and will have to ask for forgiveness when it occurs. A person who has left his fear-orientation at salvation, may still experience fear and will need to come back to restoration from the fears facing him. We can't neglect this fact of reoccurring fears by saying "You are saved, so don't be afraid." That would be the same as saying that a Christian can't sin. The evangelist John expressed this in his letter when he spelled it out clearly that we don't live in sin, but as Christians we still sin (1 John 1:6–8).

A person saved from a fear-orientation needs a church able to answer the need of this cultural worldview. Such a church must be sensitive to fellowship needs and must present a holistic view of salvation. I have heard many people ask how can we explain the concept of sin and transgression of the divine law but I have never heard anyone ask how to explain Christ as the answer to fear? It should be natural to contextualize the theological answer in this way to see Christ as the answer to fear, but it should also be our goal to see the church contextualized as the answer to fear as well. The question should be can we see the church as the answer to fear?

A fellowship functioning in a fear-oriented culture needs to address holistic salvation in different ways and with different tools. A Christian fellowship should have the goal to be more like heaven, being a pre-taste of heaven. In a similar way that a church in a sin-guilt-oriented culture preaches on staying close to the Father, living a holy life, and avoiding sin, a church in a fear culture should preach on security in the Father, living in the light, and living with trust and faith. I deliberately avoided negative descriptions of what fear is as they bring our attention to problems and challenges. When focus is on the negative it is like teaching how to avoid a mine field, and all attention is on how to avoid darkness and shadows of death. Instead we should raise our eyes to the light and trust that staying in the light is the power. A focus on the positive teachings about living in the light builds up security and shalom. As our fellowship is Christ's body and family, we need to be able to express what it should be and not just what it shouldn't be. In light of this, I take it for granted that we do avoid the darkness, just as we don't need to walk into temptation, but in the power of Christ we can walk through it safely, though we normally avoid it.

Power manifestations are part of fighting areas of fear. Jayson Georges points out in *The 3D Gospel* that Charismatic and Pentecostal churches have had more success in fear-oriented cultures. The same can be said among some Tibetan churches where the response has not taken the shape of traditional Pentecostal churches, but has focused on prayer for healing and bravery in facing opposition. These manifestations are part of making the fellowship a place of power and security. They help insure that power encounters are not merely one-time occurrences but part of the daily life of the community of faith.

Part of ministry to the unreached Tibetan is prayer for the sick. Breaking through fear results in a demonstration of the power of God. At the same time I want to stress that the church is like a pre-taste of heaven, God's people on earth already now and still not yet. Douglas Webster expresses that "because the very power that raised Jesus from the dead is accessible, the church should live differently—as 'a colony of heaven'" (2012, 158). That means we can fight fear with power. This is not merely about power over spiritual manifestations, it is the power over death itself. This is what leads to the place of security, the spiritual home. The opposite of fear is a haven of safety, a fortress of salvation, and that should be our goal for the church too. Grenz stresses that we as a church should live in accordance with our new home,

> Christ established the church not merely to be a mirror of original creation but to be the eschatological new community, living in accordance with the principles of God's new creation and thereby reflecting the mutuality that lies at the heart of the triune God. (2005, 286)

A church in a fear culture should practice exercises that make the church and the fellowship a safe and secure home for believers. The first step should be to focus on prayer; prayer is fellowship with God and in this is a place of safety. But prayer should also include the power bestowed upon us by being God's children. Knowing that prayer is a mighty weapon, it should also be exercised in ways that give opportunities for manifestations of the Spirit, such as healings and miracles.

In some of the existing Tibetan churches experiencing spiritual power is a critical part of their communal life and comes quite naturally to a people expecting spiritual wonders. Dreams are also common, and the Scripture states that this is one way God chose to talk to us. In this way the church should encourage and expect God to speak through dreams also.

Let us not believe that prayer and supernatural happenings, as important as they are to daily Christian life, are the only components necessary to making the church community a safe place for those in a fear-oriented culture. Two others components for counteracting fear are trust and faith. Teaching and encouraging trust in God means believing in God in all situations, seeking His kingdom first and believing that he cares for all our needs all the time. Another important component is faith, the shield in the heavenly armor. Paul tells us that the shield of faith can extinguish all the flaming arrows of the enemy (Eph 6:16). When the arrows are gone, that place is now safe and fear is gone. This means that trust and faith are keys in fear-oriented cultures. Both need to be taught well and also exercised. This resounds well with Psalm 21:7 where we affirm that through trust in the Lord we will not be shaken.

The third area in the midst of a fear culture is to be a safe haven, letting the church be a place of normal care, empathy, and comfort for each other. The first big earthquake on the 25th of April 2015 in Nepal occurred on a Saturday morning (church services are held on Saturdays on their day off in the Hindu tradition) during the time of church services. Due to the severity of the multiple earthquakes and the many aftershocks people were very afraid and didn't dare to stay under their rooves for many weeks. It was interesting to listen to the rumors of predictions and interpretations of the earthquake. The Christians were blamed for the earthquake by the Hindus and the Buddhists since the first earthquake happened during the common church service time. The cause of the earthquake was expressed to be spiritual. Even though the churches cared for people in many ways, everyone was afraid. One way the churches cared was to make shelters and safe havens in the yards around the church buildings. These places were great for fellowship, for sharing and caring for each other and were also safe places where tears could flow and comfort be found. A true Christian fellowship functioning as a place to face fear with comfort and care, is a church of shalom. Shalom here should be interpreted in its wider meaning to include peace, health, and wholeness as expressed by C.L. Feinberg in the Evangelical Dictionary of Theology: "The primary and basic idea of the biblical word 'peace' (OT *šālôm;* NT *eirēnē*) is completeness, soundness, wholeness" (Elwell 2001, 896).

I have not heard of any church working specifically on the concept of shalom as the opposite to fear, but it is a common part of church ministries among the Tibetans. Prayer life is a strong part of these churches, but also the mutual support and feeling of strength from the fellowship. To stay close to God and strong in the fellowship are encouraged and can easily be seen as part of the daily life, exemplifying trust and faith. In all this we can see how relationships with each other are very important since all of this functions in the context of a community.

As we have said earlier, salvation needs to be an answer to all three cultural orientations: guilt, shame, and fear. The church must also answer the challenges of each one. As a starting point, the main cultural orientations should be the dominant focus. Since the Tibetan culture is both strongly fear- and shame-oriented, the church should also provide a strong answer to these worldview needs and make them a priority for the church community.

A church in a shame culture has to work on fellowship as well as sharing and giving honor. The first step toward this would be not to shame each other. Unfortunately, it is common when sin and guilt is the cultural orientation of a particular fellowship for regulations of sin to become the focus of that church. In a church we visited in a Thai context, the pastor forbid the engaged couple to get married with full wedding attire and festive decorations in the church because they had lived together for some time. To live together is common in the context, but shouldn't happen in the church and therefore the pastor took measures to show this was not accepted and shamed the couple. Instead of expressing forgiveness as a core value, shame was used to control church members making it very hard for the couple who wanted to rectify their behavior. There is a lesson to consider here when determining whether shame should be used to coerce people into following rules, or to build up the fellowship. A positive use of shame culture would be more effective and would follow the gospel model too, Jesus didn't shame the sinner but gave them mercy and forgiveness.

A church in a shame-oriented culture has a great working advantage if it will use the precious gift from Christ, which is the "fellowship of saints," the body of the church. The opposite of shame is honor, and as there is no shame nor honor without relationship it is in the very core of relationship we find honor. Honor should therefore be a core value of the church, not honor of the worldly type, but the honor that belongs to the children of

God. The people of God are described in many honorable terms in Scripture and this stems from being God's people. It is an honor coming from belonging to the one most honored. All glory and honor are given to Christ and we are His body and therefore honored in the same inseparable way as Christ. From this I want to stress that the concepts of the honor bestowed upon us through Christ, be taught well and often.

Community is very strong in shame-oriented cultures and it must be a strong value in the church as well. One of the main reasons for backsliding is the lack of community, or too much pressure from the surrounding non-Christian society. This is an important issue the church needs to pay attention to if it is to grow dynamically and function well. Size helps to make the community stronger and more dynamic but is not the most important factor. Recently, I visited a Tibetan fellowship which had the strength of a community that gave honor to its members, but was also dynamic and growing fast. It was not a standard church but it exemplified the values in an honor setting. This fellowship had grown from just a few, to eighty people in around five years. It was more of a discipleship training school with businesses to support its members in the midst of a hostile society. They described themselves as focused on training and running businesses as the basis for outreach. But in my eyes, they were functioning as a church, they were a fellowship of believers who belonged to one another. They also lived like a fellowship with services, times of teaching, and communion. They had a strong commitment to sharing the gospel with each person in the area and were not shy about their Christian identity.

This church had a strong commitment to the task and to the group. It had a purpose. In addition to Christ-focused discipleship training. This church's purpose was outreach within a geographical area. Each member contributed to the purpose and to the group; roles were important and it gave a strong sense of belonging. They also had an open attitude about sharing and caring, with clear roles, not excluding anyone but welcoming all. During my discussion with the senior leader it was easy for members to join in and contribute to the conversation. The leader did not take exclusive control as the only one talking about the situation or the strategies. (Private conversation, November 2015). It was an inclusive group, easy to join and feel a part of; both new and old were important to the group. Several members had suffered beatings from the surrounding Buddhist society, but they shared and cared for each, encouraging one another to be strong, and to take honor in suffering for Christ as His beloved children.

My simple analysis and conclusions from meeting this fellowship summed up in a few words are: each one contributed to the group and purpose, they belonged, they honored the members, and they were inclusive and caring. Most of all, the way this fellowship worked, brought them together in unity.

Honor can be given in many ways in a group and doesn't need to be avoided for fear that it appear to be too worldly. Honor should be given for a good purpose in the family of Christ. And I can see even in the western culture how important it is for the children to be honored in church by, for example, receiving a Bible publicly, or to be cheered upon for singing or playing or for a testimony to be well received. We could share more examples of giving honor, but the key is to give honor to the various contributions and to let each one contribute to the fellowship in different ways.

It can be too easy for a leader or a small group to be the main active part of a fellowship, and to make others feel less important or like they don't belong in full. This would, of course, be a loss of face, and it would be harmful to the fellowship.

A sin-guilt cultural orientation has been the basis of much discipleship training. It is also the motivation to encourage regulations, forgiveness, and disciplined holy living. In our near history in the West it has been the dominant teaching to build up mature believers. I can see how the concept of a 3D gospel can help to build more stability and regulate faith, as a good source of help when times are shaking and challenging. Instead of trying to start explaining sin, it would be more effective to start in the dominant culture and grow into the other cultures' foci. In this way the understanding of salvation will be stronger, deeper, and wider. In this way the church will grow into the full understanding of salvation and fellowship in heavenly likeness.

Working hard on the community and its values ought to be a priority in any of these cultures, but even more so for those in a shame-oriented culture. We can take examples and lessons from different groups and functions, but most of all we should be reminded that as believers we are a family. Families each have several special traits. First a healthy family is united, and strongly committed to helping and supporting each other. Members of a healthy family will make mistakes, but forgiveness is easy to find. Family members are also happy for the success and progress of others. There is much more to say about fellowship, but this short chapter only suggests a few first steps toward a more conscious way of presenting a wider understanding of salvation in a church in a fear-shame culture. A wider understanding and a holistic view of transgression, sin, atonement, and holiness should be pursued.

WHAT DOES IT MEAN TO THE CHURCH?

When we are establishing churches and shaping Christian leadership in Tibetan contexts, teaching and spiritual formation need to pay close attention to the full understanding of reconciliation. Allow the culture be a starting point for understanding but also work on a wider understanding to grasp the other aspects of reconciliation that may be lacking in your culture. It is the nature of salvation to have a personal relationship with God being reconciled as an individual but it is in the context of fellowship that we grow and live as His children. This means that we bring the understanding of cultural aspects of reconciliation to model and shape the fellowship too.

A fellowship shaped by the culture, giving different aspects of reconciliation is the soil for good growth in faith. But understanding comes from the deliberate work of teaching and living as a fellowship. For a fellowship in a fear-oriented culture it is important to be a church shaped and formed by the following:

- *Prayer.* Prayer for staying in the light of the Father and knowing that he is providing safety. But also prayer of manifestation and power, for the members of the fellowship to understand more of God's power, and practically understand that God is bigger than anyone who is against us.
- *Teaching.* Teaching the fellowship to also know God, not just experience God's might and power.
- *Caring and supporting each other.* The fellowship should function as a family, in caring for each other and also in protecting each other as a community.

Another aspect critical to ministry within a shame-orientation culture that the fellowship needs to pay attention to is how it encourages one another. To make fellowship members understand more of the width and depth of salvation they will find part of the answer in fellowship. Fellowship should help members feel valuable, gain a sense of honor, and maintaining good relationship between sisters and brothers.

- *Unity.* The fellowship should understand that unity is about how we belong together. Making the fellowship work and function as a real community is an essential part of the focus.
- *Contribution.* The fellowship should work to make each person feel important and that they have something to contribute to the community.
- *Relationship.* Relating to each other should be natural but intentional. It should aim to function as a family. Relationships should give honor in many

different ways such as celebrating anniversaries and other important moments.
- *How the fellowship fits* in to the wider society is a question left to each situation, but the question should not be neglected as it is an important part of who we are in the society as well.

For a church to be whole, the aspects of sin-guilt culture should not be ignored. This should be done through teaching, and clear directional leadership. One clear response in sin-guilt culture is discipleship training, helping new believers understand confession of sin and forgiveness. There should be an understanding of rules but always through the knowledge that the work of the law is completed.

A new reconciled being and a restored fellowship need to embody the practices of God's riches in the aspects of the different cultural orientations. One cultural orientation can be the starting point and emphasized in the early stage, but the goal is to bring each believer into this holistic understanding. Fellowships desiring to serve as places where answers can be found for the different orientations should emphasize:
- Power and security through fellowship and prayer.
- The importance and need of every individual.
- Honor and encouragement of steps toward progress.
- Care for one another.
- Teaching that builds a good foundation of faith.
- Striving for unity.

A fully flowering Tibetan church is one that is reconciled with God, thrives through prayer, is made up of members who feel safe and whole, and is a place of shalom. It is a fellowship that nurtures relationships, gives credit and honor to all church members, and allows all to contribute and bring important things to the table. When we start to see this, I believe backsliding will disappear, and a momentum will grow, resulting in many being saved by the power of God, by the relationship of the saints and in the forgiveness of transgression.

References

Bell, Sir Charles. 1946. *Portrait of the Dalai Lama*. London: Collins.

Bridges, Jerry. 2012. *True community*. Colorado Springs: NavPress.

Elwell, Walter A., ed. 2001. *Evangelical dictionary of theology*. Ada, MI: Baker Publishing Group.

Georges, Jayson. 2014. *The 3D gospel: Ministry in guilt, shame, and fear cultures*. Timē Press. Kindle version.

Grenz, Stanley J. 2005. "Biblical priesthood and women in ministry." In *Discovering biblical equality: Complementary without hierarchy*, edited by Gordon Fee, Rebecca Merrill Groothuis, and Ronald W. Pierce. Downers Grove, IL: InterVarsity Press.

McGrath, Alister E. 2007. *Theology: The basics*. Oxford: Blackwell.

McIntosh, Amy. 2015. *Story of Drolma—Daughter of Tibet*. Chiang Mai: Central Asia Publishing.

Merriam-Webster. 2015. "Sin," accessed December 5, 2015. http://www.merriam-webster.com/dictionary/sin.

Norbu, Jamyang. 2015. "The Lhasa ripper." Shadow Tibet, March 22, 2015. http://www.jamyangnorbu.com/blog/2015/03/22/the-lhasa-ripper/

Stott, John. 1984. *The cross of Christ*. Downers Grove, IL: InterVarsity Press.

Tsering, Marku. 2005. *Sharing Christ in the Tibetan Buddhist world*. Chiang Mai: Central Asia Fellowship.

Watters, David. 2011. *At the foot of the snow*. Seattle: Engaged Faith Press.

Webster, Douglas D. 2012. *Living in tension, 2 volume set: A theology of ministry*. Eugene OR: Wipf and Stock.

10

Seeking Social Reconciliation for India's Dalits Through Buddhism

Sunil Sardar

India's caste system is a three thousand-year-old system of divinely sanctioned slavery. Hinduism's earliest texts, the *Vedas*, describe the creation of man into a four-part hierarchy. At the top is the *Brahmin* caste, the priests. Below them is the *Kshatriya* caste, the warriors. Next is the *Vaishya* caste, the merchants, and last is the *Shudra* caste, who are the slaves. Translated from Sanskrit, the *Purush Suktra*, (a hymn from the Hindu scripture the *Rig Veda*), says,

> When they [the gods] divided the Man, into how many parts did they apportion him? What do they call his mouth, his two arms and thighs and feet? His mouth became the *Brahmin*; his arms were made into the Warrior [*Kshatriya*], his thighs the People [*Vaishya*], and from his feet the Servants [*Shudra*] were born. (Doniger O'Flaherty 2000, 31)

Existing outside this four-fold division is the rest of humanity, including non-Indians, whom the *Vedas* derogatorily call *Mlecchas* (impure barbarian), along with the remainder of Indians, deemed so low that they are not even in the system. These Indians are called *Dalits* (broken people), formerly called the "Untouchables."

DEHUMANIZED CONDITION OF DALITS

These Dalits have existed for thousands of years through the worst form of human slavery the world has ever seen. They are segregated outside of the village. They clean sewage with their bare hands. They dispose of dead bodies, human and animal, and they make leather and other "unclean" products. For all their service to India, they are denied education, denied entry to temples and public facilities such as drinking water wells, denied access to more lucrative jobs, and denied access to personal luxuries and forms of dignity. Declared to be sinners and polluted at birth, they are persecuted and raped by the caste Hindus as a just punishment for all the sins they had committed in their previous lives, sins for which their birth as a Dalit is evidence enough.

> Those born into the subordinated castes are supposedly being punished for the bad deeds they have done in their past lives. In effect, they are living out a prison sentence. Acts of insubordination could lead to an enhanced sentence, which would mean another cycle of rebirth as an Untouchable [Dalit] or as a Shudra. So it's best to behave. (Roy 2014, 25)

Shrewdly, the Brahmins who created this system also created a solution for the problem of the sin-birthed Dalits. That solution was the perpetual propitiation of the gods through sacrifices and offerings, all paid for by the work of the Dalits, yet carried out by the pure and holy of the caste system—the Brahmins themselves. This constant reminder of their inferiority and polluted state enslaves them to both fear and to the Brahmin. The Brahmin, to the Dalit, holds the keys to their salvation and thus no expense should be spared to coerce this "upper caste" into performing the rituals necessary to purify them. Doniger explains how Manu, the author of the *Shastras* (Hindu scriptural texts), describes the birth-based pollution, segregation, and discrimination to which the Dalits should be religiously subjected.

> They [Dalits] are economically exploited, victims of social discrimination, and permanently polluted ritually. The only way out, says Manu, is by "giving up the body instinctively for the sake of a Brahmin, or a cow, or in the defense of women and children." (2011, 313)

Kancha Ilaiah says Dalit parents "teach the children that 'they must shiver and shake before the upper caste master' . . . but a pretense that starts at an early age becomes part of a person's behavior during a lifetime. Fear of the upper castes is gradually internalized" (Ilaiah 2009, 10–11). They address everyone they meet with respect and humility. They take their shoes off when walking around the high-caste parts of town. Fearfully, they beg for their own wages earned from the landowner whose farm they worked, often to be simply beaten and turned away. They capitulate to Brahminical standards of living, which force them to live in poverty, to remove all possessions that could be seen to inspire jealously among the privileged castes, to refrain from succeeding in work or business, and to refrain from even attempting to work a job of dignity. They name their children degrading names to pacify the Brahmins who name their children glorious names. They make donations freely to the Brahmin, who then stop them from coming near while commanding them to leave their gift at the Brahmin's foot so he won't be polluted by their presence. Fear of the gods, but more specifically fear of the Brahmins, keeps the Dalits in poverty, humility, hopelessness, and shame (*India Untouched* 2007).

A PROPHETIC DALIT VOICE

Arising from this condition in the late nineteenth century, a young boy named Bhimrao Ambedkar went to school, where he was forced to sit outside the classrooms because he was Dalit. Against all odds, he graduated from his high school and became the first Dalit to enroll in Elphinstone College. From there, he would go to Bombay University, earning a degree in economics and political science, and then to Columbia University in New York, where he earned a PhD in Economics. He then continued on to Gray's Inn in London to pass the Bar, and finally to London School of Economics for his second PhD in Economics (Jaffrelot 2005, 3).

Ambedkar returned to India as a champion for the Dalits. He led several forms of protest against the injunctions of Hinduism against Dalits, such as leading several thousand Dalits to a public well to drink the water there, and leading thousands more to burn copies of the *Manusmriti*, the Hindu law code that describes how to treat the Dalits (Mani 2015, 351–2). He purposely planned this protest on December 25th, the birthday of the person he considered to be the greatest liberator in the world: Jesus Christ.

His fight for dignity and freedom for the Dalits would eventually bring him into conflict with Mahatma Gandhi. Gandhi was a staunch Hindu and supporter of the caste system.

> Gandhi was consistently emphatic that an individual's caste was ascribed at the moment of birth, and not to live by one's caste was "to disregard the law of heredity" because "[the caste system] is inherent in human nature, and Hinduism (had) simply reduced it to a science." . . . Gandhi's "politics of piety" was driven by the political expediency to include the Dalits in the Hindu fold to form a Hindu majority (Ibid., 341).

The actions and counter actions of Gandhi and Ambedkar would prove vital to understanding the role of Buddhism as an instrument of protest and, just as importantly, what they were protesting against. The first time Gandhi and Ambedkar came into conflict was at the Round Table Conference in London. In 1932, fifteen years before India's Independence, the British began working with the leaders of India's many fractured and divided groups to discuss what a free India would look like. They called a Round Table Conference to bring these leaders together in London to discuss among themselves what India's Constitution would contain. Ambedkar went as the representative of the Dalits. His primary demand was the same as the demand of many other groups, including the Muslims, Anglo-Indians, Sikhs, and Christians. They each demanded a separate electorate for their communities. This would mean that only Dalits would be able to vote for who represents the Dalits, only Muslims for Muslims, Sikhs for Sikhs, and so on.

The reason for Ambedkar's demand for the separate electorate was that the Dalits were minorities behind the caste Hindus, namely the Brahmins, Kshatriyas, Vaishyas, and Shudras. There was an affirmative action program, named "Reservations," that was in place, but that only guaranteed that the representative of predetermined districts would be a Dalit. The people who would choose which Dalit were the caste Hindus. Ambedkar correctly feared that the upper castes would simply elect stooges from the Dalit castes in each reserved district and when that Dalit started to disobey the upper castes, they would replace him. Ambedkar eloquently argued his point that even under Reservations, real representation would be denied to the Dalits. The British agreed with him and awarded a separate electorate for the Dalits.

Gandhi was fine with Reservations, but when he heard about the decision for the separate electorate, he was furious. In his mind, all Dalits were Hindus. Therefore, giving Dalits a separate electorate would divide a united Hindu people. He approved of

Muslims having a separate electorate, but Gandhi's belief system could not support Dalits that were not Hindu. He therefore took action, meeting with the British and with Ambedkar to repeal the award. Neither was willing to give in, so Gandhi responded by fasting until death. He did this while he was in a jail in the Indian city of Poona.

Ambedkar knew what would happen if Gandhi died on this fast. He believed that there would be a significant retaliation of the caste Hindus against the Dalits, because the Dalits had refused to listen to the Hindu leader, and he had died because of them. Fearing this massive loss of life, Ambedkar gave in to the demand and relinquished the separate electorate. In return, more seats in the Parliament were reserved for Dalits. This agreement came to be known as the "Poona Pact." The newspapers celebrated Gandhi's altruistic heroism in increasing the seats reserved for Dalits. The repeal of the separate electorate was censured. More information about the Poona Pact can be found in most biographies about Ambedkar. One of the most in-depth narratives is included in Dhananjay Keer's, *Dr. Babasaheb Ambedkar*, pages 136–92.

However, the return of the awarded separate electorate was not Gandhi's full intention. This process had made him aware of what the Dalits were doing. They were distancing themselves from Hinduism, and Gandhi needed the Dalits within that system. He knew he therefore had to prevent the Dalits from leaving Hinduism, so he embarked on a two-year mission to bring the Dalits back into the system. He called the Dalits *Harijan*, meaning children of *Hari*, who is the Hindu god who upholds the caste system. This is a term the Dalits rejected then and still do today.

Gandhi then went on to found the *Harijan Sevak Sangh*, or the society for the service to *Harijans*. He appointed Ambedkar to the board of the society, but Ambedkar quickly quit, citing the uselessness of the society. Ambedkar sought civil rights, civic education, political awareness, and similar benefits for the Dalits.

Gandhi wanted them to stop drinking alcohol, stop eating meat, and start worshipping the cow. Ambedkar wanted Dalits to lead the organization. Gandhi viewed untouchability as a sin of Hinduism and felt that since upper castes were guilty of committing the sin of untouchability, it was they who should take the lead in fighting against it (Mani 2015, 365–70). In Gandhi's ideology, Hinduism and the caste system could and should exist without untouchability. In Ambedkar's ideology, untouchability was inseparable from the caste system and Hinduism, a concomitant production of the system. The only way out was to eradicate the caste system and to completely reject Hinduism.

RELIGIOUS PROBLEM, RELIGIOUS SOLUTION

In many ways, Ambedkar's dispute with Gandhi was that which finally drove the Dalits away from Hinduism. Ambedkar categorized himself as a Hindu. In fact, four years after the Poona Pact and the Harijan Sevak Sangh, Ambedkar famously said, "I was born a Hindu, and have suffered the consequences of untouchability. I will not die a Hindu." His fight for the emancipation of Dalits took a drastic turn. Whereas before, he was focused on civil and political rights, now he was focused on getting the Dalits out of Hinduism. He had come to the awareness that the problem of untouchability was primarily a religious one, and required a religious solution, a solution that Hinduism was unable to provide.

Ambedkar searched twenty years for a new religion. It was during this time that he penned the Constitution of India. It is important to note that Ambedkar's goal for India was a modern, successful nation, and he did everything he could to build it. Many people focus solely on his political achievements, like drafting the Constitution, his economic philosophy, or his "upliftment" of Dalits. Ambedkar wasn't a leader of the Dalits, he was a Dalit who was also a leader, a Dalit national leader, who worked tirelessly to build a new nation. He is thus worthy of the title that Americans use to refer to similar people in their history, "founding father."

While Ambedkar was studying Christianity, he said to a missionary friend of his,

> When I read the Gospels, the Acts of the Apostles, and certain passages of St. Paul's Epistles, I feel that I and my people must all become Christians, for in them I find a perfect antidote to the poison Hinduism has injected into our souls, and a dynamic strong enough to lift us out of our present degraded position. But when I look at the Church, many of my own caste have become Christians and most of them do not commend Christianity to the rest of us. What sort of people are they? Selfish and self-centered. They do not care a snap of their fingers . . . so long as they and their families get ahead. (Adeney 2009, 197)

He ultimately picked Buddhism as his religion, to be the perfect antidote to the poison Hinduism has injected into his people. But he didn't accept the traditional form of Buddhism that existed throughout the world. To understand the reason for this requires an understanding of what happened in India 2,500 years previously.

Buddha was born in India and lived there his whole life. His formation of a new religion was a revolt against the caste system and the form of Hinduism that existed then. Superstitions, sacrifices, black magic, sacred languages, tantras, and mantras—these were all creations of Hinduism that had no basis in reason or logic. Buddha rejected them all (Mani 2015, 100–4). This new religion spread quickly and found many adherents among the Shudras and Dalits. After just two hundred years, India's king, Ashoka, converted to Buddhism and brought nearly all of India along with him (Thapar 2002, 180). Much like Christianity in Rome, Buddhism became the state religion and engulfed India.

However, Buddha's new religion wasn't strong enough to withstand the gradual corruptions inflicted on it by the upper caste Brahmins, and it soon began to accept and promote the very things Buddha had fought against. By the time Buddhism was ready for export, much of the superstitions, mantras, tantras, and the sacredness of a single language had crept back in and corrupted Buddhism. Once its power had been effectively removed, the Brahmins led a nation-wide purge of Buddhism from India (Mani 2015, 135–38). Until the British came to India, Buddhism was an unheard of religion in its home country.

> Centuries of brahmanic-feudal dominance had completely wiped out all traces of Buddhism in India, so much so that as late as the 1820s the Buddha's historicity and Indian-ness was being debated among scholars, and as great a Buddhist king as Ashoka was absolutely unknown till 1837 when James Prinsep, a British official in India, deciphered the script used on the Ashokan rock and pillar edicts. (Mani 2007, 5)

Therefore, the Buddhism that existed in the world when Ambedkar made his decision was a corrupted Buddhism, almost entirely indistinguishable from Hinduism, and a Buddhism that Ambedkar couldn't accept. He therefore recreated Buddhism for India, even writing its central text, *The Buddha and His Dhamma*. On the day Ambedkar converted, 600,000 of his fellow Dalits converted with him, making it the largest mass conversion in world history. Millions more have converted since then, and Buddhism (or at least a form of Neo-Buddhism) has made a startling comeback in India.

The fuel for this comeback has been the discrimination the Dalits have suffered under Hinduism. Though the caste system is taught only by Hinduism, every religion in India practices it. Therefore, religions that should become sanctuaries against caste discrimination, like Islam and Christianity, instead undermine themselves and prove themselves to be no safer than Hinduism. Buddhism, being accepted by the greatest Dalit leader in Indian history, is the only religion that has proven to be one that does not practice caste. Therefore, it is the major recipient of Dalit conversions in India.

Ambedkar's conversion gutted many of the central doctrines of Hinduism that kept the Dalits in fear. He created twenty-two vows to which he and his followers all pledged and which were inscribed on a pillar at the place of his conversion. These vows call on his followers to reject all Hindu gods, to reject Brahminical rituals, to reject any ceremony (including weddings and funerals) preformed by a Brahmin, to reject the inequality of mankind, and to forcefully reject Hinduism itself. The twenty-first vow specifically says, "I consider that I have taken a new birth" (Omvedt 2003, 261–62). Or, as I translate it from the original Marathi, "Today I am being born again."

This "being born again," out of the pollution-based Hindu caste system into a life free from rituals, Brahmins, and demanding gods, set the Dalits free to pursue the very things they had been denied under Hinduism. After Ambedkar's conversion, and much more so after the process of Liberalization in 1991, when India switched from socialism to capitalism, Dalit entrepreneurs no longer lived in the fear of making the Brahmin jealous with their success (Kapur et al. 2014, 1). India saw a dramatic increase in the presence of Dalits in schools, including the elite universities. Before, Dalits were required to stay illiterate. Now, they view education as their salvation. Dalits have started to speak with authority, demanding the same respect that they've shown others for millennia. Without Ambedkar's conversion and the self-respect Dalits obtained, we wouldn't see even the limited success that we currently see among the Dalits.

WAS BUDDHISM THE CORRECT CHOICE?

What was Ambedkar looking for in a religion? What did he expect a religion to do for him and his people? If we know the answers to these questions, then can we argue from the Bible that Christianity satisfies Ambedkar's expectations? Sixty years after Ambedkar's conversion, has history proven that Ambedkar made the right choice, choosing Buddhism?

On May 15, 1936, Ambedkar was scheduled to give a speech he entitled "Annihilation of Caste" at a program of Hindu social reformers, called the "Jat-Pat-Todak Mandal." As early as December of the preceding year, the Mandal had received a copy of the speech Ambedkar intended to give. From December of 1935 through May of 1936, Ambedkar and the Mandal exchanged several letters and postponed the date of the speech several times. Eventually the reason for the hesitations, exchanges, and postponements were clear: Ambedkar intended to denounce Hinduism as the religion that creates, justifies, and maintains the caste system, while also announcing that he would leave Hinduism. The Hindu reformers couldn't allow him to say that from their platform, so they cancelled the program. Ambedkar printed the speech on his own, but by that point the climax of his speech—his intended conversion—was well known throughout India. Sixteen days after the intended date of the speech, on May 31, 1936, Ambedkar gave a speech to a mass gathering of *Mahars*, Ambedkar's caste. This speech was entitled "What Path to Salvation?" During the speech, Ambedkar justified his announced conversion, called upon all *Mahars* to convert with him, explained what conversion would do for them, and revealed what he expected to find in his new religion.

> The religion which preaches what will happen to your soul after death may be useful for the rich . . . but what of those who, by remaining in a particular religion have been reduced to the state

of dust, who have been denied the basic necessities of life such as food and clothing, who have not been treated even as human beings, and have since completely lost the sense of being human? . . . Are they expected to look at the sky and merely pray? (Ambedkar 1936)

This quote came at the end of Ambedkar's speech, but it begins our discussion of the Christian preaching on forgiveness of sins. A typical salvation message from a Christian might include, "If you believe that Jesus died for your sins, then God will forgive you of your sins, and you will go to Heaven to live with him forever after you die." The fact that Ambedkar mentions "what will happen to your soul after death" makes it clear that that type of message was commonly given and widely known. Ambedkar's critique is that such a message is of value for the rich, but the poor, such as the oppressed Dalits, do not benefit with this message. Ambedkar is not arguing that the central dogmas of Reformed Christianity, such as justification by faith and forgiveness of sins, are irrelevant. But he *is* saying that their immediate benefit should be preached, such as it was in the Protestant Reformation, which tore down many of the sinful slaveries of the corrupted Roman Catholic Church.

"Convert yourselves to get human treatment. Convert to get organized. Convert in order to become strong. Convert to secure equality. Convert to attain liberty. Convert so that your domestic life should be happy . . . This path of conversion is the only right path of freedom, which ultimately leads to equality . . . Our aim is to gain freedom . . . The Untouchables [*Dalits*] are in need of social liberty" (Ambedkar 1936). These quotes from Ambedkar's speech make clear what he expected to find in his new religion: dignity, organization, strength, liberty, and freedom. These are the qualities he wanted for his people now, not in the afterlife. We then need to ask ourselves if Christianity offers these things, and if so, how then we can communicate them?

PREACHING A LIFE-GIVING GOSPEL

"God created man in his own image, in the image of God he created him; male and female he created them" (Gen 1:27). The Christian creation story is the polar opposite of the Hindu creation story, stated earlier in this paper, when man was created into four castes. The image of God in all human beings demands the inherent equality of all human beings. Although that image is tainted and marred by sin, it is still there. It's still the primary difference between man and animals. It is the reason all humans have dignity. However, sin has corrupted mankind, and thus the image of God is not recognized among God's image bearers. Does the New Testament give commands and reassurance that Jesus' followers are to live according to the truth of God's image in all mankind?

> If anyone has material possessions and sees a brother or sister in need but has no pity on them, how can the love of God be in that person? (1 John 3:17)
>
> Whoever claims to love God yet hates a brother or sister is a liar. (1 John 4:20)
>
> From now on we regard no one from a worldly point of view . . . if anyone is in Christ, the new creation has come: The old has gone, the new is here! (2 Cor 5:16–17)
>
> With it [the tongue] we bless our Lord and Father, and with it we curse people who are made in the likeness of God. From the same mouth come blessing and cursing. My brothers, these things ought not to be so. (Jas 3:9–10)

There are, of course, many others, but these should suffice to prove that Christianity not only teaches the dignity of all human beings through their creation in the image of God, but it also teaches that we are to respect that image and love the people in whom that image dwells. To not do so is a rejection and hatred not of the image bearer, but of the Creator of the image they bear.

The ideal Christian life, which, of course, has been the subject of much research and investigation by theologians and skeptics alike, in theory provides what Ambedkar wanted. Love—existing, active, and growing among Christians—unites Christians in dignity and liberty. Unlike Hinduism, which teaches segregation from those of impure birth, Christianity teaches the universal love and acceptance of people (providing that such people aren't Christians who are an extreme state of unrepentant sin, a very specific context). "You shall love your neighbor as yourself" (Mark 12:31). "God shows no partiality" (Rom 2:11). "Judge not, and you will not be judged; condemn not, and you will not be condemned; forgive, and you will be forgiven" (Luke 6:37).

> I wrote to you in my letter not to associate with sexually immoral people—not at all meaning the people of this world who are immoral . . . in that case you would have to leave this world. But now I am writing to you that you must not associate with anyone who claims to be a brother or sister but is sexually immoral . . . (1 Cor 5:9–11)

Such a life builds strength through community, through a love for each other, which is one of the primary benefits Ambedkar foresaw through conversion.

So what, then, should be the message Christians should preach, to present the life, death, and resurrection of Jesus Christ as a means through which the primary needs of the Dalits can be met? Our solution is this: We were all created equally in the image of God, but sin distorted that image and caused us to hate one another. God loved us so much that He sent his Son, Jesus, as a sacrifice to set us free from sin. With our faith in Jesus' resurrection, we're made into a new creation. Now, as children beloved by God, we are free to regard each other as a new creation in love; the old hatreds and prejudices have died, the new creation of love and reconciliation has arrived. And from now until forever, we will live in the eternal love of God and his children.

But the realities of the caste system and caste discrimination still exist even between Dalits. Ambedkar acknowledges this in his "What Path to Salvation?" speech.

> It cannot be denied that the castes included in the Untouchables the practice of untouchability [against each other]. But equally, it is false to say that they are in any way responsible for this crime. The Caste System and untouchability originated not from the Untouchables, but from the high-caste Hindus. And if this is true, the responsibility for this age-old tradition falls on the caste Hindus and not on the Untouchables. While practicing untouchability and casteism, the Untouchables merely follow the lesson taught by the caste Hindus. (Ambedkar 1936)

This is where the gospel, we believe, has the greatest power to glorify the cause and purpose of God.

> All this is from God, who reconciled us to himself through Christ and gave us the ministry of reconciliation: that God was reconciling the world to himself in Christ, not counting people's sins against them. And he has committed to us the message of reconciliation. We are therefore Christ's ambassadors, as though God were making his appeal through us. We implore you on Christ's behalf: Be reconciled to God. (2 Cor 5:18–20)

> There is neither Jew nor Gentile [we also say caste nor caste], neither slave nor free, nor is there male and female, for you are all one in Christ Jesus. (Gal 3:28)
>
> There is one body and one Spirit, just as you were called to one hope when you were called; one Lord, one faith, one baptism; one God and Father of all, who is over all and through all and in all. (Eph 4:4–6)

FRATERNAL FREEDOM AS GOAL

Ambedkar's goal of freedom meant freedom from a vile religion, but what he wanted most was freedom from the social tyranny that religion erected. There are many aspects of Hinduism that, while most westerners would view them as horrendous, they don't even merit mention in Ambedkar's grievances against the Hindu religion. He sought dignity for his people, social intercourse with fellow Indian citizens, mutual respect and trust, and a brotherhood that broke the bonds of caste. The word Ambedkar used frequently throughout his writings was "fraternity." We find what Ambedkar desired in one of the most beautiful discourses the Bible gives on reconciliation:

> For he himself [Christ] is our peace, who has made the two groups [Castes] into one and has destroyed the barrier, the dividing wall of hostility, by setting aside in his flesh the law with its commands and regulations [*Manusmriti*]. His purpose was to create in himself one, new humanity out of the two [the fraternity Ambedkar wanted], thus making peace, and in one body to reconcile both of them to God through the cross, by which he put to death their hostility. He came

and preached peace to you who were far away and peace to those who were near. For through him we both have access to the Father by one Spirit. (Eph 2:14–18)

God's purpose of reconciliation has universal application. As the Bible says, "God was reconciling the world to himself in Christ" (2 Cor 5:19), and it is the entire world to which this message should go. Reconciliation is only fully possible "in Christ" and it's the most powerful revolutionary ministry in the world. Reconciliation is so uniquely Christian that, in India, Muslims and Hindus don't even have a word for it. But from the Dalits of India to the Rohingya of Myanmar, the Kurds to the Jews of the Middle East, and the Shia of Saudi Arabia to the Sunni of Iran, the promise of reconciliation to each other and to God through the death and resurrection of Christ provides immediate and long lasting life, liberty, and dignity. Forgiveness is the beginning of the reconciliation process and it's the only thing that has the power to break the downward spiral of oppression that leads to bitterness that leads to revolution over and over again. Christ's application of forgiveness leading to reconciliation is the required beginning of any process of true liberation, be that for an oppressed people group, as India's Dalits are, or for an individual enslaved to sin.

References

Adeney, Miriam. 2009. *Kingdom without borders*. Downers Grove, IL: InterVarsity Press.

Ambedkar, Bhimrao. 1936. "What path to salvation?" translated by Vasant W. Moon. Columbia University. Accessed May 9, 2016. www.columbia.edu/itc/mealac/pritchett/00ambedkar/txt_ambedkar_salvation.html.

Doniger, Wendy. 2000. *The Rig Veda*. New Delhi: Penguin Books India.

———. 2011. *The Hindus: An alternative history*. New Delhi: Penguin Group.

Ilaiah, Kancha. 2009. *Why I am not a Hindu: A Sudra critique of Hindutva philosophy, culture and political economy*. Calcutta: SAMYA

India untouched: Stories of a people apart. 2007. DVD. Directed by Stalin Kurup. India: DRISHTI Media, Arts, & Human Rights.

Jaffrelot, Christophe. 2005. *Dr. Ambedkar and untouchability*. New Delhi: Permanent Black.

Kapur, Devesh, D. Shyam Babu, and Chandra Bhan Prasad. 2014. *Defying the odds: The rise of Dalit entrepreneurs*. Gurgaon, Haryana: Random House.

Keer, Dhananjay. 2009. *Dr. Babasaheb Ambedkar*. Mumbai: Popular Prakashan.

Mani, Braj Ranjan. 2015. *Debrahmanising history*. New Delhi: Manohar.

———. 2007. *Resurgent Buddhism*. New Delhi: Critical Quest.

Omvedt, Gail. 2003. *Buddhism in India: Challenging Brahmanism and caste*. Thousand Oaks, CA: Sage Publications.

Roy, Arundhati. 2014. *Annihilation of caste: The doctor and the saint*. New Delhi: Navayana.

Thapar, Romila. 2002. *Early India*. New Delhi: Penguin Group.

II
Reconciling to Self, Others, and God?
The Gospel Responding to Fear, Guilt, and Shame in Thailand

Daniëlle Koning

One question preoccupied me from day one as a missionary in Thailand. What does the gospel bring to people with a Buddhist background? What does it add to their lives? Does it improve people's well-being? Can it be depicted as bringing more "abundant life" to them, and if so, in what ways? What does "salvation by Christ" look like in Thailand? Don't get me wrong. I knew what the gospel meant for me. I knew what it meant for my Christian friends, most of whom came from Europe, America, and Africa. But I was endlessly fascinated and concerned about the question of what the gospel would and could mean and "deliver" in Buddhist Thailand. This is why the topic of this conference was very exciting to me. Analyzing how the gospel heals and helps people in the areas of fear, guilt, and shame gives a tangible focus to these questions that I have been wrestling with. In this paper, I will investigate the ways in which Christianity addresses (or fails to address) fear, guilt, and shame in the lives of Thai people.

So let's start with a basic question. What is the gospel? There are infinite ways to answer this question. Depending on their circumstances, needs, and worldviews, gospel believers may variably depict the gospel in terms of power, healing, freedom, grace, forgiveness, community, moral development, eternal life, etc. In this paper, I adopt the framework that the gospel is a source of reconciliation for brokenness. Within this framework I distinguish three levels:

1. Reconciliation within oneself: to move from a) a negative self-image and suffering to b) a positive self-image and holistic well-being;
2. Reconciliation between oneself and others: to move from a) selfishness and broken relationships to b) other-centeredness and healthy, loving relationships;
3. Reconciliation between oneself and God: to move from a) an untruthful view of God/the spiritual world and self-oriented ways of relating to this to b) a truthful view of God/the spiritual world and devotional ways of relating to this.

The ways in which the gospel establishes reconciliation on any of these levels depends on how it is mediated through human individuals and society. Different types of reconciliation are harder or easier to accomplish for different types of cultures, personalities, and value systems. In this paper, I will explore the ways in which reconciliation via the gospel happens or fails to happen in the context of Thailand. I will embark on this exploration by looking at the reconciliatory impact of the gospel in relation to three different cultural orientations all-present in this complex country:

1. Fear-orientation: powers, spirits, or other forces influence and perhaps even dictate success in life and must be appeased continually;
2. Guilt-orientation: correct action and productivity are highly valued and self-esteem is based on one's innocence;
3. Shame-orientation: honoring others holds high priority, and great care is taken to avoid one's own and other people's loss of face.

This paper is organized as follows. First, I will give an overview of how fear-, guilt-, and shame-orientations play out in Thai society. Subsequently, I will analyze how the gospel responds to these orientations in Thailand. Further, I will zoom in on how the gospel's response to these orientations contributes or fails to contribute to reconciliation on the levels of self, other, and God. I will conclude by offering a perspective on the overall reconciliatory impact of the gospel in Thailand, arguing that Christianity in this country seems to have a stronger impact on the relationship within oneself and between oneself and others, than on the relationship between self and God. The data and analysis are based on my fieldwork among both Christians and Buddhists in the city of Khon Kaen, Thailand, as well as literature study.

FEAR-ORIENTATION IN THAILAND: MANIPULATING SPIRITUAL POWERS

Fear-orientation is prominent in Thai culture. The bulk of Thai religious practices are fear-oriented in the sense that they center on the pursuit of power and blessing via the manipulation of spiritual powers. The underlying logic of these practices is animistic: the universe is formulaic. People can access and manipulate the world around them to their benefit if they know how to tap into (secret) strings of formula. Spiritual beings or the "singsaksit" (anything holding sacred power) relate to humans in a system of manipulation or reciprocity mediated through correct form: you give the spirits what they like (e.g. cigars, elephant statues, etc.) and they will (have to!) give you want you want (health, money, etc.). It can also be reversed: you promise to give the spirits something that they like if they fulfill your request ("bon")—once they have fulfilled it, you give them what you promised ("kee bon"). Examples of this animistic-formulaic logic of blessing are countless: wearing purple on Saturdays, beating a sacred drum, walking through a dragon sculpture, offering red Fanta to a spirit shrine, having a monk draw Khmer symbols in your new car, etc.

The good fortune or blessing that Thai people strive for involves all areas of life. McDaniel suggests that "protection" and "security" are key topics (2014). Other recurring themes that Thai people seek spiritual help with, as I have witnessed them in various contexts (TV spiritual hotlines, shrines, ceremonies, etc.), are health, wealth, work, money (winning the lottery!), love, family, safety, fertility, beauty, old age and more generally happiness, prosperity, and luck. The materialistic nature of many of these themes must be understood in the context of the hyper capitalistic nature of the Thai economy, which translates into commodified, highly utilitarian, prosperity-oriented forms of religion.

GUILT-ORIENTATION IN THAILAND: MAKING A MORAL EFFORT FOR GOOD KARMA

The best way to understand guilt-orientation in Thailand is to look at the influential concept of "karma." Though Thai and other Asian cultures have been commonly depicted in terms of shame instead of guilt, I would argue that there is a guilt-orientation in Thailand as well. The central concept of karma, indeed, is more akin to notions of guilt than notions of shame. Karma is not in the first place about presentation (the looks of things) or relationship (the way one is embedded in networks), both of which are connected to shame-orientations. Rather, karma is about the moral status of the individual: it is centered on ethics (not presentation) and the isolated person (not social ties). With all the diversity in Buddhist styles in Thailand, the idea of karma is one of the most persistent ones—people who reject notions of spirit beings and ritualistic manipulation still maintain the basic idea that people's lives are both products and producers of karma.

In the logic of karma, the universe is made up of lines of cause and effect. An individual's action is the cause of the things he or she experiences in this life and the next. This is the realm of the Thai mantra "to do good is to receive good, to do bad is to receive bad." This logic adds a moral dimension to the pursuit of good fortune—it basically says that it is not enough to wear an expensive amulet or to be sprinkled with holy water. Here, the amount of good fortune in this life and the next is dependent on the moral effort one makes in life—taking care of one's parents, feeding street dogs, being calm, staying away from alcohol, sweeping the temple grounds, etc. Individuals who make such moral effort are highly valued and depicted as "good people" ("khon dii").

SHAME-ORIENTATION IN THAILAND: INVESTING IN PRESENTATION

Shame-orientation is a powerful dimension of Thai culture. It is expressed in high investments in the good presentation of the self (avoiding loss of face). Thai society runs on "presentation"—polite, non-offensive, pretty, non-intimate exchanges (see Mulders 2000). Mulders proposes that "presentation" equals "substance" in Thailand—externals are what social relationships are made up of, which explains the strong emphasis on physical appearance. Komin refers to the importance of presentation as the "smooth interpersonal relationship orientation," explaining: "This orientation is characterized by the preference for a non-assertive, polite and humble type of personality . . . as well as the preference of a relaxed, and pleasant interaction which accounts for the 'smiling' and 'friendly' aspects of the Thai people" (1991, 143).

The focus on presentation or shame-avoidance is related to the discouragement of expressing one's inner world, even among close friends. Komin, for example, connects the Thai value of fun to the importance of "easy-going, relaxed, and superficial interaction, with limited revelation of the individual psychological depth" (Ibid., 193). Deep negative feelings are hard to talk about—a Thai-American lady felt deeply guilty after her brother died, but said: "I cannot talk about it to my family in Khon Kaen, in our culture we keep things inside." Emotional expression is discouraged. Being calm, letting go, and not worrying too much are virtues. Thai people value avoiding arguments and keeping disagreements inside. This type of emotional repression has psychological and social advantages, but in Mulders' view, it is not without cost. Mulders observes serious mental health problems in Thailand and analyzes that all the stifling of emotion leads to uncontrolled outbursts in other, unhealthy ways, pointing to the Thai high murder rate and alcohol abuse as examples. Emotional repression, in his view, is connected to low self-discovery, low self-respect, and low self-esteem, producing vulnerable, easily hurt egos.

The focus on presentation or shame-avoidance is further related to honoring hierarchy. Social status is profoundly important in Thai society. Important status markers are wealth, profession (doctors/lawyers/teachers), religious status (monks), relationship to the royal family, ethnicity/nationality (shades of skin color), and age. It could be said that this social hierarchy is present in a quiet way—big people don't need to do much to establish their status, and Thai people are very sensitive to get the picture and behave accordingly. Cohen calls Thai competitiveness "covert" and "masked by a pervasive concern with 'appropriate' and decorous deportment and a constant preoccupation with the preservation of 'face'" (1991). Thai hierarchy, then, might be described as "passive-aggressive," it is soft-spoken, but very tangibly present, and few would dare to disregard it. Though on a macro-level this deeply engrained system of social hierarchy seems to go largely uncontested (people prefer trying to climb the ladder over trying to unsettle the system), on a micro-level individual Thai people do experience frustration about it and sometimes complain about it being unfair.

THE GOSPEL ADDRESSING FEAR: MIRACLES AND BLESSINGS

Thai Christianity addresses the fear-orientation in Thai society by adopting the wider societal emphasis on seeking prosperity and Christianizing this pursuit. Cohen provides an insightful window into the historical development of this emphasis. He analyzes how evangelistic strategies centered on "power encounters," rather than on theological/ philosophical confrontations between religious systems, became predominant in Thailand (1991). In his view, nineteenth century missionaries were quite ignorant of the huge ideological gap between Theravada Buddhism and Protestant Christianity. They had many uninformed prejudices about Buddhism and relegated the whole country as a place of darkness ruled by Satan.

Over time however, missionaries began to gain more understanding of Thai religious expressions. They began to sympathize with much of Buddhist teaching, but at the same time also realized "the complete disjunction" between Christianity and Buddhism. In response, they resorted to a strategy of avoidance. They focused on bringing the good news without criticizing Buddhism. They also considered adherents of a more philosophical Buddhism "practically unconvertible." Instead, they decided to focus on those they could reach—the animist Buddhists, especially the tribal and northern people. Here the focus was not on showing the "soteriological superiority" of Christianity but simply on showing "the greater efficaciousness of Christianity to deal with the powers which threaten the daily existence of the farmer and the hill tribesman." In this way, the main theological strategy in Thailand became what Cohen calls the "contest of power" (spiritual encounter), rather than the "battle of the axes" (ideological confrontation).

Contemporary Thai Christianity, indeed, reveals the central role of spiritual power and blessing in many ways. In Thai Buddhist-Christian conversion stories, for example, power encounters play a dominant role. In his thesis on Protestant church growth in Thailand, Visser found that "miracles were the most important experience for 21% of all people who became Christians" (Visser 2008, 137). In a series of YouTube videos portraying the conversion stories of the members of a charismatic church in

Khon Kaen, the turn to Christianity was primarily depicted in terms of miraculous experiences—converts had been saved from diseases, floods, addictions, accidents, etc. Of course, like Cohen said, being saved from the power of spirits is a key motif in many conversion stories too—especially in rural areas.

Taylor substantiates the centrality of spiritual power and blessing by analyzing the predominant sermon themes in Thai churches, which he identifies as: 1) power encounter—the power of God to help you with your problems is what "95% of the Thai are interested in," and 2) "relief from, or understanding of, suffering (since many Thai Christians find their understanding of God challenged by the fact that He allows them to suffer)" (Taylor 2003, 102). Clearly, the core salvation theme here is being delivered from troubles, not from sin. A survey of Thai Christians showed that "While most missionaries rated 'forgiveness of sins' as the major reason for the importance of religion, Thai Christians rated it as seventh in importance out of a possible ten options. Power, not the atonement, is at the heart of the Gospel for many Thai Christians" (Dahlfred 2011, 14).

The emphasis on miracles and blessings helps us understand the relative success of charismatic types of Christianity in Thailand. Churches know this is what people want and intentionally promote Christianity as the road to blessings. For example, a local off-shoot of one of Thailand's most successful churches, "Hope for Bangkok," renamed itself Chiwit Suksan (happy life) and promotes the identity of its people as *khon heng phra-phon* (people of blessing). Churches are not afraid to claim that they have answers to people's problems. A new church in one of the established Khon Kaen neighborhoods promoted itself by walking around the area and asking people "Do you need healing from diseases? Come to our church!" The priest in the Khon Kaen Roman Catholic parish emphasized during a mass that their patron saint was especially skillful in solving fertility issues. Lay people naturally share the gospel with their friends and family members by emphasizing how God has blessed them in tangible ways.

In sum, the fear-orientation of pursuing power and blessing via spiritual forces is central in Thai Christianity. It emerged in the interaction between foreign missionaries and Thai society and recurs in Thai-led churches as a conversion motif, sermon theme, and evangelistic strategy.

THE GOSPEL ADDRESSING GUILT: PROMOTING MORAL LIVING

Christianity addresses the guilt-orientation in Thai society by sharing in and even adding to its strong emphasis on ethics. In fact, there seems to be a demand for new forces of morality in a society that is challenged by corruption, which gives Christianity a new potential of appeal. It is indeed common for Thai converts to frame Christianity as a morally elevated alternative.

Converts in our church in Khon Kaen say things like: "All religions teach people to be good people, but Christians are really serious about sin"; "Buddhists make merit at the temple, but Christians actually wash their hearts"; "Buddhism these days is not what it used to be—there is drinking and smoking—but Christians don't do that." It seems that in this sense Protestant Christianity in Thailand has a similar voice and type of appeal as Buddhist reform movements that promote a morally disciplined, de-materialized form of spirituality in the context of prosperity-oriented religiosities. Christianity provides moral resources that some feel are in limited supply in a rapidly changing country.

THE GOSPEL ADDRESSING SHAME: EXPRESSION AND EQUALITY

Christianity addresses the shame-orientation in Thai society by subtly counteracting it in two ways. First, Thai Christianity seems to encourage emotional expression. In some churches, this takes flamboyant public forms in dance, cheerful song, and speaking in tongues. In other churches, it takes more introverted forms in the emphasis on introspection ("search my heart oh God"), small group intimacy and confession, and prayer and prayer requests as a means of publically expressing one's heart.

Second, though Thai Christianity continues to be hierarchical (e.g. by putting pastors and church leaders on a pedestal), it has a subversive element in that it promotes an egalitarian philosophy of brother- and sisterhood in the context of common dependence on Father God. A CD made by Isaan Christian musicians seems to point to this idea. It includes a song entitled "Jesus is my parinyaa jay," which could be translated as "Jesus is my diploma." Some of the lyrics on this CD refer to Christ's acceptance of all, whether high or low in society, presenting Christianity as the great equalizer. One church communicated Christian egalitarianism to its members by combining two types of dance and song in a Christmas service, expressing the coming together of "high" and "low" social classes.

EASING FEAR: THE HAPPY SELF

Thai people who are drawn to Christianity often have an experience that demonstrates to them that this religion provides answers to real life problems in a more powerful way than other spiritual "methods" or forces. In this sense, the gospel has an important reconciliatory impact as it decreases fear and suffering and enhances the holistic well-being of individuals.

A good example of this is grandma Pew in our church. Grandma Pew experienced a great deal of suffering in her life. She became a widow four times—losing her husbands for a variety of tragic reasons. She lost her only child at a young age. She now lives in very poor circumstances. She has no husband or children to take care of her, and receives only a meager pension from the state (seven hundred Thai baht, roughly twenty dollars, a month). Often she does not have enough money to buy food and relies on free food services at a public institution, which closes down during holidays. She is embarrassed as she struggles to participate at funerals in her neighborhood, as it is customary to support the family of deceased acquaintances with a financial gift to cover the high funeral costs. She lives with her sister in an almost empty home where many basic attributes have been sold to be able to buy even more basic essentials like food. She has a difficult relationship with her sister and often does not feel comfortable to be at home because of that.

On top of all that, she struggles with various diseases and needs to visit the doctor regularly, though she does not have sufficient income to pay for a taxi to the hospital. In short, grandma Pew's life is full of concern and worry. The anxieties in her life, however, were addressed in a powerful way when she started joining our church community. Our local pastor and his wife, who live in the same neighborhood, built a strong relationship with grandma Pew. They provided meals for her. They took her to the hospital. They brought her to church, where eventually she was baptized. In the church community, her needs are met in a variety of ways. Church members support her financially. They bring her food and help her take her medications. The pastor takes her everywhere he goes, so she has time away from her lonely home and the ability to see interesting places. Grandma Pew has gained a large number of "sons" and "daughters" in the church community, people who like to chat and pray with her—and who she loves to joke around with. Grandma Pew has found new happiness in her life—the gospel has brought her a release of stresses and improved well-being in holistic ways.

BECOMING AWARE OF AND OVERCOMING GUILT: THE PURE SELF

For many Thai Christians, the ethical emphasis of the gospel provides an enhanced positive self-image. There is frequent use of terms like "boorisut" (pure, clean, innocent) to refer to oneself as a Christian in comparison to oneself prior to being a Christian. People take great joy in knowing that they have moved what they view as a transition from being "bad people" to being "good people"—people who don't drink anymore, are kind to others, and have stopped cheating.

Kung is a good illustration of how the gospel inspires a view of the self as morally developed. Kung is a lady in her late forties that accompanied her European husband to our church. Within a short period of time, she began to say that she was very impressed by the community dynamics in the church. She loved the experience of people smiling at her, treating each other as equals, and helping each other out in practical ways. As she continued to be exposed to biblical teachings and the lives of churchgoers, she developed a profound awareness of her own sinfulness and a deep desire to change her life. She wanted to become "pure," and follow the moral instructions of the Bible. She started doing things that she had never done before. Selling clothes at a local market where relationships were highly competitive, she started helping other sales women decorate their booths, much to their surprise. Kung shared her clothes with people who had limited income. In one case her landlord had invited Brahman priests to bless his apartment building. Such events usually involve large amounts of food preparation and dish washing. Kung decided to help out with the dishes. When a friend of the landlord found out that Kung is married to a foreigner (which raises her status) and yet chose to do the lowly work of washing dishes, she was impressed. "How come you are such a good person?" the friend asked. Kung, full of conviction, answered straightforwardly: "Oh, that is because I am a Christian. That's how we do things at my church. Giving makes you happy." Kung's way of living has changed in many ways. And with that, her idea of herself has changed. In her words: "It is strange, but it seems that my heart was so narrow-minded in the past. I never helped other passengers who needed a seat on the bus. But now, I'm changing. I think I am so much purer now."

REPLACING SHAME WITH HONOR: THE VALUED SELF

The gospel has a reconciliatory impact in relation to the shame-orientation on the level of the relationship with oneself, in the sense that its encouragement of self-expression as well as its egalitarian philosophy promote a positive self-image, in particular for lower status individuals. People who are at the bottom of the social hierarchy in terms of ethnicity, profession, physical appearance or wealth receive a new source of valuing the self by learning that they are accepted into a mixed-status community and that they share the same loving Father with all other people.

In our church community, for example, there are several young people that in some ways are on the low end of the social spectrum. In church, however, they have the experience of people being interested in them and accepting them as they are. One of the teenagers lives with her alcoholic grandmother in a village outside of Khon Kaen. Her parents work and live in Bangkok and give her only limited attention. She does not have a lot of natural mentors in her life. In church however, she is invested in. She has often received the feedback that she has the potential to become a leader. She receives free music education and is asked to help with the music for worship services. The church environment gives young people like her an experience of being valued individuals.

RELATIONALIZING GUILT ORIENTATIONS: LEARNING TO SERVE AND OFFERING AN ALTERNATIVE COMMUNITY

The focus on being a good person in Thai Christianity has reconciliatory consequences for the relationship between oneself and others. People report the ability to forgive other people more readily than in the past, being more attentive of needy people in their surroundings, and being less easily angered at others.

In our church, there is an intentional effort to stimulate service activities. For example, the church will go out to serve a meal at a home for the handicapped, or offer a program and gifts at an orphanage. At the same time, the value of serving is picked up by non-Christians who interact with our community. During the week we have a music school that is completely run by Christian teachers. Parents who come to the school have said things like: "Everybody is so nice to each other here. This school is like a dream land." Some point out that the school and the teachers offer them a view of another kind of society, one in which being positive and kind are key values. They experience the lived gospel as a refreshing alternative to the individualistic and materialistic values that wider society promotes. In this way, the gospel has the double effect of training believers to be more other-centered through service, as well as offering non-Christians a view of an alternative lifestyle in which community is prioritized.

SANCTIFYING SHAME-ORIENTATIONS: EMERGENCE OF MIXED-STATUS RELATIONSHIPS

The deeply hierarchical nature of Thai society in some ways is reproduced in Christianity, but there is also evidence of an impact of the gospel's anti-hierarchical values.

In our church in Khon Kaen, the way people are received kindly irrespective of social status has impressed newcomers.

Highly educated people play with children from lower class neighborhoods and serve food to our toothless grandmothers who only had a few years of elementary school education. Prior to celebrating the Lord's Supper, it is our custom to engage in feet washing. This in itself is a revolutionary practice in a society that considers feet to be very lowly—Thai people tend to apologize for even pointing to their feet. It becomes even more countercultural however in that people of high and low classes in society will wash one another's feet. The shame-orientation is here sanctified in the sense that honoring people is practiced in a way that cuts across social class.

ADDRESSING FEAR WITH PROSPERITY: PRIORITIZING THE SELF

In the above, we have seen two ways in which the gospel brings about reconciliation between the self and others. However, the blessing-oriented focus in Thai Christianity that is nestled in the wider Thai understanding of religion as a prosperity-producing force brings a countercurrent to the impact of the gospel on this level. This is because the prosperity focus often gets centered on self. As one lady was discipled in our church, for example, it was an eye-opener for her that she could and should engage prayer to plead for the well-being of others aside from her own family's well-being. So from this perspective, there is a countercurrent in Christianity's contribution to bring about another-centered focus or more loving relationships.

FEAR-INSPIRED THEOLOGY: THE ANIMISTIC GOD

In the relationship between oneself and God, the gospel as it addresses the Thai fear-orientation provides reconciliation in one particular way: the self moves away from other gods to the biblical God as the source of help. However, I would say that reconciliation between self and God here is still limited. This is for two reasons.

First, there is often a lingering untruthful view of God. God seems to be approached as an animistic spirit, who can be manipulated on the basis of correct form rather than approached as a Sovereign Person who decides to bless when, who, and how. I found that both young and established Christians had preoccupations with correct form as a way to guarantee blessings and avoid curses. Some showed a strong concern about using the exact right words (which is very important in Thai folk Buddhism, e.g. *kaathaa* [spells]). They strained themselves to apply the royal vocabulary that is common in Thai Christian prayers but uncommon in daily life. They strictly corrected each other to move from "Buddhist" to "Christian" terminology—e.g. to not say bun (merit) but *phra-phon* (blessing), or to not say *suat mon* (the term Buddhists use for chanting/praying) but *athithaan* (the mainstream word Thai Christians use for prayer). One convert said *khoop khun phracaw* (thank God) with such frequency as she related her experiences that it seemed to be a magic formula to her. In addition to language, I saw a tendency to approach Christian rituals with a strong focus on form. New believers seemed to not primarily be interested in the meaning of rituals, but were very concerned about knowing what the right actions were that they were supposed to do. Sometimes there was a rigid holding onto certain procedures that in themselves are not salvific—such as the Thai pastor that insisted on an exact sequence of detailed actions during the Lord's Supper.

Second, the relationship with God often remains on the level of self-oriented ambition rather than devotional union. I observed that for many of the Thai Christians I met, the focus of their spiritual experience was not so much on developing a growing love and understanding of God as it was on preparing the conditions to receive blessings from God. In fact, when the blessings stop, there is a tendency to leave. We already saw that many Thai people become interested in Christianity because of an experience of the efficacy of praying to the biblical God. However, such power encounters do not necessarily lead to a permanent, exclusive bond with God. This reality must be understood in the wider context of the cultural feature of "reciprocity" in Thai society.

Reciprocity means that there is a system of give and take—often set in patron-client type relationships, both in the social and spiritual realms. In this system, to receive something implies the obligation to give something in return. Thai Christians apply this same idea, i.e. that they need to "repay God" for a blessing. One of our church grandmothers, for example, brought a one hundred baht bill to the pastor when she found her lost wallet in response to a prayer. Indeed, one study showed that Thai Christians scored very high as compared to British Christians on the felt need to repay God. However, according to the reciprocity principle, one is released from the obligation to repay after one has fulfilled it, especially when new gifts don't seem to come in anymore. As one long-standing missionary put it: "You thank God and then move on." So people can leave a patron (whether a human or a spiritual being) when they feel they have repaid him or her, or when they feel that he or she doesn't take good care of them anymore. Loyalty to gods and spirits depends on their usefulness, not on the intrinsic worth of the relationship or an absolute sense of devotion. This is one of the reasons why there is a high drop-out rate among Thai Christians (according to some up to 80 percent).

In sum, it seems that the reconciliation between the self and God in relation to the Thai fear-orientation is limited since pre-conceived cultural notions reproduce a) an unbiblical image of God, casting Him in the role of an animistic spirit or conditional patron, and b) self-oriented rather than devotional forms of relating to the supernatural world.

LOW-SHAME THEOLOGY: THE LEGALIZED GOD

An ideal reconciliation between the self and God from a shame perspective would conceptualize the entire God-human relationship in terms of honor and shame. Some missiologists have sought to develop honor-shame oriented theologies, e.g. Jackson Wu's *Saving God's Face: A Chinese Contextualization of Salvation through Honor and Shame* and Christopher Flanders' *About Face: Reorienting Thai Face for Soteriology and Mission*. In this line of thinking:

1. God's honor is very important—the gospel is not just about human salvation. Jesus is depicted as saving God's face through his shame. Sin is depicted as a violation against God's honor. Sin makes God lose face. It dishonors God; it puts shame on his name.
2. Human honor is depicted not in terms of personal effort but in terms of what God has done for humanity and how humanity responds to that. God honors us through creation and by being made in the divine image. God honors us (gives us "face") by accepting us freely. Sin is loss of a state of honor, a total loss of face before God. Ultimate sin is ingratitude toward the God that honors us. Faith is recognizing the worth of God. Face calculus (considering what to do to save face), well known from interpersonal relationships, is redirected primarily to God.

This gospel-derived honor-shame conceptualization of the God-human relationship has high restorative potential as it offers a truthful picture of God (the honorable One) and humanity (being dependent on God for honor) and promotes devotional attitudes (gratitude). In my experience however, I have rarely seen lay believers actually approach the gospel in terms of such restorative honor-shame lenses. Instead, the more legal language of God "forgiving" your "sins" or "cleansing" you from "guilt" is commonly used. This, however, does not mean that guilt is a central concern in the relationship with God, as we will see in the next section.

INDIVIDUALISTIC GUILT: THE MORALIZED GOD

Reconciliation in relation to the Thai guilt-orientation in terms of one's relationship with God would ideally mean an understanding of God as the One who forgives, the One who takes guilt away, and the One who empowers people to act morally. In other words, rather than approaching ethics from a strongly individualistic point of view, as is the case in the logic of karma, ethics would become primarily relational: God is the One who makes people innocent, God is the One who makes people good. I found, however, that this type of reconciliation between oneself and God is largely absent. It seems that ethics continue to be understood from a highly individualized perspective in which one's own intentions and efforts, rather than God's grace and forgiveness, determine one's moral status. I will illustrate this by looking at interpretations I observed among Thai Bible students in regard to two key biblical events: the Fall and the death and resurrection of Jesus Christ.

The story of the Fall reveals that sin is not an abstract, individualized category of simply doing something wrong. Rather, sin is a relational category: sin is breaking the relationship with God, sin is violating the law of God. Genesis 3 points to the origin of sin and depicts it in these relational terms. My Thai Bible students, however, read this text from a different, e.g. karmic perspective. After repeated reading and discussion, the most obvious conclusion for them was that prior to Genesis 3, evil already existed in the world. The Fall did not change anything substantial about the nature of reality—it was just another instance of human beings doing the wrong thing. Evil in their view therefore does not have its cause in the breaking of a relationship (Adam and Eve not trusting God), but in a trans-historical reality (evil/sin as an intrinsic part of life). In this way, evil remains an individualized category (sin as "bad deeds," or de-merit) rather than becoming an interpersonal category (sin as man's disobedience to God; sin as humans breaking the God-human covenant).

If sin in this sense is seen as individual and not as interpersonal, it would seem that its solution would also be seen as individual and not as interpersonal. This is exactly what I observed in my Bible students' perspective on Jesus' death and resurrection. From a biblical perspective, the Fall created a gap between God and humanity that humanity is not capable of restoring. God took initiative to restore the relationship with humanity by sending his Son to this earth. Jesus' death and resurrection made it possible for human beings to choose allegiance with God again. The ways in which I heard Thai Christians process the significance of Jesus' death and resurrection, however, did not center on its implications for a restored relationship with God. Rather, they framed it in two ways:

1. Jesus' death showed that He was highly moral—even though He was innocent, He did not get angry with the people that killed Him but remained impressively calm;
2. Jesus' resurrection from death showed that He was/is extremely powerful.

The events of Jesus' death and resurrection were therefore not seen as the necessary solution for sin offered by God. They were not read as restoring the broken relationship between humanity and God. Rather, Jesus' death was seen as a moral example and His resurrection as a demonstration of power, two things that provide strength and inspiration for people's individual journeys to being good people.

These interpretations of the Fall and Jesus' death and resurrection point out that sin tends to continue to be understood with karmic eyes of individual responsibility, rather than with a renewed understanding of God as the one who releases people from guilt.

CONCLUSION: HORIZONTAL MORE THAN VERTICAL RECONCILIATION

In this paper I have explored the ways in which the gospel has or fails to have a reconciliatory impact on the three levels of self, relationship with others, and relationship with God in relation to the fear-, guilt-, and shame-orientations of Thai society. In this conclusion I will synthesize the findings.

In the introduction, I defined reconciliation within oneself as moving from a negative self-image and suffering to a positive self-image and holistic well-being. It seems that Christianity in Thailand offers reconciliation on this level in a strong way, as it had a positive engagement with all three cultural orientations. In relationship to the Thai fear-orientation, Christianity can be said to decrease suffering and enhance the holistic well-being of individuals. In relationship to the Thai guilt-orientation, Christianity can be said to boost a positive self-image by a new experience of the self as pure and innocent. Finally, in relationship to the Thai shame-orientation, Christianity promotes an improved self-image by encouraging self-expression and a view of human beings as egalitarian and highly valuable.

Reconciliation between oneself and others was defined as moving from selfishness and broken relationships to other-centeredness and healthy, loving relationships. The reconciliatory impact of Christianity in Thailand on this level was less strong as it was on the level of reconciliation within the self, but still strong. Reconciliation on this level was seen in relation to the Thai guilt-orientation: Christians experience their relationships as growing in moral strength, e.g. care and peace. Reconciliation was also seen in relation to the Thai shame-orientation:

Christianity encourages the formation of relationships across social status. However, reconciliation was not clearly visible in relation to the Thai fear-orientation: here Christianity seems to reproduce a self-oriented type of spirituality focused more on receiving blessings for oneself than on caring for others.

Reconciliation between oneself and God was defined as moving from an untruthful view of God/the spiritual world and self-oriented ways of relating to this to a truthful view of God/the spiritual world and devotional ways of relating to this. We found that Christianity had the least impact on this level. In relationship to the Thai fear-orientation, the Christian God often was understood and approached as an animistic spirit or conditional patron, and the emphasis of religious life was more on personal ambition than on devotion and service to God. In relationship to the Thai shame-orientation, a gospel-derived, restorative honor-shame conceptualization of the man-God relationship was rarely adopted by lay believers to replace legal language of "forgiveness" and "sin." Finally, in relationship to the Thai guilt-orientation, the Christian God was not so much understood as the One who sets people free from guilt but more as the One who gives people a moral example and impetus for their individual journeys into goodness.

In sum, we may conclude that the reconciliatory impact of the gospel in Thailand plays out primarily on the horizontal level of human beings: within the self and between the self and other human beings. The vertical dimension of reconciliation, that is restoring people to a truthful image of and devotional attitude toward God, seems to be least impacted by the gospel in Thailand.

References

Cohen, E. 1991. "Christianity and Buddhism in Thailand: The 'battle of the axes' and the 'contest of power.'" *Social compass* 38 (2): 115–40.

Dahlfred, K. 2011. "Animism, syncretism, and Christianity in Thailand." http://2sowers.com/Assets/Animism.pdf

Flanders, C. 2005. "About face: Reorienting Thai face for soteriology and mission." PhD diss., Fuller Theological Seminary.

Komin, S. 1991. *Psychology of the Thai people: Values and behavioral patterns.* Bangkok: National Institute of Development Administration.

McDaniel, J. 2014. *The lovelorn ghost and the magical monk: Practicing Buddhism in modern Thailand.* New York: Columbia University Press.

Mulders, N. 2000. *Inside Thai society: Religion, everyday life, change.* Chiang Mai: Silkworm Books.

Taylor, S. 2003. "A prolegomena for the Thai context: A starting point for Thai theology." PhD diss., International Theological Seminary.

Visser, M. 2008. *Conversion growth of Protestant Churches in Thailand.* Zoetermeer: Boekencentrum.

Wu, J. 2012. *Saving God's face: A Chinese contextualization of salvation through honor and shame.* EMS Dissertation Series. Pasadena, CA: WCIU Press.

www.ingramcontent.com/pod-product-compliance
Ingram Content Group UK Ltd.
Pitfield, Milton Keynes, MK11 3LW, UK
UKHW022236230426
12048UKWH00018BA/1301